INTRODUCTION TO MARXIST THEORY

Introduction to Marxist Theory

BY HENRY B. MAYO

NEW YORK   Oxford University Press

1960

PRINTED IN THE UNITED STATES OF AMERICA

Preface

MARXISM may be studied today for at least two good reasons. In the first place, Marx was one of those pioneers, like Darwin or Freud, who changed the tenor of man's thought; and every student of history and society must sooner or later come to terms with him. His work may be riddled with ambiguities and inconsistencies, but it remains one of the landmarks of human thought, and the critical appraisal of any great system is one way of extending our knowledge. Marx's insight was never so constructive as it was analytic and critical; and certainly his influence has not been wholly beneficial. Yet much the same could be said of the founders of many other systems.

There is a second, but no less important, reason for studying Marxism. Marx's theories have often been refuted, but they are now the official beliefs of a third of the world's population. Hence to discuss them systematically is no mere academic diversion: urgent questions of domestic and international policy compel us to inquire into what the communist part of the world believes, or professes to believe. The democrat ought to know the case of his chief opponent, its strength and its weakness. To reject communism is not enough; it must be rejected soberly, and on the right grounds, with knowledge of what it does and does not contain.

To explain Marxism has naturally involved an examination of the writings of both Marx and Engels, since it is from these two men, joint authors of the *Communist Manifesto* in 1848, that the ideas of modern communism are largely derived. If our study stopped with Marx, however, we could hardly understand modern communism, which differs in many important respects from what Marx taught. Communism today is firmly cast in the Russian mold, and it has thus been necessary to examine also the chief additions and alterations to Marx's thought made by Lenin and his successors. Marx once wrote that Russia always runs after the most extreme ideas the West has to offer. In some particulars, indeed, Russian communism, although paying tribute to Marx, flatly contradicts some of his theories.

Other modifications of Marx's original ideas have of course been made by other schools of Marxists, including Trotskyites and some of the theorists of the European Social Democratic parties. It is even conceivable in the light of recent history that a number of 'national communisms' may develop — for example in Yugoslavia or China — some of them differing somewhat from the Moscow version. But I have concentrated upon what may be called the Moscow orthodoxy, with only occasional references to other strands of communist thought.

Although the democrat ought to understand communism, it is even more desirable that he should understand his own philosophy and system. Theories of democracy are distressingly vague and conflicting. If democracy is to be defended it should be for the right reasons, with knowledge of what we do and do not mean by it. At many points throughout the analysis of Marxism, references have been made to democracy in order to contrast the two theories, and in the last chapter I have confronted democracy with Marxism in a more systematic manner, and raised some of the current policy problems which are raised by the conflict of these two systems.

On such great issues it is not easy to be original or impartial. The books on Marxism are as the sands on the seashore, so that any contemporary writer is bound to repeat much that has been said before. Yet communist theory is living and changing; there can be no definitive analysis, and so it must be repeatedly examined afresh.

As for neutrality, the present political divisions of the world make it almost impossible, and a writer has a duty to state the point of view from which he writes. Mine is openly that of a democrat as I understand democracy. Although he is committed to a particular system, the democrat places a high value upon integrity and intellectual honesty, and he must make the effort to treat his material as objectively as possible, or we might as well give up any pretence of searching for truth and frankly acknowledge that we hold our opinions because they flatter our prejudices or further our interests.

> Naturally a lot of people, and people who are not only good but able and intelligent, will disagree here . . . They have Faith with a very large F. My faith has a very small one, and I only intrude it because these are strenuous and serious days, and one likes to say what one thinks while speech is comparatively free: it may not be free much longer.*

I am rather less pessimistic than Mr. Forster. We can, if we are alert, determined, and courageous, maintain a free society against assaults both from the wave of communism and from the angry flood of reaction against it.

The greater part of this study was formerly published under the title *Democracy and Marxism* (Oxford University Press, New York, 1955). The chief changes are: Chapter 1, which is entirely new; the first portion of Chapter 7 and parts of Chapter 9 have been rewritten; one chapter of the former edition — that on 'The Theory of Democracy' — has been omitted; while the Bibliography has been revised.

H. B. M.

Columbia, S.C.
December, 1959

---

* E. M. Forster, *Two Cheers for Democracy*, London, 1951, p. 85.

Contents

Contents

INTRODUCTION TO MARXIST THEORY

'. . . in an age that produces such masters as the great Huygenius and the incomparable Mr. Newton, with others of that strain, it is ambition enough to be employed as an under-labourer in clearing the ground a little, and removing some of the rubbish that lies in the way of knowledge.'

JOHN LOCKE,
Essay concerning Human Understanding.

He [Marx] believed that the future lay in the hands of an immense class-conscious proletariat imbued and saturated with the principles of Marxism. He believed it with the faith of a fanatic in things not seen.

The fanaticism of Marx's belief matched the bleak outlines of his character . . . Marx is the outstanding example in history of the truth, which is sometimes ignored or denied, that fanaticism is as easily compatible with intellect as with emotion.

E. H. CARR.[1]

1

Karl Marx:

The Man and His Work

I

IT IS WORTH STATING the main facts about the life and work of Karl Marx for two reasons: first, because to do so will throw some light on the sources and nature of Marx's thought, and this in turn will help us to understand Marxism; and second, because too many crusaders for democracy have all too often given a distorted view of the character of the man. To call Marx stupid or to dismiss him as an angry man with carbuncles, as some have done, is no way to refute Marxism or to defend democracy. It is also a dangerous way of arguing in this case, because it leads to evasion of Marxist theory, and hence to a serious underestimate of the strength of the appeal of Marxism.

1. E. H. Carr, *Karl Marx, A Study in Fanaticism*, London, 1935, pp. 61–2.

Karl Heinrich Marx, the son of a middle-class Jewish lawyer, was born in the small town of Trier in the Rhineland in May, 1818, and came of a long line of rabbis on both sides of the family. Karl was the second child in a family of seven, and the only child in any way remarkable. The family name had earlier been shortened from Marx Levi to Marx, and in 1824 when the boy was six years old the family was officially received into the Evangelical (Lutheran) church. Heinrich Marx, the father, was a deist and rationalist of the eighteenth-century type, so that it was not religious enthusiasm which led to the wholesale family conversion. He seems to have been far more German than Jewish, one of those amenable and prudent persons who join the State Church for social and business reasons and because they like to go all the way in conforming with their fellow citizens.

The young Marx enjoyed a normal and happy upbringing. The father's influence was strong, and his humanitarian and rationalist characteristics, but not his obliging and respectful manner, were also to appear in the son. The other great personal influence in Marx's childhood was that of his cultivated neighbor and future father-in-law, the Privy Councillor Baron Ludwig von Westphalen. He took a friendly interest in Karl, who was obviously an alert and clever child; treated him as an equal, and encouraged his literary and speculative tastes; and it is almost certainly from von Westphalen that Marx derived his taste for romantic literature and his lifelong regard for such authors as Shakespeare, Dante, and Schiller, and for the ancient Greeks.

School teachers commented favorably on his abilities and his seriousness, but deplored his handwriting and his preference for an involved style of expression. From school in Trier Marx went as a youth of seventeen to the University of Bonn, nominally to study law; but after a year transferred to the more exciting and cosmopolitan University of Berlin. At Berlin he abandoned law for the study of philosophy and history, and earned a deserved reputation among his acquaintances as an able controversialist and philosopher. Soon, following a course common in young manhood, he shed his religious views, and well before taking his university degree he had become a militant atheist and an ardent materialist. He continued all his life in these views, an example which has been faithfully copied by most of his disciples. He attended a variety of lectures, but chiefly studied by himself, and lived the typically intellectual and half-dissipated life of the student of those days, although he was careful not to take part in any forbidden politics. His only clash with the authorities had occurred at Bonn, where he once earned a day in jail for being drunk at night and disturbing the peace.

His father, who both admired and worried over his brilliant and erratic son, died when Marx was twenty. Marx now thought seriously of his future, and so set to work on his doctoral dissertation, the subject of which was a comparison of the philosophies of Democritus and Epicurus. Three years later he submitted his thesis to the University of Jena, and in 1841 at the age of twenty-three duly received his doctoral degree.

While in Berlin, Marx was naturally affected by the influences playing upon that generation of students. The philosopher Hegel had been dead for five years, but 'the dead generations weigh heavily on the living,' as Marx once wrote; and intellectual life was dominated, some would say disastrously so, by Hegel's romantic and highly speculative views of nature, history, the state and the individual, views in sharp contrast to the empiricism and rationalism of the preceding Age of Enlightenment. Despite its elements of greatness, the philosophy of Hegel will always remain one of the best armories whence weapons may be drawn by anyone who wishes to launch an attack upon liberty, reason, and the individual. If people can be permanently spoiled by too much bad philosophy in their youth, then Marx is a prime example.

There were in fact two main streams of Hegelian influence: the orthodox professorial views — Hegel was almost a Prussian 'cult' — and a more radical stream, or Hegelianism of the Left as it was called. The latter was popular with the younger men who used Hegel's logical methods to produce radical conclusions, instead of the conservative and nationalist conclusions of Hegel. It goes almost without saying that it was the latter stream which affected Marx, and he moved rapidly to an extremist position in religion, philosophy, and politics. Since political action was well-nigh impossible because of the tightened Prussian autocracy, the great controversies were confined to religious and philosophic issues. Accordingly it was in these fields that Marx displayed his revolutionary attitudes. He was being autobiographical when he wrote shortly afterward, 'Criticism of religion is the foundation of all criticism.'

What is known as the Higher Criticism — i.e. the application of the ordinary methods of scholarship and historical inquiry to the Biblical texts — had recently come into vogue, and among those who had taken it up was a Bonn lecturer named Bruno Bauer, an older friend of Marx. Bauer was later dismissed from his post because of his views on religion, and his works were confiscated, the authorities fearing that dangerous thoughts on religion might take a more serious political turn. Bauer's dismissal put an end to Marx's hope of a university position. Who can say whether the course of world history would have run differently had Marx settled down as an eccentric but respected professor, involved in nothing more revolutionary than academic politics?

Although the association represented an important stage in the development of Marx's thought, this did not prevent him from later denouncing Bauer in the most savage terms. Throughout his life one of Marx's less pleasant characteristics was a readiness to heap some of his choicest invective upon his former friends. If they had been useful to him in his mental pilgrimage he tossed them aside when he had learned what he could from them. The habit of denunciation was an essential part of Marx's stormy character, yet at the same time it stemmed from a genuine conviction of intellectual differences. So his former associates were attacked for their 'erroneous' views, and often also on personal grounds, since it always came naturally to Marx to impugn the motives of those who disagreed with him. His biting scorn was vented not only upon Bauer and a number of young Hegelians in his polemical work *The Holy Family* (an allusion to Bruno Bauer and company) but also later upon newspaper colleagues such as Rutenberg and Ruge; upon socialists such as Weitling,

Proudhon, and Lassalle; upon Harney and other English Chartists, and upon many others. Indeed he was sometimes more lenient to those who did not pretend to be communist than he was to those communists who did not see eye to eye with himself. The same behavior is characteristic of modern communists, whose settled dislike of the bourgeoisie is almost a friendly feeling compared with their attitude toward social democrats, Trotskyites, Titoists, and other 'traitors, and deceivers of the proletariat.'

Marx was declared unfit for compulsory military service, and with an academic post out of the question he turned toward journalism. He became, rather surprisingly, editor of the *Rheinische Zeitung,* a Cologne paper recently founded by a group of businessmen to be an organ of moderate liberal reform and business interests. The enemies were clericalism and 'feudalism.' The Rhineland had been joined to Prussia only after the Napoleonic wars and, thanks to its different history and the French heritage, was a good deal more liberal in outlook than Prussia itself. The Prussian censorship was also more lenient there, since the government was careful not to antagonize the inhabitants too much. It was therefore possible for Marx to carry on for some time, especially since there was no socialism in the paper. He has been called the first noteworthy German journalist, and certainly he and his colleagues engaged the Prussian authorities with great vigor.

His first journalistic experience contributed much to Marx's development. He made a strong impression on friends and opponents alike, and gained confidence in his ability and in his mastery of the art of controversy. His interests shifted from philosophy to social and economic questions, and he became aware of the deficiencies in his knowledge on those subjects. The newspaper was suspended after a year or so (at the request of the Russian government) as it was sooner or later bound to be, for Marx, never a tactful man, wrote with a fine disregard of any consequences. With some of his colleagues he decided to carry on the literary fight against German reaction from a safer base in France. It was at this time, in the summer of 1843, that

he married, and later in the year went to Paris to live. For the
rest of their lives the couple lived abroad as exiles, and paid only
short visits to Germany.

When he was a youth of eighteen Marx had fallen in love with
Jenny, the daughter of his friend Baron von Westphalen. During the early part of his courtship he was given to writing
romantic poetry, of no special merit, and he presented Jenny
with three volumes of his poems, which she treasured all her life.
She was four years his senior, and returned his affection, but it
was seven years before they could be married. Some of the Westphalen relatives had objected to the match on social grounds,
while at the time of marriage Marx had no job, little money,
and poor prospects. None of this daunted him, however, for he
had more than his full share of the self-confidence common to
young men and lovers.

Jenny was an intelligent and charming woman, inevitably
dominated by Marx's forceful character, while he in turn was
proud of both her beauty and brains and also, oddly enough, of
her aristocratic ancestry. By all accounts the marriage was a
happy one and the couple remained devoted to each other and
to their children through all the illness and hardship that were
to shadow so much of their lives. Most people who met him
found Marx irritating, condescending, and arrogant, and only
within the security of the family circle, with his children and
grandchildren and with his close friend Engels, was he able to
unbend and show a gentler side of his character.

II

On arrival in Paris late in 1843, Marx and his friends embarked on the publication of a radical philosophic periodical,
the *Deutch-Französiche Jahrbücher*. This German-language venture, to which the poet Heine was the best-known contributor,
was a complete failure and made only one appearance, in March
of 1844. The sojourn in Paris, however, set Marx much further
on the road to the evolution of his final doctrines. Paris in the
1840's was in truth the intellectual capital of Europe, and the

atmosphere was chaotic, idealistic, and exhilarating. As Bakunin said: '. . . two months on the boulevards was usually long enough to change a liberal into a Socialist.' [2] The city was swarming with radicals and revolutionaries and Marx met a number of them, especially among the German and Russian emigrés. He was brought into touch with revolutionary political thought as never before, particularly among socialists and communists (the words were then becoming popular) of several varieties. There were, for example, several 'Utopian' or French schools of socialist thought, e.g. of Fourier and Saint-Simon; and the 'true' or German kind, the latter of which Marx attacked in *The German Ideology;* as well as the anarchism of Michael Bakunin himself. Above all there was Pierre-Joseph Proudhon, who may justly be regarded as the chief prophet, if not founder, of the anarchist and socialist tradition with its strong ethical bias. His book *What is Property?* had given the shocking and unforgettable answer: 'Property is theft.' To him Marx owed much and at first gave high praise. It was from Proudhon that he received the idea of interpreting Hegel in economic terms, an idea which was later to form the central concept of the whole Marxist system. But Marx's admiration for these schools of thought did not last long, and most of them were later subjected to withering attack in the pages of the *Communist Manifesto;* while a complete book, *The Poverty of Philosophy,* was written to expose Proudhon and his fatal ignorance of the dialectic. During this Paris period Marx read and studied prodigiously in politics, history, and economics, on the last of which he had hitherto been comparatively ignorant.

Perhaps the most important event in this phase of Marx's life was his meeting with Friedrich Engels. They had met briefly once before, in Cologne, but the real friendship dates from the Paris days. Engels, the son of a textile manufacturer in northern Germany, and later clerk, manager, and part-owner of a cotton business in Manchester, was in many ways a remarkable man.

2. G. P. Maximoff (ed.), *The Political Philosophy of Bakunin: Scientific Anarchism,* Glencoe, Ill., 1953, p. 37.

Although not of the intellectual caliber of Marx, he was highly talented and versatile — a linguist, soldier, journalist, businessman — and practical and efficient in all that he undertook. He was gay, musical, fond of good wine, of fox hunting and other sports; kept an Irish mistress, Mary Burns, to whom he was deeply attached, and after her death lived with her sister Lizzie, whom he later married. (Engels tried vainly all his life to prove that these Irish girls were descended from Robert Burns.) Engels seems almost the only likable and fully human of all the saints in the entire communist calendar. From the meeting in Paris onward, he yielded to the spell of the masterful personality and genius of Marx and became a disciple. But he was no mere Boswell to Marx's Johnson; he was also a colleague and collaborator who supplied many of the qualities lacking in Marx himself. It is almost impossible to overestimate his contribution to that partnership, which has been called 'the most famous literary partnership of the nineteenth century, and perhaps of all time.' [3] Engels supplied Marx with first-hand information on social and economic conditions in England resulting from the Industrial Revolution; and himself wrote a book on this subject, *The Condition of the Working Class in England* (1844).[4] Through Engels too Marx was later brought into contact with the English radicals — the Chartists, Owenites, and others. Indeed Engels, through an article on political economy, first put Marx on the track of the idea that capital and labor were the necessary but dialectically conflicting elements in the economic process. The profuse correspondence carried on for many years by the two whenever they were separated gives us a great insight into the characters of the two men, as well as many illuminating comments on their doctrines.

After little more than a year in Paris, Marx, with many other critics of the German authorities, was expelled from France at the request of the Prussian government, and the Marx family

3. R. N. Carew Hunt, *The Theory and Practice of Communism*, New York, 1957, p. 11.

4. F. Engels, *The Condition of the Working Class in England*, trans. and ed. by W. O. Henderson and W. H. Chaloner, Oxford, 1958.

moved to Brussels, where they lived for the next three years, 1845 to 1848. By the time he left Paris, Marx, a young man still in his twenties, had roughed in the main outline of his system of thought. The method was dialectical, an approach taken over from his undergraduate studies of Hegel; this was combined, however, with the rigidly materialist outlook which had also been acquired as a student, and which had been strengthened and further developed by his study of Ludwig Feuerbach. He had turned away from philosophy to social and economic questions, and was much more concerned with the application of the dialectic to history and to capitalist society; and these he conceived in terms of the class struggle and the opposition of capital and labor. The massive system of historical materialism, which professes to reveal the iron laws of history by reference to the underlying economic forces, was thus laid down long before Marx undertook his monumental researches in the reading room of the British Museum. His subsequent work merely added the corroborative detail and provided the factual 'proof' for his intuitively formulated hypotheses. The well-known judgment which describes Marxism as a blend of German philosophy, French socialism, and English economics is not far from the truth, as Lenin was fond of emphasizing.

In Brussels, Marx took an interest for the first time in political activity of a sort; helped to found a German Workers' Union — characteristically for Marx, without any working men in it — and read papers at their meetings. Other groups of a similar kind existed in Europe for the study of radical social thought, but were only loosely linked until 1847, when at a meeting in London they were joined together in an international Communist League, with Engels as secretary. Marx was asked to draft a statement of principles — and so the *Communist Manifesto* was born. Engels had already drafted a statement, in the question and answer form of a catechism,[5] but in consultation with Marx agreed that it would be better to draw up a Manifesto, since such a form would be likely to have more lasting

5. F. Engels, *Principles of Communism,* a new translation by Paul M. Sweezy, New York, 1952.

historic value, and would give scope for a more elaborate theoretical exposition of their views. The name communist was appropriate, partly because the *Manifesto* was to be the official statement of the Communist League, and partly because it served to distinguish their views from the German and Utopian types of socialism which they so much despised, while 'communist' also had a more specifically working-class and revolutionary connotation, whereas the word 'socialist' was more respectable and bourgeois.

Marx was clearly looked upon as being solely responsible for the *Manifesto,* although it was published under the joint authorship of Marx and Engels. Engels moreover always insisted that to Marx belonged most of the credit, especially for the central thesis; and this is probably true, although Engels was always a modest man where collaboration with Marx was concerned. In one sense certainly it was a joint production, for by this time the two friends has evolved a large fund of ideas in common, and had arrived at common conclusions.

The *Manifesto* was first published in London late in February 1848; too late to have influenced the February revolution in France in that year, or even the later German uprisings. The circulation for the first month or two was among members of the League in Brussels and London. The first English edition appeared in 1850, and the first American in 1870. Today the *Manifesto* is published in practically every important language in the world, and it is the best known and most readily accessible of all Marxist writings.

The Communist League itself, which inspired the *Manifesto,* soon faded away, split by internal dissension, and was finally given the *coup de grâce* by Marx himself, who arranged the transfer of the executive to Cologne, where it could not operate because of the censorship. The only convincing reason for this fatal transfer is that Marx could not tolerate the rival leadership and policies of Schapper and Willich, and since he could not lead alone, thought it better that there should be no League at all. A repetition of the same attitude and tactics in Marx is seen later on with respect to the First International.

The *Communist Manifesto* is undeniably one of the world's historic documents, and is usually compared in influence to such other classics as Magna Carta or the American Declaration of Independence. This, despite the fact that most of the workers of the world have neither read its forty-odd pages nor adhered to its doctrines, and that its major prediction regarding the impending doom of capitalism failed to come true.

The *Manifesto* is provocative, rhetorical, and powerful, full of brilliant generalizations and savage invective. Marx had in general little use for the secret societies with their ritual and paraphernalia so dear to the revolutionaries of his time; he believed that communists should operate in the open, and here was to be the definitive statement of their theory, aims, and methods. It was in fact four things: (i) an interpretation of history to serve as the theoretical basis of the movement; (ii) an analysis of contemporary capitalism; (iii) a critique, often quite unjust, of other 'false' socialist doctrines; and (iv) a stirring call to action, which included an outline both of ultimate aims and of an immediate program. The writing is a sample of Marx's style at its best: vivid, ironical, passionate, and free of dialectical confusions; and it is by far the easiest to read of his systematic writings, for although Marx often wrote well and clearly, many of his works, especially where the thought is vague or where he tries to use the dialectic, are in the turgid and involved style of the German intellectual which comes so easily to a disciple of Hegel. The *Manifesto* has a vigor and emotional drive quite lacking in Engels' first draft.

The year 1848 was an exciting year of revolution and ferment in western Europe. For a time it seemed that liberty, nationalism, and constitutional democracy might sweep away all semi-feudal and absolute governments. Made fearful by events in neighboring France, the Belgian authorities took no chances. Marx was arrested and deported from the country where he had lived for three years and went straight to Paris, then in the throes of a confused revolution, where he thought himself sure of a welcome. But Marx and his emigré German colleagues of the Communist League were hardly noticed, and played a very minor role, their most dramatic action being to issue a futile call to Germans to emulate the rising of their French comrades.

Events in Germany appeared promising, and Marx hastened to Cologne to carry on propaganda from the editorial chair of another recently established newspaper. Here his idea was to telescope the bourgeois and proletarian revolutions into one, but publicly to stress only the former, because of its popular appeal; an idea which he expounded at greater length, together with minute instructions on tactics, in his famous *Address of 1850*, a piece of doctrine which later figured so prominently in Lenin's Bolshevik theory and practice. He soon became angry over the gradual frittering away of all hopes of reform by the Frankfurt Constitutional assembly — that 'cloud-cuckoo land,' that 'Assembly of old women,' that 'Parliamentary cretinism.' The effects of his disillusion with the Frankfurt experiment clung to Marx all his life and reinforced his deep skepticism of 'democratic' parliaments. He became less and less moderate in his writing, financial support for the paper fell off, and after a few months he was arrested with several others and tried for sedition. He conducted his own defense, and achieved a considerable personal triumph when he and all the accused were acquitted by the middle-class jury, the foreman of which thanked him 'for an unusually instructive and interesting lecture by which they all had greatly profited.' [6] Marx's paper was soon closed down, the last edition being printed, as a defiant gesture, in red ink; and Marx was forced to leave the country once again.

He returned to Paris, while Engels went to take part in some real soldiering in the insurrection in Baden. But in Paris too the revolution was over. As Marx saw it, the bourgeois republic which had succeeded to power was mere camouflage for a royalist reaction, and it was plainly evident that the day of the proletariat had not yet come. Marx took part in a street demonstration, and was given the choice of leaving France or settling in what he called 'the Pontine Marshes of Brittany.' The latter was impossible to one of his temperament and he chose to leave

6. I. Berlin, *Karl Marx, His Life and Environment*, London, 1939. p. 156.

France and go instead to London, that celebrated haven of political refugees, where no matter how revolutionary his opinions might be, his personal liberty was assured. In the autumn of 1849, then, the Marxes and their three children settled in London, which was to be home to Marx for the rest of his life.

III

Marx's private life in England for the first twenty years was hard and often pathetic. He never held a position which paid enough to support a family in moderate comfort. Indeed, he appears to have tried only once to secure a steady job, and in that instance — when he applied for a post as railway ticket clerk — he was turned down because of his handwriting! He had a great abhorrence of being turned into 'a money making machine,' and his family paid dearly for his high-minded principles. Sporadic journalism, small legacies, numerous loans from relatives and friends, and subscriptions among sympathizers: these constituted one stream of his income. The other was the constant flow of money, sometimes in small amounts, sometimes in large, from the ever helpful Engels. It is impossible to see how Marx and his family would have kept alive without the help of Engels, the only friend from whom Marx could take assistance without feeling the bitterness of charity received, and the inevitable animosity toward the giver.

For many years the Marx household suffered at intervals all the privations and indignities of extreme poverty, especially trying to a family as bourgeois as the Marxes: insufficient food, poor housing, pawnbrokers, dunning tradesmen, and evicting landlords. Three more children were born (making six in all), two of whom died in infancy while another, the only surviving boy, died at the age of eight, leaving Marx almost inconsolable. "The house seems deserted and empty . . . ,' he wrote, 'I have suffered all sorts of misfortune, but now I know what real suffering is.' For several years his wife Jenny was a chronic invalid, and on top of everything else Marx himself fell ill and was often

plagued by boils and carbuncles which were so bad and in such
awkward places that he was forced to do much of his writing
standing up. 'I hope,' he once wrote to Engels, 'that the
bourgeoisie as long as they live will have cause to remember my
carbuncles.' Afflicted with all of Job's trials he lacked any of
Job's god-fearing patience, as he himself pointed out. Marx and
his wife were not very good family managers, and it was the
devoted German servant, Lenchen Demuth, who was the
practical spirit of the household. It says a great deal for the
devotion and character of the Marxes that throughout this long
period of domestic worries the family life remained unshaken
and on the whole happy. Where he could dominate, as in the
family circle, he was quite gentle and kind, with a marked
puritanical strain. (Although he could be blunt, even vulgar, in
his writing, he hated anyone to use bad language before ladies.)
The festive moments in his life were few: an occasional party
with friends, or a pub-crawl — during one of which some street
lamps were broken — and perhaps brightest of all, Sunday ex-
cursions to Hampstead Heath when troubles were forgotten and
Marx and his children played gaily together.

For a time after his arrival in England Marx could hardly
bring himself to believe that the proletarian revolution was not
imminent. In 1850 he turned once more to politics through the
medium of the moribund Communist League, for whose General Council he wrote his now famous *Address;* but that organization was doomed to futility, banned in some countries and
everywhere split by doctrinal and personal divisions within its
leadership. It was at this time that he engineered the move of
the executive to Cologne, where after a spectacular trial in which
the government relied on evidence forged by its own agents, the
sentence of seven of the leaders brought the League to an end.
Not until the 1860's did Marx again take part in another international organization; meantime he launched jointly with Engels
another publication to promote the cause of revolution. But this
too was a failure, and with their funds exhausted the pair separated, Engels returning with some reluctance to work in his
father's cotton business in Manchester.

Any effective revolutionary activity on the Continent was ruled out. Absolute rulers were more firmly in the saddle than ever in Germany, Austria, and Russia; and in France the *status quo* had been stabilized in 1851 by the coup d'état of Louis Napoleon, who organized a plebiscite for himself and was naturally returned to office for a further ten years. With returning prosperity the fires of revolt were dying down. Marx therefore turned his attention to England, which, being further along in the Industrial Revolution, had in the Chartists the only considerable proletarian movement in Europe. The Chartist movement had passed its heyday, but Marx and Engels hoped to use it as a vehicle for the propagation of their views, and to reconstruct it on the basis of militant communism. But the British workmen remained annoyingly indifferent to the self-appointed messiah and his new gospel. In any case Marx's personality made the project almost impossible; he quarreled fiercely with George Julian Harney, but managed for a few years to keep up his connection with Ernest Jones and his Chartist newspaper until the latter, like Chartism itself, gradually petered out in the 1850's.

In the early 1850's Marx wrote two of his more vigorous booklets: *The Class Struggles in France, 1848–1850,* and *The Eighteenth Brumaire of Louis Bonaparte.* They show Marx, with great effect, following the clue of class and economic interests, to disentangle and make sense of a confusing political period. As with all of Marx, the simplifying generalizations are usually too sweeping, the stark colors unrelieved by finer shades; but there is no denying the biting and eloquent journalism, or the incisive and often helpful nature of his analysis.

Driven by necessity to find a regular source of income, Marx was lucky enough during this time to secure a paid journalistic assignment. He was always, of course, a frequent contributor to minor radical journals, but such organs, like scholarly journals of today, are seldom noted for making cash payments. In 1851 he was made European correspondent for the *New York Tribune,* at that time perhaps the best newspaper in America, edited and managed by Horace Greeley and Charles A. Dana. Many of the people connected with the *Tribune* were Fourierists and literary-circle socialists of various kinds — Dana for instance was one of the patrons of the Brook Farm utopia — and the paper was decidedly radical in tone. In addition it was strongly critical of most foreign governments, and the American public was fond of that kind of criticism.

As correspondent Marx for the first time became really interested in foreign affairs and in English domestic politics. But so handicapped at the outset was he by ignorance of his subject and of the English language that for the first year the obliging Engels came to his aid and wrote all his articles for him. Later, as he acquired facility in the language, Marx wrote most of his own articles, those on English politics and politicians often being astute analyses of the real issues at stake, and always enlivened by his caustic wit. In foreign affairs the Crimean War, and what is known as the Eastern Question — involving the fate of Turkey and its enmity with Russia — had just come to the fore and this engaged Marx's keen attention for several years. Here too his articles were at first written for him by the versatile Engels. Largely influenced by the eccentric pamphleteer David Urquhart, Marx came to hold very strong Russophobe and pro-Turkish opinions on the subject, and only toward the end of his life, when to his agreeable surprise his work was taken up by a number of admiring Russian revolutionaries, did he soften his hostility to the Slav peoples. Anti-Slav views have always come very easily to Germans, while in addition Russia was, rightly enough, regarded as the very epitome of a backward autocracy.

Other writings of Marx at this time consisted mainly of more personal and ephemeral pieces. Marx was seldom at a loss for enemies, real or imagined, and always threw himself with zeal into literary warfare, so that many of his works were written as attacks upon opponents. Nor did he mix much with the common run of emigrés in London, or become deeply involved in their perpetual quarrels and ingrown sectarianism. He lived, as Engels remarked, in 'a certain isolation.' In this period too he relieved his exile by a trip to Germany, during which he visited his aged mother for the last time.

Throughout most of the 1850's Marx's chief interest outside of journalism lay in his studies. These he pursued with great regularity, often spending the entire day from ten in the morning to seven at night, reading in the British Museum. He was one of the first to tap that great source of economic and social history, the official government reports, and much of the material was later incorporated in his volumes of *Capital*. (He was not of course the only pioneer in this field. Disraeli, for instance, had explored the same territory in the 1840's to gather material for his novel *Sybil*.) Marx also drove his followers on the same hard road of study, and it is interesting to recall the advice he gave in later life, advice all too often neglected, that his followers should not adopt his conclusions and make them a substitute for their own hard work and exact scholarship. By 1859 he had progressed sufficiently to produce his first systematic work on economics, the *Critique of Political Economy*.

Early in the 1860's Marx's decade of regular journalism came to an end with the severing of his connection with the *Tribune*. Greeley had come to dislike some of Marx's views, notably those critical of Russia, and in any case the onset of the Civil War led the American reader to transfer his interest from Europe to internal affairs. Henceforth Marx was forced to rely on Engels for his chief means of support.

IV

The best known of Marx's political activities concern his relationship with the First International. French and English trade unionists had been moving toward closer co-operation in the early 1860's and a major meeting was called in September 1864 in London, with representatives from several countries. There the decision was made to set up a permanent organization, to be known as the International Working Men's Association, a kind of federation with a membership comprised of individuals, trade unions, and other organizations. Marx was among the fifty-five delegates on the General Council, and was also on the committee to draft a constitution. In truth he dominated the committee, as he always found it easy to dominate meetings of working men, by virtue of his superior education, his eloquence, and his forceful and autocratic manner — a fact of which he himself was well aware. Beside greatly influencing the rules, he prepared an *Inaugural Address* which contained much of his philosophy, set forth in a Marxist review of working-class history in the nineteenth century, together with a plea for international proletarian action. Although brief it remains one of the best of Marx's pamphlets.

From then on, the International, with whose early and respectable beginnings he had no connection, became increasingly dominated by Marx, mainly from behind the scenes. His constant purpose was to make the organization properly Marxist in outlook and policy, as opposed to the divided and sentimental socialism of the French, the nationalism of the Italians and Germans, the sober objectives of the English trade unionists, and the flighty mysticism of anarchists such as Michael Bakunin.

The importance of the First International was greatly exaggerated alike by its enemies and its friends. For the most part it was a harmless enough body, and besides passing many high-sounding resolutions at its annual meetings, even on occasion performed some useful pieces of work. It was in no sense a party, and Marx conceived its function to be that of promoting class consciousness and proletarian solidarity on the basis of the Marxist social analysis. This it did to some extent but perhaps its greatest use has been as a legend or myth in the history of communism. Although it had attracted some attention in the first years of its existence, not until 1871, when the International became associated in the public mind with the Paris uprising which put the revolutionary Commune government in power for a short time after the defeat of Napoleon III in the Franco-Prussian war, did it earn world-wide notoriety for itself.

The Franco-Prussian war naturally caused some trouble within the ranks of the International, as national sentiments have always done for communists. Even Marx at first felt some stirrings of German patriotism, although he regarded both Bismarck and Napoleon III (Louis Napoleon) as deadly enemies of the proletariat. While he did not at first approve of the Parisian Communards, once they had achieved power he wholeheartedly supported them and saw them as the first historical instance of the dictatorship of the proletariat. When at the end of a brief two months' rule the Commune fell, its supporters butchered wholesale by the troops, Marx paid tribute to it in *The Civil War in France* — an outspoken communist pamphlet fathered by the General Council of the International. These connections earned gratifying publicity for Marx, but needlessly alarmed much of the solid citizenry of England and the Continent, who mistakenly attributed to Marx and the International a share in shaping events in Paris. Some of the members of the International happened to be also members of the Commune, and this, together with Marx's bold defense of the Commune, was the only foundation for the public hysteria. The British government, however, refused to be shifted from its phlegmatic stand even by official German protests, and since neither Marx nor the International had taken any illegal action both were left alone. The organization, never boasting a large membership, suffered from the adverse publicity, and many supporters fell away.

It was, however, Marx's personal and doctrinal quarrel with Michael Bakunin, perhaps the greatest antagonist of his career, which finally led to the collapse of the International. The dissension had gone on for years, with Marx as always suspecting the worst of his adversary, and had overshadowed the many other schisms and disputes that were always threatening to disrupt the International. In 1872 the great struggle between the two factions came to a head, and Marx took the initiative in arranging the transfer of the headquarters to New York, where it would be beyond the reach of his enemies. This piece of sabotage was indubitably the finishing blow, since although the organization might have lingered on in Europe, in New York it was well beyond the reach of effective action. Bakunin was also expelled from the International at Marx's instigation. There is no doubt that Bakunin as a person was extremely trying, sly, and conspiratorial; while as representative of a half-cracked brand of impracticable anarchism mixed with Proudhonism he could only harm the International. A rival International was set up in Europe by the Bakuninist dissidents, but both petered out, the American section soon being formally dissolved. Other Internationals were later formed, but not until after Marx's death.

The *Critique of Political Economy,* which Marx had brought out in 1859, was merely a fragment, a preface to the great work he had planned on economics in general. His journalism, his perpetual controversies, and his preoccupation with the International must have interfered greatly with production. The first volume of the long awaited *Capital* did not come from the press until 1867, and this is the volume of which most people have heard. (Like the Bible, however, Marx's *Capital* is one of those works to which everybody refers, many occasionally glance at, but which few have seriously studied.) The remaining two volumes of the trilogy were never brought out by Marx himself, but were put together by Engels from the drafts and manuscripts which Marx left behind, and were not published until 1885 and 1894 respectively. The entire work was meant to reconstruct the 'science' of political economy from the ground up, and to serve as the irrefutable proof of his thesis on the nature of capitalism and the class struggle. It is possible that Marx was not altogether clear on many ideas in his thesis and that this accounts for his failure to complete his ambitious project. He was the sort of man who writes freely on a superficial level, but who accumulates mountains of notes for his scholarly work and seems terribly inhibited in putting them into publishable form.

After the effective end of the International in 1872, the last eleven years of Marx's life were not very productive, but were spent in comparative quiet. The financial position of the family improved, thanks to Engels, who settled an annuity of £350 on his friend, so that for the rest of his life Marx lixed as a comfortable bourgeois rentier. The family moved to better quarters and Engels, having sold out to his partner, came to London to live and to be near Marx. Jenny Marx recovered reasonable health, and domestic life became more placid. Of the remaining children, two daughters married and went to live in France; the third and youngest was dissuaded from marrying a suitor of whom Marx disapproved, and remained with him as his prop and stay.

Marx continued intermittently with his studies and his wide reading although in some fields, notably the scientific, he never ventured very far. But he lacked the zeal and working capacity of his early years. Perhaps the oddest feature in the life of this otherwise consistent man was his entry into business. Together with partners he launched an enterprise to exploit a printer's patent, the invention of one of the partners; but the project was unsuccessful, among other reasons because of quarrels among its sponsors.

Marx dropped almost entirely his few connections with the genuine proletariat and their organizations, and for the most part kept in touch with only a handful of disciples and friends, of whom Engels was the foremost. He became the 'Sage of Soho,' but the circle of friends was small, considering the mental stature of Marx and the number and variety of the people he had known. Most of his former colleagues were by this time dead or else completely estranged. He took little part in politics, with one important exception in 1875 when the Social Democrats and the Worker's Union of Germany met at Gotha to unite their forces in the great German Social Democratic Party, which grew to be the largest socialist party in Europe until its destruction after the accession of Hitler. The Social Democrats had been more Marxist in outlook while the Worker's Union had inclined more to the principles and tactics of Lassalle, the flamboyant and popular German Socialist leader who more than anyone else built the party in Germany but whose ideas had been anathema to Marx, and with whom there had been the inevitable quarrel, with rather more than usual personal abuse from Marx, before Lassalle's untimely death in a duel. Marx was roused to one final outburst of anger by the Gotha program: it was intolerable that there should be any compromise of his principles or that any ideas of Lassalle should prevail, or that Lassalle's memory should be linked in terms of equality with that of Marx. He wrote a violent, lengthy, and sometimes childishly petty criticism of the Gotha program. (The views

which Marx expressed in his criticism figure largely in modern
communist theory, because of the importance which Lenin attached to them.) Out of deference to Marx a few minor changes
were made, but the union was carried through by the two groups
despite his protests and on their own terms. Several years later
he roused himself for a controversy with Bismarck's government,
the last of his political activities.

All through his life Marx had sought for signs that the inevitable revolution was about to break out, his hopes often
rising and falling with the state of trade and employment. He
continued to the last believing in the impending and inevitable
downfall of capitalism, despite the fact that many of his past
predictions had proved wide of the mark. He followed with great
interest the course of economic development in the United
States throughout the 1870's and foresaw — like many others —
that capitalism there would make tremendous strides. Unluckily
for his reputation, he also expressed the view that the proletarian revolution would occur first in the United States. It is
only fair, however, to point out that occasionally he showed
a tendency to modify the rigidities of his analysis, and once or
twice he conceded the possibility of a peaceful overthrow of
capitalism in certain countries — England, Holland, and the
United States.

In the last few years of his life he worked little and turned
more and more toward family interests. His constitution must
have been basically sound to withstand the abuse he gave it: the
sedentary life, overwork, irregular habits, and the rank cigars
which he smoked constantly. Yet toward the end his health gave
way and he developed a disease of the liver. He followed his
doctor's prescription and accompanied by his daughter went
the rounds of the English and German watering-places with
the best of the bourgeoisie. His wife died in 1881, a serious blow
to the now ailing Marx. He suffered a bad attack of pleurisy
shortly afterward and never fully recovered. The death of his
eldest daughter in France in January 1883 was a further blow
deeply felt, and he died quietly in his sleep on March 14, 1883,
just under sixty-five years old. By this time he had achieved

world fame. On the one hand he had become the Grand Old Man of Communism, honored in many countries except in England, which always remained perversely indifferent to this strange foreign genius in its midst. On the other hand he was also the 'best hated and most calumniated man of his time.'

He was buried next to his wife in an unconsecrated section of Highgate cemetery. Engels made a short speech at the interment, in which he paid tribute to the master, to his devotion to the cause of the workers and to his ability: 'the greatest living thinker has ceased to think.' He compared Marx's economic interpretation of history with Darwin's law of evolution — a comparison of which Marx had been fond — and predicted that his name and work would live on for centuries.[7]

V

How shall we sum up the character and work of this strange and fanatical genius? One conclusion seems safe enough: Marx was not one of those people who become enemies of the established order because of a thwarted or unhappy childhood. Nor are psychological interpretations based on the fact of his Jewish ancestry anything more than guesswork. It has been elaborately surmised, for example, that because of his origin and appearance Marx had a 'Talmudic' mind, or that he suffered from feelings of inferiority for which he compensated by becoming an extreme radical. This kind of explanation is of very little help except perhaps to throw light on some personal whims such as his derogatory references to many Jewish contemporaries. But then, Marx disparaged nearly everyone. Again, the handling of the dialectic can scarcely be called rabbinical; it is much more justly called German or Hegelian.

7. Engels himself lived until 1895, and when he died left large legacies to Marx's two surviving daughters. These two left no children, but the oldest daughter Jenny (who died before Marx) left three sons and a daughter, and through these there are present-day descendants of Marx. One of Marx's grandsons through Jenny Longuet became the leader of the French Socialist left wing, and a great-grandson was in Morocco in 1940 agitating against French rule.

When all is said and done, a critic of society is not to be explained away by psychoanalysis. The fault may lie not in the Hamlets, but in the times, which really may be out of joint. In any event, such psychological explanations of Marx are quite irrelevant to the truth or falsity of Marxism, and it is that question which should be our greatest concern.

Marx possessed a brilliant, fertile, and restless mind, and was a prodigiously hard worker with an immense capacity for reading and digesting his material. While on his honeymoon he read and made notes on nearly a hundred books. He aspired to be a scholar and a man of action, but was never completely at home in either role. All the time he nursed the bitter and corroding knowledge that he was obviously superior in ability to other more popular and successful figures. Personally disinterested in his lifelong campaign on behalf of the proletariat, he was — like most intellectuals more interested in ideas than persons — basically unable to make contact with those to whom he devoted his life. Vain, immensely pugnacious, given to impatience and intolerance especially when confronted with opposition or rivalry, he was, as Bakunin said, 'as autocratic as Jehovah the god of his fathers.' He was one of those men who are respected or hated as the case may be, yet are never liked as persons, except by a few intimates. Except for Engels and his immediate family he neither understood nor cared for people as individuals, and there was, throughout all his life, a lack of warmth in his human relationships. There is fundamental though not uncommon incongruity between his high plans for mankind as a whole, and his almost inhuman attitude to individuals who stood in the way. Always suspicious of trickery and intrigue, he even suspected a conspiracy of silence among the bourgeoisie in regard to some of his books because they did not sell or receive wide review. Hating all traces of servility and sentimentality, he had nothing but contempt for those who appealed to vague principles of love and justice instead of sharing his own conviction of the inevitability and rightness of the proletarian victory. Above all he was tenacious, fanatical, and sublimely confident of the truth and rightness of his own theories. Perhaps only a personality such as Marx possessed could do what he did. Another type would have lacked the drive, the single-minded persistence, the absorption in a set of fixed ideas.

Is the Marxist system of thought an original construction? Such a question about any thinker whose works are a landmark in the history of ideas is usually difficult to answer, and the case of Marx is certainly no exception. No doubt all of Marx's main ideas may be found in one part or another of the socialist and non-socialist literature of the period, and scholars have been able to trace exactly the ancestry of every strand of his thought. But that in itself neither disposes of Marxism, nor makes Marx less a genius. What Marx did was to select a number of appropriate ideas, develop them in detail, fortify them with illustrations, and weave them into a coherent and challenging body of theory. He combined, summed up, documented, and gave life to a system. It is thus the system as a whole which is original, for Marx in his thinking was first and foremost a system-maker, and in this respect resembles other great architectonic theorists such as Aristotle, Aquinas, or Hobbes. John Locke's modest ambition was to help in 'clearing the ground a little, and removing some of the rubbish that lies in the way of knowledge.' But that was not Marx's way: like Hegel he was satisfied with nothing less than uprooting and cultivating afresh the whole field of knowledge. Almost everything is woven into his *Weltanschauung:* a general philosophy or metaphysic, a theory of knowledge, a philosophy of history, economic and political theory; and all is brought to a focus in a practical program for action.

Not all of these elements are to be found, of course, in the *Communist Manifesto,* or in any single work of Marx. Even when all his works are taken together they present no methodical exposition of his thought. Yet granting the lack of order and the unequal treatment of different topics, the whole adds up to a remarkable and grandiose system which compresses the past and the future within the scope of a few pungent generalizations.

In his politics Marx achieved little, for except at rare moments he led no exciting revolutionary life, nor was he ever a popular leader. Everything he accomplished was through his personal associations, particularly with Engels, and above all through his writings. Over a great part of the globe his theories, often distorted, have hardened into dogma, while the advanced capitalist countries for which he wrote have sharply rejected him, but have nevertheless been profoundly affected by him.

> *We Germans are of a terribly ponderous* Gründlich-
> keit . . . *Whenever anyone of us expounds what
> he considers a new doctrine, he has first to elaborate
> it into an all-comprising system. He has to prove
> that both the first principles of logic and the funda-
> mental laws of the universe had existed from all
> eternity for no other purpose than ultimately to
> lead to this newly-discovered, crowning theory.*
>
> ENGELS.[1]
>
> *Dialectics cannot be despised with impunity.*
>
> ENGELS.[2]

2

Dialectical Materialism:
The Philosophy Underlying Marxism

I

THERE IS A COMMON impression abroad, even among non-
Marxists, that Marx formulated his theories as a result of his
studies in economic history. But Marx did not in fact arrive at
his theories in that way. His main ideas were formulated early
in life and purely by a process of *a priori* reasoning. He was still
a young man in his twenties when the main outline of his system
of thought was laid down. The elaborate study of the fact of
economic history came later, and these were used to document a
case, the conclusions of which were already present in his mind.
The sentence on capitalism came first, the verdict and trial then
followed.

1. In *Karl Marx, Selected Works,* 1942, I, p. 138.
2. *Dialectics of Nature,* New York, 1940, p. 309.

The first part of the Marxist system to be laid down was the general philosophy. This he formed while a student at the University of Berlin; it was materialist in substance and dialectical in manner. Although Marxism is a revolutionary philosophy whose practical outcome is utterly different from that of Hegelianism, the two systems are alike in much of their terminology and in their reliance on the dialectic as a key to unlock the whole of human history.

Like Mesopotamia, dialectic is a blessed word. No one can hope to understand either Hegel or Marx unless he is prepared to explore its mysteries. It is probably the most overworked word in the Marxist vocabulary, and can always be trusted to confuse and overwhelm the ordinary person.

Perhaps the most enlightening, if not the simplest, approach to the dialectic and to the Marxist theories in general is through Marx's philosophy of materialism. Hegel was an idealist, not of course in a moral sense but in a technical, philosophical sense, and it is hardly distorting his views too much to say that he believed the external world, or what we usually call reality, to be merely a reflection or embodiment of ideas. This he put in the form of the apparent paradox: 'All that is rational is real.' Marx took the exactly opposite view that matter existed independently of, and prior to, ideas; and that ideas are merely the reflection or embodiment of matter. This view he called materialism, although perhaps a better name for it, and certainly one less likely to arouse strong emotions, is common-sense realism. Materialism is a label that covers many philosophies, and it is important to realize that to Marx it had only a neutral meaning, without any moral or immoral flavor.

Marx and his disciples have nowhere attempted a systematic refutation of philosophic idealism, but they abuse it with great vigor, usually taking it to mean that 'nature exists in our minds.' By contrast Marxist materialism or realism, up to this point, is only a simple acceptance of the evidence of the senses, combined with a firm belief in the existence of the external world independent of any observer. Marxists dislike any skepticism about sense impressions as much as they dislike idealism (or, if one prefers the word, phenomenalism).

This common-sense view is all very well, but a philosophy based upon it must put forward a theory of perception to explain just how the mind is related to the external world. Marx himself said very little on this important subject and, once having taken up a realist, or materialist, position, was not deeply interested in perception or cognition or in any other of the stock problems of philosophy. Usually he was content to adopt the reverse of the Hegelian position — that is, that ideas are a reflection of matter — but sometimes he made room for the activity of the mind in the process of knowing, and allowed for an interplay or reciprocity between mind and matter. Such a recognition of the active part played by the mind is again merely common knowledge and does not take us very far. It is a statement of the problem, not a solution, yet it remains as one of the ambiguities in the foundations of Marxism.

Engels and Lenin tried at greater length to explain the nature of perception, but both of them were much less subtle than Marx, and usually reverted to a more old-fashioned kind of eighteenth-century materialism. Lenin spoke repeatedly of ideas being a reflection (or copy, or photograph) of matter, which presumably reduces mind to a quite passive and mirror-like function — a notion that is clearly not borne out by even an elementary knowledge of the psychology of perception.

The notion that ideas are a mere reflection of matter is, however, in full agreement with a purely determinist outlook, and this after all is what Marxism sets out to prove for the social behavior of mankind in the mass. If the active share of the mind in the process of perception is stressed too much, then one may have to admit that ideas have a kind of independent power and perhaps may even stir men to mass action, so that men may shape events as well as be shaped by them. This of course cannot be permitted in a strictly determinist social theory, which sets forth a predictable outcome for the future of society, regardless of the desires or thoughts of men.

Now in practice Marxists obviously display a firm belief in the power of ideas, as witness their intensive propaganda efforts to make converts and influence events. In their own actions they thus throw determinism overboard, but once that is done, the way is opened for the undermining of all necessity in history; so whatever the Marxist practice may be, the theory generally tends to be purely deterministic.

Marx's social theory was meant to serve as a guide for action, and so were his theories of knowledge and truth. At times what he seemed anxious to assert was the impossibility, as well as the use-lessness, of contemplative knowledge, of idle curiosity, or of knowl-edge for its own sake. His attitude in this respect was thus closer to pragmatism, or instrumentalism, than to a philosophic material-ism based on natural science.

His argument in so far as it is pragmatist may be put thus: the mind is not merely passive but knows the external world only by acting upon it; the very nature as well as the purpose of knowledge is for action. The knowing-and-action is a single process which, like the labor process in production, changes the world and man, too, at the same time. It follows from this that thinking and knowing cannot be disinterested: all understanding is for control. 'The question whether objective truth can be attributed to human thinking is not a question of theory but is a practical question. In practice man must prove the truth, i.e. the reality and power, the "this-sidedness" of his thinking.' [3] Problems of philosophy are thus solved by social practice and can never be solved by a mere spec-tator or by the philosopher in his study. Such is also the meaning of the many references in Marx to the unity of theory and practice, references that remind one so strongly of the remarks on the in-separability of faith and works in Christian thought. Marx's view does more than reject theories that may be fanciful and remote from reality. It is an emphatic statement that if by the use of our theory we can make things work, or take action that is successful, then our theory has been proved true.

Although this is the best face that can be put upon Marx's theory it would be wrong to suggest that he systematically ex-pounded or adhered to this or any other theory of knowledge, for there are indications in his later writings of some changes of views on the subject. Lenin, as usual, carried Marx's views to the extreme and wrote: 'non-partisanship in philosophy is only a contemptible cloak of servility to idealism and fideism,' and 'pro-

3. Marx, *Theses on Feuerbach.*

fessors of economics are nothing more than scientific salesmen of the capitalist class, and the professors of philosophy are scientific salesmen of theology.' [4]

Inasmuch as Marx's theory of knowledge is pragmatist there is no need to marshal in any detail the usual arguments against that position. Only one or two things need be said. There is an unbridgeable gap in logic between saying that we believe what is useful or satisfying, and concluding that therefore the belief is true; and there are several ambiguities surrounding the use of a criterion for 'success' in the case of any applied social theory or personal belief. If the experience of the holder is the test, by this test all faiths may be proved true, or false, depending on whether we take the experience of the true believer or the apostate. Further, if the mind selects only those facts which satisfy or 'work,' then all hypotheses should work — which is obviously absurd. Nor, if we make our own truth, can facts ever thwart our purpose — which is also absurd. Whatever else truth may be — and here we raise another of the classic disputes of philosophy — its test is not purely that of success or working, any more than it is emotional satisfaction or expediency. Such theories, then, are only partial truths, although it is undeniable that the test of 'working' — used perhaps in a more publicly verifiable sense — is often applied in scientific experiments with fruitful results, whatever its shortcomings may be when applied to social theory or personal beliefs.

Marx did not of course intend any of his theory to apply in a purely personal and subjective sense, the sense that 'my truth' can be different from 'your truth,' toward which pragmatism always inclines. Lenin, too, would tolerate only an element of relativism in his materialism: to allow more would, he thought, be subjective and idealist. Marx meant his theory in a public, one might almost say in an absolute, sense. That is why, although he approached pragmatism and even positivism at times, these labels would be inaccurate descriptions of his whole thought, and are all repudiated by Marxists as indignantly as they repudiate idealism and 'agnosticism.' (Agnosticism, in this usage, means to doubt the existence of the external world and the evidence of the senses.)

4. *Materialism and Empirio-Criticism,* New York, 1927, pp. 296, 308.

To summarize the foregoing: at the very basis of the Marxist theory of perception there is a set of ambiguous meanings, and no one theory is consistently espoused. Marx sometimes allowed a more active share to the mind in forming ideas than did Engels or Lenin, but the theories always have a strong tendency to revert to determinism, in which ideas are wholly derived from matter. The net contribution of Marxism-Leninism to the theory of perception is precisely nil: an understandable result since psychology is not one of the strong points of Marxism. (Marxist writers, especially in the U.S.S.R., despise all forms of what they call 'bourgeois psychology,' including the Freudian. Seldom, if ever, do they condemn Western psychology without grave distortion of its findings and theories.)

The Marxist contribution to theories of knowledge and truth is also negligible, Marxism tending sometimes toward pragmatism and always to the view that truth can never be objective but must by its very nature serve partisan purposes.

II

Marx professed materialism but generally tried to distinguish his views from the mechanical materialism which regarded man as a machine, or which reduced all human behavior to the laws of physics and chemistry. The difference lay in the dialectic nature of his materialism.

The meaning of the dialectic may best be examined in the light of its original usage. To the Greeks, dialectic was merely the art of discussion according to a special pattern. The dictionary (Concise Oxford) describes it as the art of debate, or the 'art of investigating the truth of opinions, the testing of truth by discussion, logical disputation.'

A statement is made, say by the teacher, and then by a process of question and answer the teacher draws out another statement which contradicts the first. An attempt is then made to arrive at a third statement which incorporates the truth of both the first statement and its contradiction. The three steps may be described as thesis, antithesis, and synthesis. The conclusion or synthesis can then be used as the starting point for another round, that is, to form a new thesis, and so the process goes on. Precisely how far it goes on is an open question.

To take a much-used example: what, for instance, is justice? The first affirmation (thesis) might be that justice is treating everyone alike. But objection may be raised to this, on the grounds that it is absurd to treat children like adults or the infirm like the physically fit. So the contradictory assertion (antithesis) might be made that justice is treating everyone differently. This in turn goes too far, and a reconciliation (synthesis) of the two statements might be achieved by declaring that justice is giving everyone his proper due. What exactly this conclusion tells us is uncertain, although many generations have thought it profoundly wise. Nor are we told how the synthesis may be used as starting point, or thesis, for another triadic voyage of discovery.

Plato used the dialectical method in his Socratic dialogues and showed great respect for it, as the method of arriving at final truth, or the mysterious reality which is said to lie behind the world of shadows revealed to our senses. It can hardly be said, however, that Plato made good his tremendous claims on behalf of his great truth-finding instrument.

By the Middle Ages the dialectic had become almost identical in meaning with logic, a description of the laws of thought. Together with grammar and rhetoric it provided the essentials of the educational method of that period, 'the lost tools of learning' to which some medievalists of the present day would have us return.

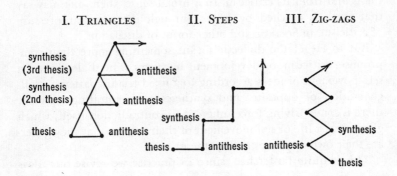

On the whole, the scholastics appear to have used the tool of dialectic with even less useful results than Plato's.

The dialectical growth of knowledge is represented by a series of circles in Hegel. Lenin stated that it might be represented by a 'curved line which infinitely approaches a system of circles, the spiral.' It may also be depicted as a triangular or other development upward, which, if twisted and drawn in three dimensions, could of course coincide with a spiral. Three flat-surface representations are shown in the diagram above.

Since it was Hegel's use of the dialectic which influenced Marx so much, a glance at Hegel's philosophy is necessary. Hegel's essential argument may be reduced to the following syllogism:

1. ideas develop by the dialectical process;
2. the external world is merely an embodiment of ideas;
3. therefore the external world develops, or moves, dialectically.

Thus stripped of all the obscurity of the Hegelian language, the core of Hegel's philosophy stands forth as an extremely dubious piece of reasoning. It must now be our business to examine this reasoning, to see how valid it actually is.

Consider first of all the major premise of the syllogism, which states that ideas develop by the dialectical process. Our ideas may indeed often change, to become both more precise and more comprehensive, by a process fairly enough described as dialectical. Conclusions are sometimes reached in the give and take of dialectical debate, although there is no reason to suppose it is the only method of discussion or even the most common. A compromise may incorporate truth from both sides, that is, from the original thesis and from its criticism. In a broad sense, then, one may say that truth is reached by stages, through the constant pressure of criticism, in Socratic and other forms of discussion.

But to Hegel the dialectic meant something more than compromise, criticism, or development by stages. The dialectic was a self-movement of ideas according to a fixed triadic pattern, a self-generation of opposites and syntheses, ever spiraling upward; there is some driving force inherent in contradiction itself, which gives ideas a life or self-movement of their own so that they generate their own opposites and syntheses.

This is quite far-fetched, since in practice we revise our ideas not because of any such mysterious quality in the ideas themselves but because our minds are critical, because we consciously try to refine our definitions, to avoid illogicalities, and to reconcile differences of meaning. Above all, we change our ideas when we find they do not harmonize with experience and the facts. And even if the force of this is admitted by the dialectician, and discrepancies between ideas and facts are allowed for, there is nothing to show that ideas and facts are brought into harmony, or higher unity, by some necessary dialectical pattern.

The last point is most important. By its very nature this kind of definition analysis — which is all that the original dialectic really amounts to — is not an instrument which can yield us any information about the world around us. It may of course suggest theories to guide our exploration, but so may any kind of analysis or thinking. There is still the old truth in David Hume's emphasis on the difference between pure reason and fact. Discussion alone is not enough, information and facts are also needed; or as the philosopher might say, we cannot get from logic to existence. Some people have held the belief that from reason alone can we deduce the world — Descartes is an outstanding example in the history of philosophy — but it still remains true that logic *by itself* can tell us nothing of facts, although the use of logic is certainly required for knowledge. It is not the method of the dialectic or any other purely logical operation which has given us our solid stock of knowledge about nature; it is, on the contrary, the painstaking and pedestrian methods of observational and laboratory science supplemented by the tools of mathematics and logical inference.

The philosopher Kant, in his use of the dialectic, pointed out that there is no limit to the antinomies, or contradictions, we may find and the synthesis we may construct if we go beyond experience and let our imagination have free play. The science-fiction writer may describe in detail a world of imaginary life on the planet Mars, and Martian society may be discussed quite logically and dialectically. But such mental exercises do not prove that Martians actually exist. In the same way the objects of wishful thinking may be nonexistent, despite Addison's proof for Heaven by our desire for it:

> *Plato, thou reasonest well!*
> *Or whence this pleasing hope, this fond desire,*
> *This longing after immortality?*

Take now the second or minor premise of Hegel's syllogism: that the external world is a mere embodiment of ideas. We can see at once that it is pure assumption, without the slightest shred of evidence ever having been offered in its favor. And it follows that if the minor premise is mere supposition, then the conclusion — that the external world is dialectical — is equally without foundation.

But Hegel was apparently untroubled by such doubts. For him the vital distinction between logic and fact drawn by Hume and Kant did not exist. The dialectic became the magic bridge between the form of thought and its content, between the logical and the real. A mental exercise in logic can give us information about the external world: we need not go out and look at it by the careful methods of science.

The absurdity of the Hegelian claim is seen when we test it by a few of the instances which Hegel gives us. By the method of the dialectic Hegel 'proved' that there were seven planets, four elements, and three continents. Clearly there is something basically wrong with such a method. Hegel also used the dialectic to justify his mixed bag of private prejudices, such as his admiration for Gothic art, his dislike of popular suffrage and of higher education for women.

Hegel was not on the whole greatly interested in applying the dialectic to the physical universe. The dialectic is nothing if not a continuing process in time, and Hegel was interested in it mainly as a means of explaining historical change. When he so applied it he was usually a staid conservative, although the method itself may, like the doctrine of natural rights, be used to serve either conservative or revolutionary purposes. It is conservative when one draws attention to the existing point reached by the dialectic of history, and justifies it as necessary. It may be revolutionary when one concentrates upon the next stage of history, since the present must inevitably give way to its successor, which in turn can then be justified. Hegel could thus say: 'Whatever is, is right,' and also: 'All that exists deserves to perish.' The clue to the paradox is that some things only 'apparently' exist: these are the things that are at the dialectical stage which is about to pass away. Thus, in France at the time of the Revolution, a critical stage of history had been reached. The *ancien régime* was swept away by the Revolution because it was only apparently real, that is, was not rational, or dialectically necessary. (But it was *after* the Revolution that Hegel discovered the *ancien régime* was not real and necessary.)

Hegel was, in a sense, not talking of the ideas of human beings at all, but of something mysterious called the 'Absolute Idea.' Accordingly, he regarded history as the progressive unfolding, or self-realization, of this elusive Absolute Idea. It is hard, if not impossible, to see what this kind of metaphysical speculation is all about, yet it need do no great harm, provided it is kept in the clouds and never makes contact with the real world of men and daily life.

Unfortunately Hegel did apply it to real life. Through the crystal of the dialectic, he surveyed German history and ventured to predict the next stage with great confidence. The next rational (dialectical) and therefore inevitable step in his day was to be, he said, the union of the several German states under a single monarchy. The new German state would then be the summit of history, 'the Divine (or Absolute) Idea as it exists on earth,' because it would be the highest point then reached in the dialectical development of history. In dialectical terms, the thesis of oriental despotism and the antithesis of Greek and Roman democracy would yield the synthesis of a German monarchy.[5]

So Hegel bestowed his philosophical benediction upon the coming German monarchy and to some extent upon the organic theory of the State: the State with its own personality and higher morality, in which war is glorified, freedom of thought is both perverse and subversive, the citizen's chief virtue is obedience, and his liberty consists of voluntary submission to the law.

Although Hegel was not a racialist, his philosophy needs only a touch of blood and soil to merge easily into the modern tribalism

5. Cf. Engels, *Dialectics of Nature*, p. 218, where he gives Antiquity (thesis), the Middle Ages (antithesis), and Renaissance (synthesis). Thus 'the New Age begins with a return to the Greeks. Negation of the Negation!'

of Hitler, who was similarly puffed up with notions of the manifest destiny and historic mission of the German people. No doubt the force of nationalism which Hegel so admired may often be linked with the cause of national independence, as today when a number of countries in the Far East have thrown off foreign rule; and more rarely, as with Masaryk and the Czechs, it may be allied with domestic reform movements; but as justified by Hegel it could and did issue forth only in reaction and despotism.

Apart from other objections the logic of the applied dialectic has one practical, fatal flaw: who is to decide whether what exists is necessary or merely apparent? When dialecticians differ, whose prescription shall we take? Unless we are willing to take someone's word for it we can only make our own diagnosis, or wait until after the event in order to be quite sure whether the event was or was not necessary. The doctrine of wait and see was indeed proffered by Hegel: 'The reality proves itself to be the necessary in the course of its development.' But if that is true it is foolish to look ahead and predict.

The dialectic as an instrument of analysis is full of ambiguities, and is hence well suited to serve the convenience of any kind of dialectician. It is especially ambiguous when used to interpret historical change, and yields different results in different hands for very good reasons:

(a) any stage in development may be taken as the thesis, depending on one's point of view, or what one wishes to prove; or, to put it in another way, an arbitrary choice must always be made to determine which stage of a continuing process is taken to be thesis, which as antithesis, and which as synthesis;

(b) any kind of difference may be magnified into a contradiction or opposite, and nothing is more obvious in Hegel, and Marx, than the wide and loose sense in which the term 'contradiction' is often used;

and (c) to any one thesis there may be a number of antitheses, and consequently a number of possible syntheses.

Neither as a method of proof for what is already known nor, still less, as a description of reality nor as a method of investigating reality to find new truth will the Hegelian dialectic stand scrutiny. This is not a surprising conclusion when we recall that the dialectic is a purely rationalistic *a priori* formula and is neither based upon an empirical inquiry nor verifiable by such an inquiry. As Morris Cohen pointed out, it is a Procrustean bed into which Hegel forced everything; but quite obviously statements are not true merely because they can be cast in the form of the dialectic, while to express some truths and problems in the dialectical form causes only obscurity and confusion.

To summarize this section briefly: originally the dialectic meant only discussion according to a special pattern, to elucidate ideas or show how they developed to become 'more and more correct.' Hegel, by assuming that nature and history are reflections of the Absolute Idea, used the dialectic to interpret both nature and history. His attempts to deduce natural phenomena by using the dialectic were absurd, since scientific methods are the only way known to man of securing reliable information about the physical universe. When he applied the dialectic to history Hegel did little more than use it as so-called proof that history was going the way he wanted it to go.

For the sake of completeness in discussing the dialectic, a note may be added: the dialectic is said to operate by three laws, or to have three characteristics.

The *first* is the transformation of quantity into quality, or the gradual accumulation of small changes leading in time to a qualitative change or a new unity. In common language this would be differences of degree becoming so great that they amount to a difference in kind or quality.

The *second* is the unity of opposites, sometimes referred to as the interpenetration or identity of opposites. When regarded in this way the dialectic is, Lenin said, 'the study of the contradictions within the very essence of things.' Contradictions (differences) appear which negate the thesis, or struggle to break the original unity; these accumulate to become the antithesis, and so we have the unity of opposites.

They continue to accumulate, the negation of the thesis in time becomes intolerable, and we reach the synthesis—which is the *third* law, or 'negation of the negation.' At this last stage, a transition or leap to a new equilibrium has been attained. The transition is always sudden, and so the leap may be described as revolu-

tionary. (Hegelians sometimes refer to four stages, the additional
one being a preliminary stage consisting of a kind of 'undifferenti-
ated unity.') [6]

III

This brief outline of the Hegelian dialectic may do Hegel less
than justice, by oversimplifying his views and sometimes treating his peculiar dialectical 'logic' as though it were syllogistic.
But my purpose has been merely to sketch Marx's relation to
Hegel, and for that end rough strokes are sufficient.[7] Marx rejected the appalling conclusions of Hegel, but was not able to
throw off with them the spell of the dialectical method, which
Lenin called that 'gem in the rubbish of Absolute Idealism.'
Marx's earlier essays are thickly sprinkled with verbal and far-
fetched paradoxes of the dialectical type.

Marx retained the revolutionary method, as Marxists say, and
applied it to reach revolutionary conclusions. Nevertheless, if
what is said above is a fair description of Hegel's method, then
there is every reason to doubt the dialectic and no reason to believe that the method is any more valid than the conclusions. For
that reason it might be thought sufficient to reject Marxism out of
hand, on the ground that any philosophy which employs such a
method is likely to be false or nonsensical.

But Marx used the dialectic with a difference, and it is the
difference which he regarded as vital. When he reversed Hegel's
philosophy and made, not ideas, but the physical world the reality, he assumed it to be a dialectical reality. Hence he described his
system as dialectical materialism instead of dialectical idealism.
His method, he said, was 'the direct opposite' of Hegel's, and:

> In my view . . . the ideal is nothing more than the material
> when it has been transposed and translated inside the human
> head.

6. T. A. Jackson, *Dialectics, The Logic of Marxism,* London, 1936, p. 107.
7. For a sympathetic account of Hegel's philosophy and logic see the two
books by G. R. G. Mure in Guide to the Literature of Marxism. An excellent philosophical treatment of dialectic materialism is given in H. B.
Acton, *The Illusion of the Epoch,* London, 1955, part I.

That is the meaning, too, of his remark:

> In Hegel's writings, dialectic stands on its head. You must turn it right way up again if you want to discover the rational kernel that is hidden away within the wrappings of mystification.[8]

But whether on its head or on its feet, there is nothing to show that the dialectic is a true description of nature. It would indeed be remarkable if automatically reversing Hegel gave a true picture of the universe: if one philosophy is false, its opposite is not necessarily true. To play the dialectical game, the opposite would be the antithesis, and we should have Hegelian idealism (thesis), Marxist materialism (antithesis), yielding a monstrosity of a synthesis.

Dialectical materialism, then, gives us a picture of an independently existing external world which is dialectical in its composition and development. Clearly, in assuming that nature is dialectical Marx has gone a long way from the simple realist belief in the independent existence of the external world and the dependence of mind upon matter.

Regarded as a theory of knowledge, the Hegelian position reversed (that is, the Marxist position) could be stated thus: nature is dialectical, and the contradictions that are formed in thought are merely reflections of those that occur in nature. This is almost exactly how Engels and Plekhanov put the dialectic. Engels, for instance, wrote: 'the dialectic of the concept itself became merely the conscious reflex of the dialectical motion of the real world.' And again, 'the dialectics of the brain is only a reflection of the forms of motion of the real world, *both of nature and history.*'[9] (My italics.)

In the moments when he inclined toward a more 'activist' theory of knowledge, Marx himself might have put it differently: the truth as we know it, and reality outside ourselves, are continually interacting, and the *interaction* might be described as dialectical. In Marxist language this would be the unity of thought and being, of subject and object; the vague doctrine that somehow knowl-

8. *Capital* (Everyman's), 1934, II, p. 873.
9. *Selected Works*, 1942, I, p. 453; *Dialectics of Nature*, p. 153.

edge and development depend upon an interaction between man and nature. But in order to provide a determinist base for his iron laws of history, Marx tended often to drop his activism and to relapse into something nearer the simpler view of Engels and Lenin that mind is a mere reflection of a dialectical matter.

At first sight it might seem curious that a person like Marx, ostensibly so hard-headed and so scornful of metaphysics, should make these large metaphysical assumptions about a dialectical nature. But it becomes less curious when we remember Marx's strenuous training in Hegelianism, and the fact that nearly every view of life, even the most robust and common-sensical, rests all unconsciously upon a set of philosophic assumptions and more often than not, as in this case, on the stock in trade of the preceding generation.

Dialectical materialism should properly speaking refer only to the physical universe and how man's mind is related to it. But Marxism regards history, too, as dialectical. Do our ideas then reflect nature or history or both? And if both, in what proportions? There is no clear answer to this in Marxism, although, as we shall see in later chapters, the emphasis shifts almost completely to history.

Meantime, let us examine more closely how Marxists try to apply the dialectic to nature. 'Nature is the test of dialectic,' said Engels, 'and modern natural science . . . has thus proved that in the last analysis nature's process is dialectical.' Or again: 'We are impelled to appeal to modern natural science as a witness for the preservation of dialectics in reality.' Lenin held the same belief:

> The latest discoveries of natural science — radium, electrons, the transmutation of the elements — are a remarkable confirmation of the dialectical materialism of Marx.[10]

The application of the dialectic to nature, or to anything apart from social phenomena, plays very little part in the writings of Marx himself, who was primarily interested in the analysis of

10. Engels, op. cit. pp. 137, 159; Engels, *Handbook of Marxism*, New York, 1935, pp. 256ff. Lenin, *The Three Sources and Three Component Parts of Marxism, Selected Works*, 1942, I, p. 55.

society in order to change it.[11] It was left therefore to Engels and later Marxists to undertake more systematic application, often with very odd and ridiculous results.

Lenin once wrote that 'oats grow according to Hegel,' and Engels, too, was fond of the example of plant growth, in which the seed is 'negated' by the growing plant, and the synthesis is the production of new seed. 'The cell is Hegel's "Being in itself" and its development exactly follows the Hegelian process.' The development of the cell, the transformation of energy, and the course of evolution — which Engels regarded as the three decisive discoveries of natural science — all proceed dialectically.[12] A modern Marxist brings the example of evolution up to date by calling Variation the thesis, Selection the antithesis, and Evolution the synthesis.[13] Engels made a ludicrous attempt to 'explain' sex by the dialectic:

> You, as a bridegroom, have a striking example of the inseparability of identity and difference in yourself and your bride. Take away the difference (in this case of sex), or the identity (the human nature of both), and what have you got left? [14]

Other Marxists also give peculiar examples, as when we are told that the skidding of a car 'negates the steering'; or the dialectic is given a moral touch, as when punishment is said to 'negate' crime.

When the emphasis is on the transformation of quantity into quality — the so-called first law of the dialectic — we are given such instances as these from Marxist literature: the gradual heating of iron until it suddenly transforms into a liquid; water changing into steam at 212°F., and into ice at 32°F.; the metamorphosis of the chrysalis to butterfly; the sudden change in the number

11. Marx's son-in-law, Paul La Fargue, said, 'In the higher mathematics he [Marx] could trace the dialectical movement in its most logical and at the same time in its simplest form.' He also noted that Marx intended to write a book on logic, and another on the history of philosophy. It is a pity we have not been given Marx's dialectical treatment of these subjects. *Reminiscences of Marx, Selected Works*, 1942, I, pp. 84, 94.

12. *Selected Correspondence of Marx and Engels, 1846–1895*, London, 1934, p. 113; *Selected Works*, 1942, I, p. 455; *Handbook*, pp. 262ff.

13. Jack Lindsay, *Marxism and Contemporary Science*, London, 1949, p. 225.

14. *Selected Correspondence*, p. 495.

series 1 to 9, to 10; and the addition of carbon and hydrogen atoms
to form new hydrocarbons. The sudden (dialectical) change is said
to occur upon reaching the nodal point, which in the case of water
to steam is 212°F. When this is expressed in the slightly different
form of the unity of opposites, or what Lenin called 'the division
of the One,' we are given: the one and the many, change and rest,
form and content, matter and spirit, substance and accident, reality and experience, and so forth almost *ad infinitum*.

Plekhanov — one of the more competent nineteenth-century
Marxists, the father of Russian Marxism, and Lenin's old teacher
— when seeking instances in nature of such sudden dialectical
change, found them not only in the processes of biological evolution but also in phenomena drawn from geology, that is, in volcanoes and earthquakes. The object of this, of course, as in Marxism generally, is to justify the use of the dialectic in social change,
and here he found the class struggle 'a striking confirmation' of
the dialectic. His examples from the past of such historical change
were the French Revolution and the revolutionizing of Russia by
Peter the Great, who brought Russia suddenly 'from its Asiatic
to its European period.' [15] One need hardly point out the obvious
fallacy in this procedure of Plekhanov, that however changes
may occur in national phenomena they have no relevance at all
to the solution of social problems.

Lenin provided a number of illustrations, drawn from nature
and the sciences, of the dialectic regarded from the other point of
view, as the unity of opposites: the plus and minus signs, and the
differential and integral calculus; positive and negative electricity; action and reaction in mechanics; and the combination
and dissociation of atoms in chemistry. And Lenin's materialism,
we are told by Moscow, was 'nothing more than the further development of the philosophy of Marx and Engels according to
the development of the sciences, primarily of the natural sciences,
in the epoch in which Lenin lived.' [16]

15. G. V. Plekhanov, *Fundamental Problems of Marxism*, London, 1941,
pp. 97–109.
16. Lenin, *Materialism and Empirio-Criticism*, p. 223. *Selected Works*, 1942,
I, Editor's note, p. 436.

Marxist scientists such as J. B. S. Haldane and J. D. Bernal in the Western world also speak highly on behalf of the dialectic in the natural sciences. Bernal, for instance, mentions 'the wealth of suggestive ideas and new tools for research and systematization that lie waiting to be used in the new methods.' Some Marxists appear to regard as dialectical all natural processes, such as food decay or escaping steam; and when these are prevented by 'artificial means' (refrigeration or a closed cylinder), the astonishing label of 'mechanical Fascism' is applied.[17] There is no evidence, however, that dialectical materialism has made any difference to the scientific work of such scientists.

Dialectical materialism is the official philosophy of the Soviet Union. That country, as much as any in the world, is also intensely devoted to natural science, which is studied and applied on a wide scale in order to raise the level of production and hence in time the standard of living of the people. A pertinent question is, then, what use does science in the Soviet Union make of dialectical materialism?

Engels once referred to the dialectic as 'our best working tool' and this is one sense in which the Russians appear to think of it: as a special tool or technique or approach, to solve problems in science, for instance, by providing various working hypotheses. This may also have been Stalin's meaning when he referred to 'the dialectical method of apprehending nature.' [18] The other main use seems to be as a method of interpreting or rephrasing the *results* of ordinary scientific investigation in order to make them more meaningful. As one Marxist has it: 'only a dialectical grasp of the facts gives a right understanding.' [19]

Far more elaborate claims are sometimes made however, as when Engels wrote:

> Dialectics is nothing more than the science of the general laws of motion and development of Nature, human society and thought.

17. J. D. Bernal, *The Social Function of Science,* London, 1935, p. 230. J. B. S. Haldane, *A Banned Broadcast and Other Essays,* London, 1946, pp. 235ff. H. Levy, *A Philosophy for a Modern Man,* London, 1938, pp. 125–7.

18. J. Stalin, *Leninism, Selected Writings,* New York, 1942, p. 406–7.

19. D. Guest, *A Textbook of Dialectical Materialism,* New York, 1939, pp. 76–7. Cf. also J. Somerville, *Soviet Philosophy,* New York, 1946, p. 204.

and when the Russians account for

> the enormous growth of technique and of the natural sciences
> in the Soviet Union, the decay of technique and of the natural
> sciences in capitalist countries,

by the use of dialectical materialism in Russia and its lack in the Western world.[20] There is support in Lenin, too, for such sweeping claims, as when he noted the interesting condition in which modern physics finds itself:

> Modern physics is in a state of confinement; it is giving birth
> to dialectical materialism. The childbirth is painful.[21]

This is a quite fantastic statement, since Lenin did not in fact know enough about the physics of his day to be able to assess what was happening to it.

The view of non-Marxist scientists who have visited Russia and seen something of Russian science at first hand, and who have followed its results as published in scientific journals, is that although rare examples may be found of Russian scientific work inspired by the dialectical hypothesis, for the most part Russian science makes no use of dialectical materialism at all; that, in short, scientific methods are the same in Russia as in the Western world. Eric Ashby, a British botanist, after a year in Russia in 1945, found this view widely expressed by Russian scientists themselves, although not of course too openly.[22]

The recent case of Lysenko and the apparently official adoption of his Lamarckian views on genetics might seem to show that Russian scientists do use the dialectic fruitfully. But the point here is that Lysenko's work in science is extremely elusive and dubious, since when other scientists repeat his experiments and follow his methods, they are unable to arrive at the same results — that is, to establish the inheritance of acquired characteristics. Among professional geneticists, who are presumably the folk best qualified

20. Engels, *Handbook*, p. 266. *Selected Correspondence*, Editor's note, p. 115. *Science at the Cross Roads*, Papers presented to the International Congress of the History of Science and Technology, by the Delegates of the U.S.S.R., 1931.

21. *Materialism and Empirio-Criticism*, p. 269.

22. Eric Ashby, *Scientist in Russia*, Penguin Books, 1947, pp. 97ff.

to judge the technicalities of the dispute, Lysenko is therefore regarded as something of a charlatan — an opinion of Lysenko common among Russian scientists themselves a few years ago.[23] (More recent reports from Russia seem to show that Lysenko's star is fading and that scientific integrity may be restored to the study of genetics.)

The elevation of Lysenko's theory to the status of temporary orthodoxy and the purge of dissenting geneticists can be explained only by reference to Russian politics and psychology, and it would be out of place here to go into full details. Lysenko's reputation as a practical agronome, and his success in convincing the political authorities that his line of research would yield quicker and bigger results in agriculture, seem to have had a lot to do with the adoption of his views. (Engels also inclined toward Lamarck, and the same tendency was observed in the early days of the Soviet Union.) [24]

It comes to this: in the opinion of Western geneticists, Lysenko has given no evidence that he or his dialectical materialism has made any contribution to scientific discovery. The whole dispute is on a par with the claims of the Nazis to a special 'Nazi science,' which, where it was science at all, consisted merely of ordinary scientific methods employed by Nazis; and otherwise was only pseudoscience, as in the case of Nazi race theories.

The grandiose claims of the Russians notwithstanding, it appears beyond dispute that modern science does not make any serious use of the dialectic either inside or outside Russia. Russian scientists, like all Russian scholars, are naturally careful to rewrite the results of their work in dialectical terms and to pay tribute to the official philosophy; this is the price they must pay if they wish to retain their positions. Are, then, the scientists who do not use the dialectic like M. Jourdain, Molière's rich grocer, who for forty years spoke prose without knowing it? Something very like this assertion was actually made by Engels and by Plekhanov. The latter asserted that

23. Ashby, op. cit. p. 114; Julian Huxley, *Soviet Genetics*, London, 1949; Conway Zirkle (ed.), *Death of a Science in Russia*, Philadelphia, 1949.

24. Engels, *Dialectics of Nature*, p. 106; J. B. S. Haldane, *The Marxist Philosophy and the Sciences*, London, 1938, pp. 94, 117.

people who have never read him [Hegel], by the sheer force
of the facts and the evident sense of 'reality,' are obliged to
speak as he spoke. One could not think of a greater triumph
for a philosopher: *readers* ignore him, but *life* confirms his
views.

Engels said much the same:

the dialectical character of this interconnection [of the system of nature] is forcing itself against their will even into
the metaphysically-trained minds of the natural scientists.[25]

Upon first reading Darwin's *Origin of Species,* Marx was struck
by the 'crude English [i.e. non-dialectical] style.' Marx nevertheless welcomed and appreciated Darwin's work, just as the Russians today are not backward in appropriating the results of
Western science, despite its 'deficiencies and decadence of method.'
The truth is that up to the present, every single scientific discovery, great or small, has been made without the aid of the dialectic
in any form, and mainly by scientists who were in all likelihood
blissfully ignorant even of its existence.

Marxists sometimes go to extraordinary lengths in their praise
of the dialectic, and appear to think that the static logic of Aristotle has been replaced by the dialectic, which they say is the only
logic capable of explaining processes, as distinct from static phenomena. Disagreeing with traditional logic, Marxists argue that
A can be both A and not A; that two contradictory propositions
may both be true. Whereas by ordinary logic it has always been
admitted that you cannot step into the same river twice — since it
has changed between the two occasions — according to the dialectic you cannot even step into the same river once. Some Marxists
— Plekhanov, for instance — have been more moderate and have
argued that the dialectic does not supersede formal logic, but
that the latter is merely a special case of the dialectic, or that the
dialectic merely deprives formal logic of its 'absolute' value.
Trotsky, too, compared formal logic with a static picture or photograph, and dialectic to a moving picture of reality. And other

25. G. V. Plekhanov, *In Defence of Materialism,* London, 1947, p. 109.
Engels, *Selected Works,* 1942, I, p. 456; *Dialectics of Nature,* p. 34.

Marxists regard dialectic logic and formal logic as bearing the same relation to each other as higher and lower mathematics.

IV

How much is really valid in all these extravagant claims on behalf of the Marxist dialectic? In venturing on an assessment we may notice first that the objections given earlier to the Hegelian dialectic are applicable also to any other use of the dialectical method. Only if taken as a description of how our ideas may change in discussion, that is, in its original Socratic use, is the dialectic at all appropriate. Sometimes, indeed, Marxists water down the dialectic to just that, as when Haldane writes: 'I hope those who disagree will point out in detail where, in their opinion, my argument is faulty. It is only by such a dialectical method we are likely to arrive at the truth . . .' [26] Here 'dialectical' is a superfluous word, and could just as well be replaced by 'critical.'

Second, consider the dialectic as applied to nature. It is no doubt easy to find instances of the so-called unity of opposites, perhaps even a struggle of opposites, if the expression is broadly interpreted. Just as in the realm of ideas it is difficult to conceive many things without some concept of their opposites — good implies evil, beauty ugliness, and so on — so in nature one may find such instances as the north and south poles, and one may even speak intelligently of a principle of polarity. But neither in ideas nor in nature is it true that opposites always generate a synthesis: in the realm of ideas, sometimes a number of conflicting theories may be discarded as wholly false; and in nature, as we see from the analogy of the poles, there is no upward triadic development, spiral or any other kind.

If dialectical terms are to be employed at all, what we often do see in nature are forces in conflict, producing together either a static or a dynamic equilibrium. This conception is at least as old as Heraclitus, with his remark that conflict is the father of all things, and as new as Havelock Ellis, who spoke highly of the insight and even serenity it gave him to conceive of the world in

26. J. B. S. Haldane, *Heredity and Politics,* London, 1938, p. 9.

terms of 'harmonious conflict.' [27] The forces maintaining an arch or the planetary system, the co-ordination of muscles in dancing, or the equilibria in plant behavior and growth, even the physiological basis of sex — all these may be thought of in terms of 'the harmony of conflict.' In psychology, too, the notion of conflict or tension may be a quite legitimate and useful way of thinking. But none of this is the dialectic — the self-generation of opposites, the trinity of continuously upward progression. The dialectic in any strict sense as applied to nature is an unwarranted metaphysical assumption. It is one of Stalin's ' "bolshevik axioms" which differ from the usual axioms in that they are anything but self-evident.' [28] Laws of nature are best regarded as generalizations about the behavior of matter, derived from, or at any rate supported by, empirical investigation. The dialectic is not such a law, descriptive of natural phenomena or supported by empirical evidence. At most it may be regarded as a vivid way of expressing an occasional truth in needlessly paradoxical form.

Third, consider the dialectic as applied generally to development or processes. As a particularly striking way of emphasizing the fact of change or development by stages — whether in nature, ideas, or society — the dialectic may not be wholly objectionable, for those who take to that kind of language. In tracing any kind of change, it is useful to look for the interaction of different factors, and for fresh syntheses and equilibria. Whitehead, for example, speaks often of interaction. It may even be possible to substantiate in nature occasional cases of the transformation of quantity into quality. Propositional or formal logic, which Marxists so much disdain, must no doubt be supplemented or at any rate cautiously used if it is to describe a complex and changing reality. (The language of the infinitesimal calculus is designed for that very purpose, to describe rates of change.) Many things are continuously changing, although examples of their producing their 'opposites' are rarer than Marxists think, unless the word is used—and it usually is so used—in an ambiguous manner.[29]

27. H. Ellis, *The Philosophy of Conflict and Other Essays,* London, 1919.
28. Ashby, op. cit. p. 98.
29. T. A. Jackson, op. cit. pp. 105, 255-9, writes: 'Thus hydrogen and oxygen are "opposites" but they can and do *unite* to form something which is

Is this dialectic logic a great deal more, as Marxists hold, than a sometimes applicable description of change? Can we employ the dialectic as a new way of thinking — a way which incidentally is not supported by what we know from psychology of the working of our mental processes — to ferret out the truth in science or society or anywhere else? The answer can only be that it is not a new logic, it is in fact not a logic at all. Aristotelian or formal logic is merely a set of rules to insure consistent thinking, and is not meant to be a description of natural processes. All Hegelians, including Marxists, subscribe to this same logic and make use of it, and do not reject, for instance, the law of contradiction. Logical distinctions could not be made without it. All the so-called contradictions of which Marxists make so much are perfectly explicable by ordinary logic.

Have the Marxist scientists produced any results which cannot be accounted for, both in their discovery and in the later descriptive accounts of them, by all the ordinary methods of science — experiment, induction, trial and error, inference, and the rest of it? The answer is meager in the extreme, and quite unconvincing to anyone who has not already as a matter of faith embraced the dialectic.

The burden of proof is upon Marxists. Granted that the dialectical method may sometimes be used in the give and take of discussion, they must show (a) how it may be applied to the worlds of nature and of history, once Hegel's idealist metaphysics is rejected; and (b) how it may be used as a method of investigation, proof, or description. They have simply not shown either of these things. Marxists merely take the truth of the dialectic for granted and beg the question entirely, as when Plekhanov cited the class struggle as *confirmation* of the dialectic. Its truth is largely a matter of acceptance or faith and one either sees it or one does not. There is indeed a strangely religious air about the whole matter: believe and you will understand; have faith and your doubts will vanish. This may be good theology, but it certainly is not science, and is precisely the kind of attitude which stands in the way of

---

not (and in that sense is "opposite" to) *either* oxygen or hydrogen.' He also cites the periodic table of the elements, and the structure of the atom itself, as dialectical.

any serious or objective study of nature or society. People who accept the full Marxist orthodoxy naturally accept dialectical materialism as part of it. One cannot be an orthodox Marxist without accepting dialectical materialism, since it is by definition part of the creed.

Even as philosophy, dialectical materialism is wholly dogmatic. Its postulates are beyond the reach of reason and critical examination: they are elusive 'bolshevik axioms.' But if the axioms are examined, the dialectic does not turn out to be a new logic, a higher thought-form, a fruitful working hypothesis, the ground plan of the universe, the clue to history, an adequate description of nature, or anything else: instead it may be seen for what it is, a purely abstract formula, a kind of secular scholasticism, or, as some prefer to call it, sheer mysticism. If development proceeds slowly or rapidly, continuously or by leaps, it is all dialectical. Nature, life, and history are cast in the form of a Socratic dialogue. Lenin's description of philosophic idealism as a 'sterile flower' may be more aptly applied to dialectical materialism itself.

Using the dialectic can also be a jolly game of playing with words, as it was with Engels' Herr Stein, 'who translated foreign propositions into undigested Hegelian language.' In adroit hands the dialectic can be used to prove anything. We may take the example of proving immortality from a recent writer on Marx: Life is the thesis, the antithesis is death, the only possible synthesis of the two being immortality.[30] Engels played the same kind of game in order to *disprove* immortality: Life is negated by death, which it always contains, in germ; living *means* dying, and therefore there can be no immortality.[31] Nothing could be neater, nothing more typical of dialectical usage, and nothing more meaningless.

Since the world and everything in it are assumed to be dialectical, Hegelians and Marxists display an inveterate tendency to force everything into the dialectical pattern in order to prove their thesis. Naturally, if the dialectic is made elastic enough, with a little ingenuity all problems may be stated in that form, and all phenomena may be brought within its scope; but its value as a

30. R. N. Carew Hunt, *The Theory and Practice of Communism*, London, 1950, p. 20.
31. *Dialectics of Nature*, p. 164.

tool then disappears. Any philosophy, if its terms are sufficiently vague, can embrace everything, as is sometimes said to be the case with Buddhism. The extraordinary feature of all this to the non-Marxist, even one who has all the good will in the world to understand it, is how little the dialectic does help in understanding anything, and how lacking in precision the examples and concepts usually are.

The very limited debt we owe to the revival of the dialectic by Hegel and Marx is merely for the emphasis on a dynamic point of view: on conflict, change, and process in nature and society. The debt would be larger and more readily acknowledged if it could be shown that it was the use of the dialectic which enabled Hegel and Marx to make their sometimes illuminating analyses of history and society. But there is every reason to believe they would both have done as well without the dialectic. Hegel for the most part had formulated his theories of history before casting them in dialectical form, and with Marx it was not so much the dialectic as his awareness of economic interest which enabled him to make an occasional shrewd analysis; while to offset the instances where the dialectic may have been useful, there are the instances where its use led Marx and Engels astray and into a wrong analysis, as it had done with Hegel before them.

The awareness of conflict, process and change is fully incorporated into Western thought and needs no dialectic to support it.

> Since 'tis Nature's law to change,
> Constancy alone is strange,

the poet had sung two hundred years before Marx, and though he was thinking of the human heart rather than of social and economic institutions, the sentiment is widely recognized as applying to these also.

In short, almost all this talk of the strict dialectic as a pattern of necessity is on the whole more confusing than useful or true; it is part of our unfortunate heritage from Hegel, who has fathered both the *enfant terrible* of the Fascist State and the illegitimate offspring of dialectical materialism.

On the other hand, if the dialectic is watered down and broadened, as it is by some Marxists, so that all change *means* contradiction; if the dialectic method is regarded merely as a dynamic as opposed to a static analysis; if it means that understanding nature or society is sometimes to change it, and that to understand continuity we must often examine conflicting trends and interactions, and above all look at things and processes, and not only at our ideas about them: then of course there can be little quarrel with the Marxists, except to deplore their terminology. The dialectic, if so broadened, then merges into the common scientific attitude of the Western world. As mentioned frequently in later chapters, when the dogma and certainties of Marxism are converted into more mundane approximations and probabilities, they are often quite useful to the social scientist.

V

At first sight it is not obvious what difference it makes to Marx's social theory whether the natural world is materialist in a mechanical or in a dialectical sense. The connection lies beneath the surface. Marx was something of a universalist and liked to subject society and the whole cosmos to the same laws. The attitude is one often caricatured as typical of German pedants, who are incapable of the simplest action without first constructing an elaborate cosmology into which the action must be fitted.

But there is more to it than that. Marx read the idea of progress into his conception of history; an idea which came easily to children of the Enlightenment and to disciples of Hegel and for that matter is still prevalent, although many people are less confident about it since the advent of the atomic era. Marx believed that beyond capitalism would be something better, not merely something different; he therefore could not regard history as an affair of mere cause and effect, or there would be no guarantee of an inevitable revolution leading to a higher stage of organized society. Now, if it is conveniently assumed that society and nature both operate by precisely the same laws, then the mechanical view of nature must be denounced as 'shallow and vulgarized' materialism, because it implies a mechanical view of history; hence the desperate attempts of Marxists to force the facts of nature into the dialectical formula. The kind of necessity that must prevail in both nature and society if the Marxist goal is to be realized must therefore be *dialectical* determinism, from 'lower to higher,' in Engels' words, and 'onward and upward' in Stalin's. And further, it must not be a gradual or evolutionary growth; it must have its leaps and its discontinuities, in order to justify a revolutionary break with the past.

Engels was definite on this: nature (matter) is dialectical and is also historical, or developing in time by 'the progressive movement from the lower to the higher, which asserts itself through all zig-zag movements and temporary setbacks'; and 'what is true of nature . . . is also true of the history of society in all its branches . . .' The dialectic meant for Engels that

> complex of processes, in which the things apparently stable
> no less than their mind-images in our heads, the concepts,
> go through an uninterrupted change of coming into being
> and passing away, in which, in spite of all seeming accidents
> and of all temporary retrogression, a progressive development
> asserts itself in the end.[32]

Stalin's argument was almost identical: in nature there are no accidents, but all phenomena are subject to laws, and since man and social phenomena are part of nature, society is also subject to laws, the same laws. The dialectic then becomes 'the algebra of revolution.'

Instances put forward to prove the law of dialectical progress in nature are not proof but, as we have seen, only selected illustrations, some of them unfortunately chosen and nearly all of forced artificiality. Even if the dialectical view of nature were true it does not follow that history is also dialectical. It is merely an assumption, and a dangerous one, to assert that human society moves by the same laws as the physical universe, that the laws of physics or of biological evolution in the animal kingdom can be applied directly to describe human societies. Engels, in one of his clearer moments, sharply criticized people 'who confused physics and economics,' and like Lenin warned against transferring biological ideas to the domain of the social sciences.[33]

32. *Selected Works*, 1942, I, pp. 452, 453, 456.
33. Engels, *Selected Correspondence*, p. 411; Lenin, *Materialism and Empirio-Criticism*, p. 284.

The real function of dialectical materialism in the closely articu-
lated Marxist system of thought seems to be this. First, it postulates
a purely material and self-sufficient nature, moving by its own
inherent dialectical laws, from which mind is totally excluded. So
far, so good. Second, this is designed to serve as a foundation for
a similar view of history in which, despite an allowance of free
choice for a minority, mankind in the mass will be subject to the
same impersonal and immanent laws as nature. Now this is a very
different proposition indeed. But since it is taken for granted, then
Marx's social analysis and all his laws of society, for instance the
class struggle, will appear to be truly scientific and thus acquire
all the prestige of natural science. Marx is not alone in perpetrat-
ing this error. Herbert Spencer and many others fell into the same
confusion of arguing from nature to society, in order to give their
social theories a scientific flavor.

Marxists are afraid that any philosophy of nature which is not
materialist will entail a corresponding explanation of history by
other than purely material forces, and that if nature is not taken
to be dialectical, neither can history be viewed as dialectically
progressive. They therefore assert that historical materialism is
inseparable from philosophic materialism, that dialectical materialism is identical with science, that the whole Marxist philosophy is, in Lenin's words, 'as a solid block of steel,' and that 'dialectics are the most generalized laws possible.' [34]

Marx himself, as we have said, was little concerned with the
application of the dialectic to nature. Assuming, as he did, that
society is moving by the iron necessity of the dialectic to the overthrow of capitalism, an air of support is lent to this law if it can
be shown, or even plausibly suggested, that the whole cosmic
process also moves according to the same inexorable law. But it
is not really necessary so to widen the sphere of operation of the
dialectic. It might be false that nature is dialectical (and it is not
so much false as nonsensical), but it could still be true (though
unlikely on the face of it) of human history, and more particularly
of capitalist society. It is not the truth of the dialectic in nature

34. E.g. 'Dialectical materialism, the world outlook of the Marxist-Leninist
Party, is a truly scientific world outlook.' M. Cornforth, *Dialectical Materialism, An Introductory Course,* London, 1952, I, p. 126.

and physics but its application to history — the dialectic as the science of society, revealing the so-called laws of social change — that is vital to Marx's system.

VI

Marx is so often abused as a materialist that it is worth noting one sense in which he was not a materialist at all. He was not the kind of materialist who believes that the only behavior of which a man is capable is the pursuit of his own selfish ends or his animal pleasures. Marx was not a psychological hedonist, or any other kind of hedonist, or even a behaviorist. Although he had many unpleasant traits — arrogance, intolerance, and abusiveness — yet within the family circle his standards of personal conduct were high, even puritanical, and he was actuated by ideals having nothing to do with his own material comfort or pleasure. His own conduct does not, of course, disprove his opinions: there is still the question whether he did imply, if not say, that human beings act and can only act from motives of economic self-interest.

Engels, indeed, did argue at times that the will is determined by economic or class interest. To some Marxists this appears to be the core of Marxism, and hence they are content when explaining human conduct merely to point out self-interested motives. Although Marx can be interpreted entirely in this way it is generally a mistake to attribute to him such a simple and extremist view.

Yet in one sense he does join hands with the classical English economists in believing that the pursuit of individual interests is the fuel that drives the social engine. The difference is that Marx believed the historical operation of the dialectic would in the end enable mankind to bring a better society into being, when selfish interests would be transcended; whereas with the economists it was natural law or the 'invisible hand' of Adam Smith which would promote the public welfare, and there was no need ever to transcend or eliminate individual self-interest.

After Adam Smith, the 'inexorable laws of economics' were used to justify a pessimistic view of society, as in Malthus and Ricardo, so that economics later became 'the dismal science,' less concerned with investigating the wealth of nations than with explaining to the masses why they must always be poor. Marx retained his optimism, however, because, as he saw it, the dialectic was on the side of a better future.

There is a good deal of truth in the economist's assumptions about human motives, and because that is so, the behavior of man in the mass is often statistically predictable — for instance, in reaction to price changes or shortages of commodities, as when bargain nylons are on sale or sugar is going to be scarce and there is a rush of housewives to the shops. And it is precisely because people act in their economic interests in the market that the wheels of industry and business keep turning. Yet such statistical generalizations do not imply necessity or determinism. No one denies that there is also room in social behavior for many other kinds of action, from choosing a wife to dying for one's country, and the assumption of the economist does not pretend to be an exhaustive account of human behavior, or to cover more than one area of life.

Similarly, Marx made room for all kinds of motives and ideals in individual behavior, as he was forced to do, since it is not hard to refute the proposition that human beings act only and always from a desire for gain. This helps to answer the old question whether Marxism is compatible with free will. At the level of the individual, the answer is yes. If we ask, is economic science in general compatible with free will, the answer on the whole is also yes. Men can, and sometimes do, act from other than economic reasons; they need not follow their economic interest in everything, but economics is built on the assumption that they usually do so in the market place. A like situation obtains in religion, which rightly enough, and on the basis of experience, regards all men as sinners, and yet teaches that sin is a matter of choice and will. Although Marxism need not conflict with a doctrine of individual free will, it must deny the influence of free will in shaping the course of history. While Marx personally conceded free will, his laws of history do not: one may thus predict the general outcome although not what any given individual will do.

Marx was logically compelled to give up the view of personal economic determinism if the gap was to be bridged between the self-interested individual and class-conscious loyalty. Yet this posed Marx with a dilemma, as we shall see later, for if there is no per sonal determinism (but only a kind of statistical probability, based on past behavior) it becomes impossible to find any iron laws in history. One can find only tendencies or probabilities, and these can work themselves out only if all other things remain unchanged. The economist is aware of this, and if he is a good economist he always qualifies his 'laws' with *ceteris paribus,* and he knows that since in real life all other things are rarely equal for any length of time, the predictions based upon a single tendency rarely come true. Marx, on the other hand, explains and predicts without qualification, and reduces all history to economic history.

In fine, Marxism mixes several points of view with regard to will and motives. Occasionally in Engels there is the notion that historical necessity arises because the will is economically determined. Often, Marx concedes that men are moved by different motives but that these do not matter; history shows a determinate social action for man in the mass. Part of the plausibility of Marxism lies in this very dualism, the combination of the individually moral and the historically necessary.

Since Marx did not believe in complete psychological determinism he avoided the error of reducing man to an isolated atom following the unchanging laws of a static human nature. He saw that man is a social product above all else and can best be explained in terms of his social milieu. It is a social rather than a genetic determinism, and of man in the mass (or class) rather than of the individual. 'It is not the consciousness of men which determines their being, but on the contrary their social being that determines their consciousness' — a proposition which Engels called self-evident and simple.[35] The Young Hegelians had also rejected psychological determinism and had enunciated a kind of social-determinist view of man. Marx took this further, narrowed its application, and, making the economic in turn the determining factor in the social milieu, gave us the economic interpretation of history.

We can now see clearly the total irrelevance of Marx's dialectic of nature, and consequently why Marxism contributes nothing to perception, philosophy, or science. To Marx the problems of the relation of mind and matter and of the theory of knowledge are unimportant, as both are usually understood. All that we are given

35. *Selected Works,* 1942, I, p. 362.

is the obvious fact that man is dependent on nature, and that there is some kind of interaction. It is the relation of ideas to the economic forces in history which really matters in Marxism and this means that, as Engels put it, the historical causes 'transform themselves into motive in the brains of the actors.' [36] The problem of thinking and being is solved by a *social* explanation, and it is the social process that is dialectical. Ideas turn out after all to be not a reflection of nature, whether nature is monist, pluralist, or dialectical, but a reflection of society, and not of all society but of only the economic ingredient. Perhaps 'reflection' is the wrong word, although it is commonly used in Marxism; the relation of ideas to society is not simple and direct, for there may be a time lag during which prevalent ideas 'reflect' the economic foundations of past society. But this problem concerns the application of the dialectic to history, which is treated in the following chapter.

36. Op. cit. p. 458.

Historical materialism is the extension of the principles of dialectical materialism to the study of social life.   STALIN.[1]

[Historical materialism is] 'that view of the course of history, which seeks the ultimate cause and the great moving power of all important historic events in the economic development of society, in the changes in the modes of production and exchange, in the consequent division of society into distinct classes, and in the struggles of these classes against one another.'

ENGELS.[2]

3

The Economic Interpretation of History

I

THE PRECEDING CHAPTER was intended to show that the Hegelian and Marxist dialectic in any philosophical sense is, as Thomas Masaryk said, the veriest hocus-pocus. If the 'principles' of dialectical materialism are extended to the study of social life we ought not, then, to expect results any more sensible than dialectical materialism itself. In fact, however, Marxist social theory is quite separable from dialectical materialism, and not at all dependent upon it. For that very reason, whatever there is of value in Marx is to be found in his analysis of history and society.

The Marxist conception of history is known by a variety of names, of which the most common are the materialist conception of history, historical materialism, the economic interpretation of history, and economic determinism. Of these the last is the least inaccurate. As in the investigation of Marx's more technical phi-

1. *Leninism,* p. 406.
2. *Selected Works,* 1942, I, p. 402.

losophy, a difficulty confronts us at the outset, since his theory of history is nowhere fully elaborated but is scattered throughout his works, so that the pieces must be taken and fitted together into a more precise pattern than Marx himself provided. The best summary of the theory, at a highly generalized level, is found in the *Preface to the Critique of Political Economy*.

Marx was interested above all in the overthrow of capitalism, and all his theories were meant to further that purpose. In the words of Engels, 'Marx was before all else a revolutionary. His real mission in life was to contribute in one way or another to the overthrow of capitalist society.' As Marx himself put it, 'the philosophers have interpreted the world in various ways; the point, however, is to change it.' [3] Yet he despised the common run of utopians and socialists of his day who were also critical of capitalism and anxious to replace it with something better. They seemed to him vague, sentimental, unrealistic, with no understanding of the economic and social forces at work, no grasp of the inner laws of history. He believed himself to be scientific and, like Hegel, able to comprehend these laws. What were they? It will be useful to have them before us in summary form before proceeding to an analysis and assessment of the separate parts.

The Marxist theory of historical materialism may be summed up in the broad statement that economic forces have determined the course of history. This is indeed all that Marxist theory means to many people; certainly it is the simplest and most plausible statement of the case, and of course it contains some measure of truth. Doubts begin to arise only when the statement is examined closely to see what it really means, and when the theory is applied to definite episodes in history.

In order to show precisely how the economic forces have operated, Marx's theory may be broken down into a number of more specific propositions.

First, when he was giving the phrase a narrow meaning, Marx called the underlying economic forces the 'modes of production,' or productive forces, and these constitute the economic foundation which is said to determine the entire superstructure of society. Included in the latter are the systems of law, politics, morals, reli-

3. Engels, op. cit. p. 17. Marx, *Theses on Feuerbach.*

gion, philosophy, and art — the whole way of life or 'culture.'

Second, corresponding to any particular set of the modes of production there are appropriate 'relations of production,' or property relations, which concern mainly the form of ownership. The modes of production gradually change and come into conflict with the existing and more static property relations. Since the modes of production always get their way, the conflict can be resolved only by the creation of a new set of property relations appropriate to the new modes of production, and thus a new dialectical synthesis is achieved. This has happened several times in the past, and

> in broad outlines we can designate the Asiatic, the ancient, the feudal, and the modern bourgeois modes of production as so many epochs in the progress of the economic formation of society.[4]

Third, the historical conflict expresses itself in practice in the form of a class struggle, so that the 'history of all hitherto existing society is the history of class struggles.' Marx thought he discerned in capitalism the last and greatest class struggle of all: a final polarization of society is held to be taking place into two ever more sharply opposed classes, the bourgeoisie and the proletariat. His economic theory fits in neatly here, to show how and why this polarization inevitably occurs.

Fourth, after a time the class struggle becomes intolerable. As capitalism ripens, with the proletariat becoming steadily poorer and more numerous, and the bourgeois class becoming richer and fewer, the conflict will end with the revolutionary overthrow of the bourgeoisie by the victorious proletariat.

Fifth and finally, after a short transition stage, the dictatorship of the proletariat — during which the proletariat consolidates its victory — there will dawn the era of the classless society and the state will 'wither away.' The process will eventually extend throughout the whole world, and when this has occurred the epochs of class history will be over and done with:

> In place of the old bourgeois society, with its classes and class antagonisms, we shall have an association in which the free

4. Marx, *Selected Works*, 1942, 1, 357.

development of each is the condition for the free development of all.[5]

Two general comments may be made before taking up the argument in detail. In the first place, Marx professed to explain much more than the workings of capitalist society; his theory is an ambitious explanation of all history. Lying behind this is the assumption that history inevitably proceeds from lower to higher stages of development, and that it does so by its own inner laws.

In the second place, it is worth recalling from Chapter 1 that Marx's theory of history is not the outcome of scientific investigations, such as any student may repeat and, by scrutinizing the same evidence, come up with the same conclusions. Marx did not *prove* his theory, but took from Hegel the formula of the dialectic, assumed from the beginning that it was true when translated roughly into economic terms, and gave it plausibility for history by an array of carefully selected facts.

Yet the Marxist construction is an imaginative hypothesis, a bold simplification of the whole of mankind's complex history, and has a great appeal to Marxists and non-Marxists alike. For that reason it must not be dismissed offhandedly, but must be treated instead as a working hypothesis and submitted to critical analysis and the evidence of the facts. To examine Marx's theory in that way is a tedious business, for it is easy to propound erroneous theories but often a difficult and lengthy task to refute them. The question that must be put to the facts is this: do they confirm the existence of the Marxist dialectic pattern, at least in the sense that they are in harmony with it? If they are not, then obviously we must reject the theory. But if Marx's theory did fit the facts then it would not be unreasonable to hold it; although as a matter of logic a theory that is consistent with the facts is not thereby proved true, *since some other theory might fit the facts equally well, or better.*

II

Marx's argument may be developed as follows. Man is not a mere product of heredity, with a constant human nature, but is

5. *Communist Manifesto.*

what he is largely because of his social heritage. What in turn has shaped the social environment of which man is a product? The answer, as a first approximation, is the economic foundation of society. The economic foundation also provides the clue to historical change, and may thus be regarded as the independent variable, so that self-induced, spontaneous economic changes are the dynamic of history. In short, the economic basis is what really counts, the rest is merely froth and bubble on the stream of history.

Can the phrase 'economic foundation' be given some precise content? Marx's reply is that man must eat to live, and his basic activity is thus the production or procuring of his means of subsistence. Marx here selected one of man's wants, the need for food, and made it the basis for his theory. The procedure of taking one element in man's make-up and basing an entire system upon it has been a common practice in the history of thought. Aristotle builds upon the fact that man is a social animal, St. Paul and Calvin upon man's sinfulness, Hobbes upon the overwhelming desire for security, and the economist upon man's acquisitiveness; the last is not far from Helvetius, who argued that man's vices and lusts are the mainsprings of progress.[6] To assert the biological truism that man must eat to live, this of itself explains nothing about man's varied history. Marx at least saw and avoided the worst pitfalls of this kind of explanation, by concentrating attention not upon the constant biological need but upon the varying economic and social expression of the need.

The processes or modes of production by which man secures his livelihood, and which constitute the economic foundation of every society, are said to be composed of three sets of factors:

The first is the natural resources available. The mere mention of these raises a difficulty, since physical resources have been much the same for any given place for long periods of history during which tremendous social changes have occurred. But in a more meaningful sense they have not been the same, for the availability

6. Engels did indeed argue that greed and the lust for power are 'the levers of historical development.' *Selected Works*, 1942, I, p. 447. In *German Ideology* Marx and Engels wrote: '[Men] begin to differentiate themselves from animals as soon as they begin to *produce* their means of subsistence . . .' *Handbook*, p. 211. Engels discoursed, without saying very much, 'On the part played by Labour in the transition from ape to man.' *Selected Works*, 1951, II, pp. 74ff.

of materials and resources depends more than anything else upon man's knowledge, especially on his scientific or technical knowledge. The resources available to the modern American, for instance, are vastly more numerous and varied than those available to the Red Indian who inhabited the same physical terrain. Marx, however, did not explain how the growth of man's knowledge comes about — it is something that was taken for granted, as emerging more or less automatically from the activities of production.

The second factor is the techniques of production, the tools and instruments used. Here the same difficulty applies as in the case of the resources, for the nature of the tools used depends largely upon knowledge. Marx treated this in the same way and took as given the fact that technological improvements occur. Emphasis upon tools and inventions alone leads to a purely technological interpretation of history and although there are glimpses of something suspiciously near this in Marx, on the whole he avoided it. Nor did he accept an explanation based on climate or geography, since these are relatively constant factors and cannot therefore explain the more rapid social changes, and, in addition, such an explanation would contradict his theory by subordinating the economic to the physical as the prime mover in history.

The third factor is less clear, and was sometimes omitted by Marx: how the work of production is organized. By this he meant man's working relations with his fellows — for example, whether he works alone or in a family unit, or as a member of a guild, or whether there is division of labor in factories. It may be taken to mean one or both of the following: (a) the forms of work organization, which are in such close relation to technology that they are determined by the materials and tools used, or (b) simply the labor applied to the resources and tools. Engels counted even 'race' as an element in the modes of production.

Since the modes of production are at the very root of the theory, unless Marxists are clear on what they mean by them the rest of the theory is bound to suffer from vagueness and confusion. Any critical reading of Marxist literature shows that the meaning of this key phrase is seldom definite or constant, but changes according to the context so that Marxists, like Humpty Dumpty, make the words mean whatever they choose. This shifting of the ground of argument puts any critic at a great disadvantage, and also stirs the suspicion that Marx's theory was not clear even in his own mind.

Marx himself summarized his theory thus: 'the mode of production in material life determines the social, political and intellectual life processes in general'; and speaking of production, said 'this one historical fact is the fundamental determinant of all history.' At times he listed the three ingredients as purposive labor activity, subject matter (materials), and the instruments. Sometimes, however, the meaning was broadened to include the methods of exchange and the means of transport, which vary according to whether production is for one's own needs or for the market.[7] Marx can be regarded as listing what are called in economics the factors of production. Whereas these have usually been given as land, labor, capital (sometimes with entrepreneurship added), Marx gives them as resources, techniques, and labor. He ignored the entrepreneurial function, and seemed usually to include capital among materials.

Stalin defined the modes of production in a rather different way, as (a) the instruments or tools of production, (b) people, and (c) labor skill, and said that they might all be summed up as the relations of man to nature.[8]

The greatest ambiguity of all in this essential phrase has already been mentioned: where are we to put knowledge, science, technology, labor skills — among the modes of production or in the superstructure? If we put them among the former as they ought to be, and as Marx sometimes put them, since scientific knowledge is obviously one of the forces of production, then the unique point of Marxist theory disappears. Marx's fundamental law may then be reduced to the statement that history is made by mankind working with nature. However true this may be, it is certainly not what Marxists usually think they mean. On the other hand, to put science in the strictly determined superstructure, as Marx and Engels sometimes put it, ignores the truth that the materials and

7. *Selected Works*, 1942, I, p. 357; *Capital* (Everyman's), I, p. 170. Cf. also T. A. Jackson, op. cit. p. 215; and V. Venable, *Human Nature: The Marxian View*, New York, 1945, pp. 88ff.

8. *Leninism*, p. 421.

tools depend for the most part on knowledge.[9] The very foundation of the Marxist theory is sapped by this uncertainty, and hence
Marxism can mean different things to different people, just as it
meant different things to Marx himself at different times. Most
expositions of Marx are thus forced to make his theories appear
more consistent and intelligible than they really were.

Now the modes of production as an independent variable, however they may be defined, clearly constitute not a single factor but
a complex of factors. Can the origin of change be narrowed down
a little further, or do all three (if there are only three) of the com-
ponents in the modes of production change simultaneously? Most
of the time Marx seemed scarcely to concern himself about where
within the modes of production the initial changes take place.
Stalin was more definite: while noting that other features such
as the geographic environment are important, he found they were
not 'determining,' but that within the productive forces the
changes occur in the first place in the instruments of production.
He then went on to give a purely technological account of history,
showing in a grossly simplified and almost certainly inaccurate
schema how the supposedly four hitherto existing types of social
structure — primitive, slavery, feudal, bourgeois — correspond to
the development of the tools or instruments used.[10] The fifth and
final form is to be the classless society, after which changes in technology will not presumably lead to any changes in the social structure.

This kind of speculation has a certain limited usefulness if carefully applied by the archaeologist, but it is not possible to grant
that only four types of *social structure* have up to now existed. Nor
is civilization described merely by describing its tools, since this
leaves out all the interesting and vital variations between the
many civilizations that have existed at the same level of productive techniques. Not only does an emphasis on tools fail to give any
invariable law of historical change, but also it is not easy to reconcile a purely technological interpretation of history with the more
usual Marxist analysis.

9. Cf. *Selected Correspondence*, p. 517.
10. *Leninism*, pp. 421–9.

In the end, then, it comes to this: the forces of production, never clearly defined, are said to determine both the course of history and the entire superstructure of society. In no sense is this an *ultimate* explanation, since how changes occur in the independent variable is as much a mystery as ever. But since the weary mind must somewhere come to rest, Marx took his stand upon spontaneous changes in the elusive modes of production. They are the mysterious self-supported tortoise holding up society and carrying history along on its back. Taking for granted a change in the independent variable, Marxism then consists in showing — more often in merely asserting — that history and society are shaped by a change occurring anywhere with the complex of factors that comprise the modes of production.

III

Historical change is said to come about, then, because of an alteration occurring first in the vaguely defined modes or methods of production. But just how *does* an initial change exercise its effect in diverting the course of history?

To try to trace the sequence of events we must recall that, in Marx's view, to any particular set of the modes of production there correspond appropriate property relations: 'relations of production correspond to a different stage of development of material forces of production.' The modes of production may be regarded as mainly technological and expressive of the relations of man with nature; yet production is at the same time a social affair and therefore brings man into relation with man; and of these social relations Marx considered almost exclusively that based on property. Stalin apparently believed that all social relations may be divided into three types — mutual, exploitive, and transitional.[11] The property relations are in short a matter of ownership of the tools and other means of production. Ownership is of great importance to Marx's theory, since it was here as well as in the productive techniques that he located the difference between capitalism and preceding societies (although private ownership of the means of production did not come into the world for the first time with

11. Loc. cit.

capitalism). The property relations of ownership are said to determine the distribution of the social product as income, and hence the entire social structure.

The relationship between the modes of production and the property relations, or 'conditions' of production, is often obscure in Marx. If the modes alone form the economic foundation or substructure we may ask the question: can two different social systems exist with substantially the same modes of production? The answer would seem to be yes, if the modes are defined as mainly technology, as they usually are. Despite similar techniques of production, slave societies have varied widely; serfdom in Russia was greatly different from serfdom in western Europe, and slavery and serfdom themselves, although quite different social systems, displayed sometimes no great differences in production techniques. It is impossible to point out any changing techniques of production which by a dialectical conflict with the property relations brought about the change from Roman slavery to Western feudalism. Similarly today, Soviet society and Western society rest upon almost identical modes of production, at least on their technical side. The conveyor belt is mass production wherever it may be found. The Marxist would doubtless comment here that the property relations in the Western world are unstable and transitional and are bound to fall into the Soviet pattern in time. In due course, he would say, the modes of production must determine the property relations. This may or may not prove to be true for the future, but the experience of the past gives no plain proof that such a determinate relationship exists.

In any case, the Marxist reply quite distorts the order of events. In the Soviet Union there was no prior industrial and technological development which forced public ownership upon the authorities. It was exactly the other way around: political power was seized by the Bolshevik Party, which abolished private ownership of such industry as existed, and then proceeded deliberately to industrialize and modernize a backward peasant economy. The Soviet Union thus affords only evidence against the Marxist thesis of economic and technological development determining the property (ownership) relations.

There is much obscurity in these 'relations of production' which are so vital to Marx's theory, and the more Marx wrote about them, the more he obscured his meaning, if indeed he ever knew what he meant by the phrase. Some social relations of production are fairly clear. A factory is organized in a certain way: there are managers, foremen, skilled and unskilled laborers. Each person has his task in the division of labor, and the tasks will change as the factory changes its machinery or its product. There is no conflict between methods of production and these particular social relations, since the latter are always adapted to the technology.

Social relations of production, in another sense, may be legal relations. Thus the factory may be owned by the state, by consumer co-operatives, by a trade union, by a single entrepreneur, by a number of scattered shareholders, or in other ways. But as we have seen, the techniques or methods of production do not necessarily determine the legal forms of ownership. Marx could give his theory plausibility by confusing social relations, as in a factory, with property relations, which are not properly speaking economic at all, but legal.

It is now time to express the theory in dialectical terms — which by strict Marxist theory is the only way it ought to be expressed. In order that there should be any parallel with the Hegelian dialectic, or with the Marxist dialectic applied to nature, the operative conflict should be found wholly within the economic foundation. How economic forces conflict and synthesize, and thus make history, is what Marx set out to demonstrate. *But this is not what he puts before us.*

As soon as we begin to study Marx we are at once struck by the fact that he applied the terms of the dialectic to history in several different ways. There is something of the same vagueness and straining of language that were noted in Chapter 2 whenever the dialectic was applied to nature. Thus, he spoke of wealth and the proletariat, or of poverty and private property, as antithesis; or of the conflict between the economic foundation and the whole of the superstructure. But in the main it appears that the really operative conflict was taken to be that between methods of production and *property relations*. In the case of capitalism, the forces of production conflict with private ownership. In Marx's own words: 'the modern productive forces and the bourgeois productive [legal] forms come into collision with one another.' [12] Later Marxists such as Stalin put the matter in substantially the same words. This, then, is the core of Marxism — the great dialectical contradiction which is counted upon to bring about the downfall of capitalism. Although it is a wholly different theory from the inverted Hegelianism with which Marx started, it is intelligible, and certainly what Marx most often adhered to.

One objection to it is this: how much do such abstractions as forces, forms, and relations actually conflict? They are not like the forces of wind and tide found in nature, since all social forces must act through the medium of persons. Marx's reply was that they act through social classes, through the medium of the class struggle. May not the human agent fail to respond automatically and so alter the conflict and its outcome? Marx hardly considered this objection at all. (Fuller treatment of the class-struggle theory is undertaken in Chapter 4.)

A second objection arises from an additional meaning that is given to modes of production. Normally this phrase is used to cover *techniques* of production but sometimes the meaning is that of productive potential, or capacity for output, and even in some cases the output itself. Engels approached this when he said, 'the expansion of the market cannot keep pace with the expansion of production . . .' and spoke of 'the mode of production rebelling against the mode of exchange,' as in the slump stage of the trade cycle, expressing some mystification about how recovery from a slump could occur.[13] All that the famous dialectical conflict comes down to for many Marxists is that under capitalism all productive equipment is not used to full capacity at all times, notably in times of trade depression. Marxist scientists think of the conflict in much the same terms, so that science is said to be 'frustrated' because every one of its countless inventions is not put to use immediately, regardless of capital requirements, priorities, obsolescence, or any of the other difficulties which any kind of economic system must meet and deal with.[14]

12. *Selected Works,* 1942, II, p. 299. M. Beer, in *The Life and Teaching of Karl Marx,* London, 1929, p. 23, put it rather differently: the thesis is private property, the antithesis is capitalism, and the synthesis is common ownership.
13. *Selected Works,* 1942, I, pp. 175, 188. *Selected Correspondence,* p. 116.
14. Hall, Soddy, Bernal, et al., *The Frustration of Science,* London, 1935.

Marx was equally indefinite when he was discussing the derivation of the whole social superstructure of society from the economic foundation. At times, for instance, he put the property relations in the basement with the economic foundation; at other times in the attic with the rest of the superstructure; and at still others he envisaged them as separate connecting links, as when he noted the three 'levels' in society — productive forces, productive relations, and ideologies. The latter observation is a shrewd one, and can almost be equated with the sociologist's classification of society into the technological basis, the social arrangements and organization, and the cultural life. Unfortunately for Marxism, however, this threefold classification does not fit into a dialectical pattern.

IV

To give a precise meaning to the word 'economic' is seldom easy. Marx made his attempt to do so impossibly difficult because he did not even keep to a *fixed* meaning.

Given the economic foundation, with or without property relations, what is meant by the key word *determines* in Marx's axiom that the economic foundation determines the superstructure of society and the course of history? If it is taken in its ordinary sense, then Marx was an economic determinist, hotly as Marxists may deny it. Without economic determinism no Marxist law of necessity can be found in history. The point is of crucial importance to Marxism and must therefore be further scrutinized.

Do the methods of production actually determine the course of history and all the way of life of society, whether dialectically or otherwise? If this question is put directly, Marxism answers both yes and no. Instances have already been given to confirm the strict determinist view of institutions as that held by both Marx and Engels, the former going so far as to write of religion as 'but the reflections of the real world.' [15] And by 'real' in this context Engels meant the world of economic forces.

If Marx were right, then to one economic foundation there

15. *Capital*, I, p. 54; and Engels, *Handbook*, p. 299.

would correspond one religion, which would be replaced as the economic foundation changed. To make a plausible case Marxists often assert that Roman Catholicism corresponds to feudalism, Protestantism to capitalism. But to what should we equate the Jewish, the Islamic, the Buddhist, and other faiths? How account for the fact that Roman Catholicism has flourished on all three of the methods of production which Marxists designate? Or that Protestantism should begin, and thrive, in semi-feudal Germany? Or that when France and some other countries became capitalist they did not become Protestant?

The Marxist often makes a fetish of this derivation from the economic, in the same way that a dogmatic Freudian might reduce everything to the sex impulse, or another person might try to deduce all a nation's culture from its climate or geography. In each case the mistake is made of riding too hard the hobby-horse of a one-factor explanation, or giving a too intensive application of an often useful and suggestive line of thought. Newton's laws, we are told, were demanded by the economic needs of the seventeenth century and so they were thereupon discovered. Plekhanov argued that in primitive society art is directly influenced by the prevalent techniques of production, as when the Bushmen of Australia imitate in their dancing their methods of hunting and food-gathering.[16] There is some broad truth in this; it would be remarkable if art were not influenced by methods of food-getting in primitive society. But influence is one thing, strict determinism is another; and as a culture becomes more complex, even the *influence* of the means of producing food becomes more remote and uncertain. How explain the minuet in eighteenth-century France? The strangely unhelpful answer given by Plekhanov was that, since France was a class society, the minuet 'expressed the psychology of a non-productive class,' and 'thus the economic is still predominant.' The low stage of development of the Red Indians in North America he accounted for by the absence of animals capable of being domesticated — a dubious proposition, which, even if it were true, is a very odd version of Marxism.[17] Plekhanov

16. *Fundamental Problems of Marxism,* pp. 61ff.
17. Ibid.

and Marx seemed to imagine there was something uniquely Marxist about the fact that the invention of a new firearm modifies the art of war.

> There are some Marxists who cannot see a flapper use her lipstick without producing pat an explanation of her conduct in terms of the powers of production and the class struggle.[18]

On the other hand, Engels in his old age was aware of the untenability of the extreme view, and several times warned against the possibility of exaggerating the importance of the economic element. 'Marx and I,' he wrote, 'are ourselves partly to blame for the fact that younger writers sometimes lay more stress on the economic side than is due it,' and he also spoke of 'the most wonderful rubbish produced by recent Marxists,' and said that 'it would surely be pedantic to try and find economic causes for all this primitive nonsense [i.e. primitive religion].'[19] Similarly, a contemporary Marxist takes Plekhanov to task for his determinism by denouncing him as 'a polemical vulgarizer,' 'a dangerous distorter' whose work is 'riddled with mechanist fallacies.'[20]

So we have an apparent retreat from the earlier strict determinism, a denial that the economic is the *sole* determining factor — whatever that may mean — and are told that only 'ultimately,' 'basically,' 'on the whole,' or 'in the last instance' does the economic foundation determine the superstructure and the course of history. There is a frequent use of such vague terms in Marxist literature.

There is no way of telling what 'ultimately' means; does it refer to underlying motives, or is it last in terms of time? Either other influences and forces play their part in shaping society and history or they do not, and, if they do, there is no determinism — dialectical or any other variety — by the single economic factor. At the very least 'in the last instance' means that the causal or functional relationship between the economic and the rest may be indirect and complex, uncertain, often not measurable or even discernible.

18. G. D. H. Cole, *The Meaning of Marxism*, London, 1950, p. 48.
19. *Selected Correspondence*, pp. 477, 482.
20. Jack Lindsay, op. cit. pp. 185-7.

If that is the case, then iron laws must dwindle into tendencies. It is often useful to have such statements of tendencies (as in the Malthusian theory), providing we do not claim too much for them, and providing we also recognize other, and often conflicting, tendencies. But a tendency is too inconclusive to serve as a guide for safe prediction and gives no rule of necessity in society or history — a familiar fact which is the despair of every social scientist.

In brief, as we may see from the later writings of Engels, common sense keeps breaking in, and although this makes Marx's theory more realistic and subtle, it also dilutes it until all sense of rigid law vanishes and we are left with conditional and tentative statements.

Many makers of theories have, in their more considered afterthoughts, modified or even contradicted their first exuberant theses. Charles Beard gave the impression in his early book, *An Economic Interpretation of the Constitution,* that the interests of the men of property (i.e. roughly economic causes) were all that mattered in 1789 in the shaping of the United States Constitution, but later he came to allow for other influences as well. Both Marx and Engels, however, in spite of some later toning down of economic influences, always came back to the determining nature of the methods of production, and argued: (a) although on the surface other influences seem to count, yet underneath it is the economic that is really effective; and (b) these other influences — legal, political, cultural, and so on — may possibly have weight if they are moving in the same direction as the economic forces, but they cannot avail if they go against the stream.[21]

Sometimes we are told to dismiss the causal relation. Marxists despise cause and effect; it is 'mechanical,' or an abstraction — a curious criticism in a system that employs such an abstraction as the dialectic. We are invited instead to think of the relation as one where the ideology '*tends* to reflect' the economic conditions. Again this is too broad, and reduces the economic to merely one among a number of influences. We are never given an explanation of how it comes about that with the same kind of methods of production quite different ideologies may flourish, or *how* the economic forces

21. Engels, *Handbook,* p. 277.

give rise to systems of ideas. Engels, for instance, noted vaguely that juridical, philosophical, and religious ideas may be *the more or less remote offshoots* of the economic relations prevailing in a given society.' [22] (My italics.)

Moreover, if the causal relation is ignored, there remains the logical difficulty of whether a dialectical interaction may not give a quite unpredictable synthesis. As noted in Chapter 2, such a result is logically quite in accordance with the dialectic but makes nonsense of the claim that the result of the interaction can be predicted. It is hard to see how one can predict a novelty.

This unresolved dualism, this attempt to have the best of both worlds of strict determinism and free will, which was found in Marx's account of the relation between mind and matter, between economic self-interest and other motives, lies here too, at the very center of the Marxist theory of history: how much importance is to be attributed to the loosely defined economic foundation and how much to the elements in the superstructure, including the power of ideas? Engels several times warned against ignoring the interaction of factors, and allowed that political power and law react back upon the economic 'to a considerable extent'; and Stalin noted that ideas are 'significant and important.' [23] But this is merely to state the obvious and, in deriving an iron law of history and society, it is ignored in favor of the overriding influence of the economic. After all, it was upon what he believed to be purely economic forces, as expressed in the class struggle, that Marx relied for a guarantee of the collapse of capitalism.

Nowadays the world is well aware of the power of ideas to influence conduct, especially when the ideas are summed up in a constantly publicized slogan or symbol. The whole art of propaganda and advertising is based upon such knowledge and techniques. Hitler was able to move masses of men to action by an astute manipulation of propaganda. Marxists, too, are fully preoccupied with ideas, as shown by their attacks upon 'false' concepts, errors, deviations, and so on; by the importance they attach to propaganda within the Soviet Union, and by their care to shield the Soviet masses from contact with disturbing ideas from the outside

22. *Selected Works*, 1942, I, p. 415.
23. *Leninism*, p. 417.

world. Marxist actions thus plainly belie the determinist theory of history which they persist in asserting.

When they are forced back from the untenable view of a strict determination of the rest of society by the methods of production, Marxists often end up in a tautology. By widening the methods of production to mean the 'material conditions of life,' and by including in the latter the methods of production, transport, ownership, income-distribution, and the whole complex of economic and social life, and by allowing as well for the interaction of ideas and the influence of man, the argument comes down to this: society, or history, is determined by everything in it. In his early work, *The Holy Family*, Marx wrote in precisely that vein: 'History is nothing but the activity of man in pursuit of his ends.'

V

When stated in the extreme form of the primacy of productive forces and the purely derivative nature of the rest of society, the Marxist thesis has, without question, been pushed beyond its proper limits. Yet something of value remains and it is important to notice this if we are to understand the appeal of Marxism, and its effect upon the world of ideas. The remainder of this chapter will assess those elements of partial truth in Marx's theory of history.

First, then, despite the exuberant distortions of Marxists, it is perhaps to Marx more than to any other person that we owe today our commonplace acceptance of the fact that economic influences extend in many devious ways throughout society. So important and well recognized is the clue of the 'economic' (including sectional interests, technology, transport, materials, trade routes, the distribution of wealth, et cetera) that Plekhanov was largely right when he said that people 'act as materialists [i.e. realists] in their historical researches' and that 'bourgeois historians and sociologists explain things in terms of the Marxist outlook.' [24] By following the clue of economic changes we can often see more clearly the problems and questions that confronted our ancestors at different times. In tracing the decline of feudalism, for instance, one must

24. Plekhanov, op. cit. pp. 59ff.

take into account the repercussions of such broad economic changes as the growth of trade and medieval towns. Similarly, attention to the economic changes taking place enlightens our understanding of the Renaissance, the rise of the modern nation-state, the American Revolution, the settlement of western Canada, and many other historical processes. It does not always work so well as in the examples just given, and by itself is rarely, if ever, sufficient. Nevertheless the concept is a penetrating one, and our understanding of historical change is enlarged by it. Non-Marxists as well as Marxists have spoken of the sense of enlightenment which it brings. It is the concept of economic history, and when all the rest of Marx's theory is forgotten he may well be remembered because he deepened and enlarged our sense of history.

In the same way, a consideration of the economic forces at work also throws a flood of light upon the institutions and ideas associated with modern democracy. Even a cursory glance at legislation, everyday customs, business practices, and the platforms of political parties will show them to be closely related to the facts of industrialism, mass production, and a mixture of private and public ownership. Indeed, if the elements in the superstructure are to have any relation to everyday life at all they must be related to one another and to the way in which the economy of the country is carried on.

Marx was thus astute enough in saying that if we want to understand an epoch, then to look no further than the 'ideology' (in the Marxist sense of the word) is like judging a person by what he thinks of himself. Such a concession is dangerous for the Marxist case, however, since if the ideology is a mere reflection of the economic, then we certainly ought to be able to deduce a true picture of society from the ideology alone. It is perhaps because he noticed this discrepancy that Lenin remarked that social consciousness gives only 'an approximate copy' of social being.

By 'ideology' Marxists usually mean the set of ideas and values put forward by a class in defense of its economic interest; while the real reason, the furthering of the interest itself, remains below the conscious level. In Engels' words: 'The real motives impelling him [the thinker] remain unknown to him, otherwise it would not be an ideological process at all.' Rationalization is the modern

equivalent of this usage. Lenin used the word ideologist in a different sense, as 'theoretician' or 'conscious leader.' [25]

More commonly today, however — and this is perhaps the best
meaning — the word means almost the same thing as a creed, that
is, a system of beliefs corresponding to and supporting a certain
type of conduct or institution, as in the ideology of Fascism, of
capitalism, or of democracy.

Even if economic influences alone are taken into account, any
existing ideology is a compound of 'reflections' of both past and
present economic factors. The American ideology of the present
day, for instance, forms a rich mixture of many ingredients including those based upon (a) the conditions of economic life in the
nineteenth century and earlier, upon small-scale and competitive
industry, the dominance of agriculture, and the western frontier;
and (b) the different twentieth-century economic order with its
mass production, trust busting, the New Deal, T.V.A., the Employment Act of 1946, the relative decline of agriculture, the rise
of organized labor, military preparedness, and a lengthening list
of similar factors. If an ideology 'reflects' the economy at all, it is
much more like a photographic negative on which a number of
images have been superimposed, so that the picture is blurred and
not closely like any single object in the real world.

It is equally true that any ideology is much more a reaction to
the *whole* environment, including geography, climate, and the
forces of nature; the facts of life and death; the historical tradition
(which Engels, like Henry Ford, called 'bunk'), the cultural inheritance of religion, philosophy, literature, and so on. In the
impressive body of modern law, for example, some of its content
is clearly recent, while some of it derives from Roman law, and
incorporates elements picked up along the centuries. The Greeks
and Romans had almost every possible form of government and
religion, resting upon the same kind of modes of production. The
greater a philosophy or work of art, the less it is dated by being
relevant only to one particular period; Greek philosophy, drama,
and sculpture are 'not of an age, but for all time.' Engels himself
had an inkling of this when he gave the entire Marxist case away

25. Engels, *Selected Correspondence,* p. 511. Lenin, *The Iskra Period,* New
York, 1932, I, p. 67.

by remarking that since ideas are the basis of philosophy, 'economically backward countries can still play first fiddle in philosophy.' [26] This sort of remark can only be regarded as an indirect defense of Hegel's dialectic and of German philosophy in general.

Marx's point of a determinate ideology also begs the question whether there is, at any one time, a single dominant ideology forming a coherent system. Only in totalitarian societies is there likely to be a single ideology. The mental life of any free society seems to be a mosaic of ideologies or sets of beliefs. Perhaps we may sometimes be able to say of a given age that there is a certain unity or affinity of economic, social, artistic, philosophic, and other assumptions, all interacting, so that no one part can be understood without reference to every other part. It is in this sense perhaps that Hegel spoke of a State as a totality, or that we speak of the Age of Enlightenment or the Victorian Age. Yet it is at the most a rough and oversimplified way of describing a culture, and the more one examines such an Age, the more diverse do the strands of thought appear, so that we begin to suspect that it is ourselves, with the advantages of hindsight, who impose unity upon a past historical period. And our suspicion is amply confirmed the more countries we examine of any particular period.

VI

Although men make their own history, it is largely from Marx that we have received the idea that they make it within limits at any given period. In Marx's words:

> Therefore mankind always sets itself only such tasks as it can solve; since looking at the matter more closely, we will always find that the task itself arises only when the material conditions necessary for its solution already exist or are at least in the process of formation.[27]

There is much ambiguity in this: opinions obviously differ on what *are* the problems, or needs, of any one time, or whether they have been solved, or met; and Stalin carried it to an extreme

26. *Selected Correspondence*, p. 483.
27. *Selected Works*, 1942, I, p. 357.

which is certainly false when he said that new *ideas* arise only when new tasks are set for society. Yet what Marx has done — and he must be given credit for it — is to emphasize that the practical limits of any historical choice are set by, among other things, the techniques of production.

Marxism gives no explanation of how or why the reformer or a new idea may arise. Thought is free, and may range the universe of both the real and the imaginary. Utopias widely different from the existing order may be constructed, although they will always bear traces of their origin. Despite this freedom of thought, some of the major problems and questions of an age are of general concern, and only some ideas and reforms are relevant. The others are barren of social results for the time being, although they may eventually come into their own when the material conditions of society have been changed appropriately.

The history of science provides examples of this. Electricity was known to the Greeks, but merely as a toy, and its practical use had to wait upon a different set of circumstances and many other discoveries — for example, in metal-working. Much the same may be said of the principle of the steam engine. Social history, too, is rich in examples of relevant and irrelevant proposals for change. Humanitarians of ancient time urged the abolition of slavery, but were ineffectual so long as slave labor was regarded as necessary to the economy; the taking of interest was condemned by the church in the Middle Ages and yet was accepted when it became necessary for production and trade; education rapidly percolated to the masses when a skilled and literate working class was required to operate modern industry.

A contemporary illustration of the same principle may be drawn from international politics. Many in the past have dreamed of world government, but until now there has been neither the technical means of easily administering such a government nor a sense of urgency powerful enough to compel the surrender of ancient prejudices and interests. With modern transport and communications available on the one hand, and the threat of scientific annihilation on the other, world government has today become possible and perhaps necessary if mankind is to survive. It does not follow, however, that world government or any other means of maintaining world peace is inevitable. Even when faced with a commonly acknowledged problem mankind is not certain to solve it. Man is not altogether good or rational, and there are many signs that destruction may be preferred to drastic change.

Engels sensed the historical irrelevance of some proposals for change when he ridiculed the view that 'if Richard Coeur de Lion and Philip Augustus had introduced free trade instead of getting mixed up in the Crusades we should have been spared five hundred years of misery and stupidity.' [28] His argument is merely a more roundabout way of saying that ideas usually get accepted only 'when the time is ripe,' or when they fit into 'the logic of events.' It reminds us that great men in public affairs often earn their title to greatness not so much because of qualities of character but because they see a little farther ahead than their contemporaries and fit into their times by setting themselves at the head of powerful and expanding movements in society. It reminds us, too, that only in a certain type of social milieu will individual initiative flourish and innovations be welcomed. The argument here, however, goes much beyond the confines of Marxism and takes into account all the factors in the total social situation without limiting itself to the economic; nor is it as narrow and fatalistic as Engels' view, borrowed from Hegel, that great men are merely the instruments of impersonal economic forces.

A sense of the economic and social limits to our immediate action also reminds us that it is of little use to sigh for the past as Carlyle, William Morris, or Eric Gill did. We must accept the fact that the kind of society we want can only *start* by being a modification of the present, which we have inherited and with which we must work. We need not be unduly disturbed about this, since the choices before us are still wide and real. The area in which free decision may operate at any one moment may be circumscribed, but small frequent shifts in direction can in time lead to quite different goals. Man is not traveling along a railway track from which he cannot stray, and which leads to a known destination, but along a forest trail which he has to hew out for himself as he travels, and the direction of which he may choose according to the goals he sets for himself from time to time.

28. *Selected Correspondence,* p. 512.

VII

When the absurd extremes of Marxism are discounted, there remains a useful reminder that man is shaped, as every sociologist well knows, by his social heritage as well as by his genetic heritage. A change of personal outlook is not in itself enough if we are to build a good society; the social environment must also be changed. Calling the individual sinner to repentance may be useful for his soul's sake, but the reformers who concentrate on changing the environment at the same time are engaged in work that is usually more effective. It is no use to try, as the Buchmanites do, to reduce the problems of society to problems of personal reform only. Society, and not only the individual, must be adjusted: a proposition that is surely obvious when we contemplate our present distracted age.

Again, the Marxist account of historical change appears even better than it actually is by contrast with other varieties on the market in Marx's day. Marx's explanation was to some extent a reaction against other views — such as the Great Men theory of history, or explanations in terms of the Divine Will, or of Chance and Fortune. The approach of the great Italian scholar Vico had been more realistic, but even he had shed little light when he classified history into three stages, savagery, barbarism, and civilization. Hegel's version of history as the unfolding history of ideas (or of the Absolute Idea); Montesquieu's theory of the relation of history to climate and racial habits; Comte's metaphysical concept of 'destiny'; explanations couched in terms of a search for political power or the influence of sea power upon history — none of these has approached the value of the Marxist account. Marx therefore may justly be regarded as overstating a fruitful hypothesis at a time when overstatement was needed to impress an age preoccupied with more fanciful and less satisfactory theories.

Nor are Marx's views as disastrous for mankind as the so-called 'racial' theories which profess to trace everything to some mysterious entity called 'blood' or 'national character.' And here for the good of our souls we should remember that it was not only the Nazis who turned their backs on sense and common humanity;

there are dangerous trends of the same kind of thought in every nation: in the Frenchman Gobineau, the Anglo-German Houston Chamberlain, or the American Madison Grant. Every time we fail to blush for instances of racial prejudice and mistreatment in England, the United States, Canada, or South Africa, we should recall that the road is a very short one from a hardened conscience to active support for an indigenous Hitler.

Neither is a serious rival to Marxism to be found in some psychological theories which profess to explain the origin of institutions and their history by reference to so-called constant and fundamental instincts of 'human nature.' Since all men are biologically alike and always have been, as far back as the records of history go, man's unchanging nature is obviously not enough to explain his varied history.

VIII

To acknowledge that in Marx's account of history there is an element of truth is one thing; to elevate it into the whole truth is another. The other side of the story is that men make their history; the economic limits, like all limits, whether set by physical nature or by our fixed ideas, merely say what can*not* be done; and all limits, in time, are almost infinitely elastic. The one kind of economic foundation can support quite different superstructures; the foundation does not create the building or the type and quality of life which is lived inside it. To use a different figure of speech, the economic basis of society may be compared to a field which may be put to many different uses. The soil may be the basis, but in the same soil many kinds of trees and crops may be grown.[29]

Societies, too, may exist with the same techniques of production but with widely differing social and cultural patterns. We know, for example, that industrial society is not identical in all countries. It may be Catholic or Protestant or Jewish or Hindu; ruthless or humanitarian; a friend to democracy, civil liberties, and the pursuit of truth, or as hostile as Soviet Russia or Franco's Spain. In the same way, although it may be said that marriage and the family

29. Karl Federn, *The Materialist Conception of History*, London, 1939, p. 100.

rest upon a biological foundation, the social institution of the family, the cultural superstructure, varies widely from one society to another.

The obvious truth of all this might give some theoretical grounds for supposing that communism, like capitalism, may vary from one country to another. Stalin once said (in another context) that 'everything depends on the condition, time and place.'[30] That is to say, the nature of communist rule may depend upon whether communism comes gradually or suddenly, whether it is introduced into a backward country or into an industrialized state, whether among people firmly attached to the democratic tradition or among people to whom repression, arbitrary authority, and the secret police are accepted as normal features of the environment; and above all whether it comes under Soviet aegis or as an indigenous movement. This point has some practical relevance today, since there are already signs that Tito is trying to build a communist society in Yugoslavia that differs in some respects from the Moscow plan; and the same divergence might occur even in China some-day, if Soviet policy should repeat its Yugoslav blunder, and if Western policy should be flexible enough to take advantage of it. (It is only proper, however, to add that the communist countries have as yet given us little reason to believe that they can diverge far from the Russian model, or that any form of communism could be tolerable to anyone who deeply cherishes personal liberty.)

All of which is to say that there is no determinism, dialectical or other, so long as men are not slot machines. Marx fell into an ancient error, and confused the notion of necessary conditions with prime or efficient cause. Windows may be essential for lighting a room, but they are not the sun or the cause of the light. Opportunity is never the same thing as a determining cause. Even if we assume — and this is true only in the very short run — that methods of production must be taken as given, like the natural environment, it is nevertheless the purposes man sets for himself and the response he makes to the circumstances that are the stuff of history. In summary then, Marx has elevated an important and universal aspect of all society — the economic, or how goods and services are produced — to the status of the aspect that is always

30. *Leninism*, p. 411.

and everywhere dominant. Engels called the economic 'a red thread' running through history. But history has as many red threads as we choose to select.

IX

Finally, it will be recalled from the discussion above that the dynamic of historical change is said by Marx to lie in the modes of production; but the property relations and the rest of the superstructure lag behind, confining and hampering the productive forces. The modes of production will have their way, and will burst the old property relations by violence, since 'with the change of the economic foundation the entire immense superstructure is more or less rapidly transformed.' [31]

Now, if we strip all this of dialectical jargon and the notion of inevitability, and express it in a tentative fashion, there is again some truth here. The idea of a kind of cultural and social lag is a familiar and pregnant one, and the Marxist contention that 'the fatal disease of capitalist culture is the divorce of theory from practice' is only another way of expressing it. Technological and economic development may make some of our old ideas, institutions, and behavior irrelevant and even a hindrance to harmonious adjustments. The material foundations of society change faster than our other institutions nowadays, and very much faster than our ways of thinking, whatever the reasons for this may be. There is also some evidence that the rate of scientific and economic change may be accelerating. We tend therefore to think in the old terms when faced with a new situation, as when France in 1939 prepared the Maginot Line for a war like that of 1914; or when in an industrialized society we talk of American democracy in Jeffersonian concepts suitable only to a nation of self-sufficient farmers; or in a world which technology and the threat of destruction have made potentially one, we continue to wear the old national strait jackets.

Modern science and technology set loose a flood of changes upon the world, more especially with the Industrial Revolution, and we

31. Marx, loc. cit.

have only partly learned how to control these disruptive influences. We are, as it were, like an African tribe which by contact with the outside world has lost the coherence of its tribal traditions, and has not yet adjusted itself to a different way of life. So evident is this cultural and social lag that a state of dynamic disequilibrium or disorganization' is said to be characteristic of the age, and to present us with all our greatest problems.

But there is a great difference between this modern sociological approach and the Marxist formula. One is empirical and causal, the other dialectical and mystifying. To Marx, man is the product of society and society in turn is the product of the methods of production. To the sociologist, man is still the product of society (genetic inheritance apart) but in society the technological, institutional, and cultural are all functionally interdependent. Changes may be initiated at any point, and non-economic factors react powerfully upon the rest. The outcome of the interaction of factors in a complex society is on the whole indeterminate, so that within wide limits the future is open.[32]

We cannot rely upon intuition, or the ancient truths which time so often makes obsolete. A scientific study of man and society is the only way by which we may reach understanding of the processes at work, and so be in a position to control the direction in which we want them to go. If no control of the direction is undertaken, the outcome of certain 'trends' may perhaps be tentatively predicted for a very short distance ahead. The Marxist formula is not, however, a tentative hypothesis to be tested and modified, and it includes much more than the concept of equilibrium and social lag. We are given something comparable to the laws of nature: the dialectical tendencies working implacably in history 'with an iron necessity towards an inevitable goal.'[33] The role of non-economic forces, especially of conscious political control, must be severely limited if any such necessity is to be found in history. When Marxists speak of the reciprocal interaction between man and cul-

---

32. Cf. G. Myrdal, *An American Dilemma*, New York, 1944, p. 78: 'In an inter-dependent system of dynamic causation there is no "primary cause" but everything is cause *to* everything else.'

33. Marx, loc. cit.

ture, of the role of leadership, and of the power of old ideas to hamper and new ideas to promote the advancing economic forces, such concessions to realism deny the very economic determinism which is the unique feature of the Marxist theory of history.

Marx offers no explanation of why a social or cultural lag should exist, and if economic determinism is true it should not occur. He merely took it for granted that private ownership which at one time favored economic and technological development somehow becomes a 'fetter' upon the forces of production at a later time. From that he went on to assume that peaceable adjustment was impossible, but that instead a class struggle was being generated which could end only in open class warfare. The next chapter is concerned with the Marxist theory of class struggle.

The general tendency of capitalist production is not to raise, but to sink the average standard of wages.

Poverty grows as the accumulation of capital grows. What the bourgeoisie therefore produces, above all, are its own grave-diggers.

For almost forty years we have stressed the class struggle as the immediate driving force of history, and in particular the class struggle between the bourgeoisie and the proletariat, as the great lever of the modern social revolution; it is therefore impossible for us to co-operate with people who wish to expunge this class struggle from the movement.

MARX AND ENGELS.[1]

4

The Class Struggle

I

IN THE PRECEDING CHAPTER discussion was centered on the broad statement that economic forces determine the course of history. The discussion also covered the first two specific means by which, Marxism asserts, the economic forces work themselves out, namely:

1. that the modes of production constitute the foundation which determines the property relations and the whole of the superstructure; and

2. that independent changes arising in the modes of production lead in time to a bursting of the old property relations and the creation of new property relations and superstructure.

In treating these propositions we have at the same time tried to

1. Marx, *Selected Works,* 1942, I, p. 337; *Capital,* I, p. 714; *Communist Manifesto;* Engels, *Selected Correspondence,* p. 376.

appraise the elements of truth they contain. The third and fourth propositions must now be examined. These assert:

3. that the dialectic has operated in history through the medium of the struggle of economic classes, and

4. that under capitalism the class struggle is sharpening, and can end only in revolutionary victory for the proletariat, after which, in due course, there will follow the final synthesis of a communist society.

Two preliminary points may be made. One is that the dialectic is expressed in two ways — as the modes of production conflicting with property relations, and as a conflict of classes. Now these two dialectical conflicts need not logically be the same, and Marxist theory makes no attempt to reconcile them. Sometimes one is asserted, sometimes the other, but more often it is merely taken for granted that they are identical, that is, that the class struggle is the human or social expression of the conflict of economic forces. To be more accurate, it is, or should be, the conflict of economic forces with legal forms.

The second observation is that the class-struggle theory is not deducible from the earlier propositions; it is a quite separate assumption. It is logically possible that the shaping of history by economic forces, and even their dialectical expression, could have taken other forms, but Marx never doubted that the vehicle had been the class struggle.

The idea of a class struggle did not, as we know, originate with Marx. Many people before him had recognized its existence and many non-Marxists today subscribe to a modified version of the idea, at least in its application to some countries. But only Marx made it the mainspring of history. The *Communist Manifesto* proclaimed with great vigor that all history is the history of class struggles, and the truth of this was thereafter never called in question.

Engels later on asserted that the class struggle was true only of 'all written history,' and not of earlier primitive societies, which nineteenth-century anthropologists had recently informed him were communistic. The most notable of these anthropologists was L. H. Morgan, whose doctrines even today are held in high esteem by the Soviet orthodoxy. It is upon Morgan's work, first published

in 1877 in his book *Ancient Society,* that Marxists base their un-
shakable belief in a primitive communism, where all property was
held in communal ownership and the proceeds were distributed
according to need. The meaning of communism as merely common ownership and sharing of income is an old one. It is the type
of communism described in many utopias,. and is found today
in some small religious communities, and (sometimes) within the
family.

In glancing back over the past Marx noted in the Manifesto that
there had always been a number of classes:

> In ancient Rome we have patricians, knights, plebians, slaves;
> in the Middle Ages lords, vassals, guild-masters, journeymen,
> apprentices, serfs; in almost all of those classes, again, sub-
> ordinate gradations.

He also recognized a number of classes in nineteenth-century
France. How then could these complex class structures be fitted
into the simple opposition of thesis and antithesis which the dialectic requires? The answer is that all classes may be reduced to
two: exploiting and exploited, 'oppressor and oppressed.' But this
easy division explains nothing and is obviously a forcing of the
facts into a dialectical framework. There seems rarely to have been
a simple one-to-one relation between technology and class lines.
Sometimes a society with a simple technology has had a complex
class structure, sometimes a simple class structure.

Marx went on to make an incidental point of some interest. The
class struggle has always ended, he wrote, 'either in a revolutionary
reconstruction of society at large, or in common ruin.' The remark
is vague, but it would seem to follow that complete ruin could
logically be a successor to capitalism. Marx never again mentioned
this possibility, however, but adhered steadfastly to the more optimistic view, the inevitable victory of the proletariat.

Since all history is viewed only as a series of class struggles,
Marxists have ransacked the past to find examples of class warfare. There is hardly a war that has not been recast as a struggle
of classes, although it does not follow from Marx's own premise that
because economic changes are brought about through class struggle, therefore all wars have been class wars. It does not even follow

that the differences between classes must always show themselves in any kind of war. The trouble here for Marxism is, of course, that since all wars, of whatever kind — tribal, national, civil, religious — have had a definite influence, whether great or small, on subsequent events, then to admit that some wars are not class wars would come uncomfortably close to admitting that other things besides the class struggle have helped to shape the course of history. Alternatively, Marxists sometimes admit the existence of non-class wars but dismiss them as irrelevant or 'of no historical significance, as, for example, the Wars of the Roses in England, and this gives the more subtle modern Marxist view that only the turning points, the points of change in history, have been marked by class wars.

The interpretation of wars as examples of the class struggle sometimes works reasonably well, sometimes badly, but more often not at all. One thinks readily of the rebellion of Spartacus or of the Peasants' Revolt as possibly fair enough examples of class fighting, but no one would assert that these have been the commonest types of war, much less that they have been turning points in history, overthrowing one social order and setting up another in its place. They fade into insignificance by contrast with great imperial struggles such as the Punic Wars, which brought down the civilization of Carthage. Only by much distortion can one fit such events as the conquests of Alexander or the militant rise of Islam into the class-struggle pattern, or thus account for the Norman Conquest, the Hundred Years' War, or the great medieval struggle of Papacy versus Empire. To talk of splits within the ruling class explains nothing dialectically. Historians have been able to give illuminating accounts of these great movements, on normal historical evidence, without reference to any dialectical class struggle. The evidence bears out what we might expect, that the gradation of classes has been one of harmony as well as antagonism, since, after all, economic interest may be furthered by co-operation as well as by conflict; and when wars have occurred the divisions have, far more often than not, cut across class lines.

The class struggle as the means by which the dialectic has found social expression is a vital concept of Marxism. Sometimes, however, this theory is laid aside in favor of the wider and more plausible statement (examined in Chapter 3) that economic forces are dominant in history. Wars are thus sometimes explained by reference to the class struggle and, since that is often impossible, sometimes by wider reference to any kind of economic interest. In Marxism there are thus two explanations of wars, as of all historical change, the narrower basing itself on the class struggle, and the wider upon economic forces which may or may not take a class form. Lenin's theory of imperialist wars, as we shall see later in this chapter, is a combination of both.

The method in the wider economic approach, which distorts history rather less, is to look for the interests that benefited or hoped to benefit from the war, or to look at the consequences of the war, and then hold these up as the cause of the war. Its logic is like that of saying because the Marshall Plan was good for American business, therefore this was the reason for the Plan. Such was in fact the communist line on the Marshall Plan, on all plans for aid to underdeveloped countries, on the Korean War, and so forth.

The method singles out the economic aspect and makes it the controlling one. It is not difficult to do this, since war, like anything else, has its business or economic side; but one may also single out any other elements usually present in war, such as patriotism, ambition, frustration, or desire for national independence or expansion. The Marxist contention denies the efficacy of all non-economic influences. If another factor seems to have been dominant in a war, say a religious issue, the Marxist case is that although the war was fought in religious terms, the masses and perhaps even the leaders were deluded, and the real cause was nevertheless economic; and in this way the Crusades and the religious wars of the sixteenth century are stretched to provide examples.

Man does often rationalize his desires and finds good reasons for his actions, a fact we can appreciate much better than Marx, thanks to Freud's excavations into the unconscious. But it is scarcely true that all wars are merely rationalizations of economic interest, that there is a cunning about economic forces which has somehow insured that they have had their way in history. Rationalization is an extremely complex process, covering much more than economic or class interest; and even when all interests are allowed for, it does not follow that systems of thought — religious, political, or whatever they may be — consist only or even mainly of rationalizations. Each case of alleged rationalization, particularly when it is said to constitute an ideology — say, as in the Crusades or in the later religious wars — must be examined on its merits, and not prejudged as in the Marxist formula.

A more serious criticism arises. In every war, as in all historical events, a number of causes and forces have been at work, non-economic as well as economic. If two or more causes are present and necessary, then there is no 'primary' cause that was 'determining'; and although no doubt an order of importance may be given in any one instance, the order will vary from case to case.[2] It is as foolish to look for *the* cause of wars, as it is to look for *the* cause of disease. Both are complex phenomena, and social-science research, like medical research, can make headway only when it ceases to apply ready-made formulas, and begins to examine the factual evidence, while never forgetting the peculiar nature of social causation.

When set up to account for all historical changes, the class-struggle explanation is even more noticeably lacking in conviction than the broader economic explanation. It does not explain, as it should do on Marxist theory, the change from ancient slavery to feudalism, or from feudalism to capitalism. If any class struggle dominated late feudal times it was not one of serfs versus feudal lords — the Marxist dialectical opposites — but landed interests versus commerce and manufacturing interests.

Neither do class wars account for the rise and decline of a civilization such as the Roman, the rise of what we vaguely call the modern Western civilization, or the impact of one civilization on another. All kinds of influences have played upon the history of mankind, and about wide areas of the past our ignorance is still so great that we can only resort to guesswork. One may of course regard history as conflict, say between man and nature, with food supply and population ever achieving and losing equilibrium. One may with equal justice regard history as co-operation between man and nature, or among men in society. But any abstraction of forces battling or co-operating in history is bound to simplify and distort

2. E. F. M. Durbin, *The Politics of Democratic Socialism*, London, 1940, pp. 166–76. Quincy Wright, *A Study of War*, Chicago, 1942, II, pp. 720–39.

life, and this is peculiarly true of the rigid Marxist abstractions of economic forces and class struggle.

The trouble with the Marxist historical case as a whole is that the labels of Oriental, classical, feudal, capitalist exhaust neither the categories of economic organization nor those of history. Within the category of ancient or Asiatic, for instance, a score of different civilizations are included. But in Marxism the empirical investigation is beside the point, since the theory at once dismisses as accidental and unimportant anything outside its own few narrow categories. Such a procedure is not confined to Marx, however, but is regularly followed by all those who first define their history, and then discard or ignore whatever lies outside their definition.

II

In a sense all that has been written here so far is a mere preamble to Marxism. Marx's wider theory of history is best regarded as a construction to lend support to his firm prediction of the overthrow of capitalism. In capitalism he professed to see the dialectic in its purest form as the thesis and antithesis of the class struggle, 'the economic law of motion of capitalism.' The picture of many classes, all mutually antagonistic, which he sketched in for the past, was put aside. The class antagonisms have now been simplified, he said, and 'society as a whole is more and more splitting up into two great hostile camps . . . bourgeoisie and proletariat,' or capitalists and workers.[3] The proletariat are those who work for wages and are forced to do so because they are without ownership of the means of production, ownership being the distinguishing mark of the capitalist.

The polarization of society into two classes was the major prediction of the *Communist Manifesto*. It is indeed the purpose of Marx's whole system to show that 'the fall of the bourgeoisie and the victory of the proletariat are equally inevitable,' and hence to invite all intelligent people to choose the side of the victorious proletariat; to ride as it were 'the wave of the future.'

Let us examine this great prophecy. The thesis of polarization

3. *Communist Manifesto.*

appeared plausible enough in nineteenth-century England at a time when even Disraeli could speak of two nations, the rich and the poor, within a single State; and when Marx could write that 'economically considered, the United States is still nothing more than a colony of Europe.' [4] The point is, however, as most of the evidence clearly demonstrates, that since then capitalist society has become less polarized into classes, in England and elsewhere. This is an argument of great importance and worth enlarging upon.

Handicraft industries, some small-scale manufacturing and peasant farming have unquestionably declined in the Western countries with the spread of modern technology, although remnants of the earlier pre-capitalist age have shown more vitality than Marx anticipated. What is far more important, however, is the rise of a new 'petty bourgeoisie' of white-collar workers — in the ever-expanding service industries, professions, technical trades, civil service, and so forth. One may therefore grant the decline of the old middle class, but the real stumbling block for the Marxist case is the growth of these new classes of clerical, administrative, technical, and professional groups, and the relatively declining numbers of unskilled workers.[5] The proletariat in the sense of unskilled manual workers is a disappearing class. And the further modern industry develops, the larger and more complex the middle class becomes, with new groups being thrown up into it all the time. The proportion of persons in the service trades (tertiary industries) is in fact a measure of the standard of living in a country, so that today even the *industrial proletariat as a whole* shows a relative decline in numbers in highly industrialized countries. It is hardly necessary to press the argument of dispersal of ownership, whether of stocks, government bonds, savings, or durable consumers' goods — the last being especially marked. It has become less and less true that the workers have nothing to lose but their chains. All this is a familiar story to the statistician and economist.

The real class significance of earlier societies is that class lines were more rigid, there was a more definite hierarchy, one's station

4. *Capital*, 1, p. 848.
5. Unskilled workers in 1910 formed 36 per cent of the U.S. labor force; by 1947 they formed only 21 per cent. Clerks and salespeople on the other hand, representing the expanding service industries, were 10 per cent in 1910 and 19 per cent in 1947. *Statistical Abstract of the United States*, 1947, pp. 144ff.

in life was more fixed. Today the structure of society is less and less on a 'class' basis; there is great fluidity, and a circulation of people into and out of occupational groups, so that it becomes increasingly difficult to draw any sharp class distinctions. This is a result which might theoretically be expected if one bears in mind the strong tendencies in society other than those making for polarization.

Far, therefore, from being a characteristic feature of the advanced industrialized countries, with their rising productivity, social services, piece-meal social and economic planning, and less rapidly increasing populations, the revolutionary class struggle is rarely observable in these countries; and on the contrary usually makes its appearance in less well-developed areas, where there are no large middle and petty-bourgeois classes to give stability to the social structure.

In his later work Marx himself showed some awareness of the rise of these new intermediate or middle classes, and appeared to think of them as outside the capitalist-proletariat schema. Although it is not clear whether he thought these groups would all be forced into the proletariat, he did appear to think they would play no part in later history. It is noteworthy that whenever Marx's studies turned up an awkward fact that did not seem to fit his thesis, he dropped the point and did not pursue his analysis. This is particularly evident in the successive volumes of *Capital,* and in the later *Theories of Surplus Value.*

These newer groups, although not fitting the Marxist categories, are nonetheless a part of society, and are becoming a larger and larger part. They are not a few small groups on the fringes of society to be ignored in any broad analysis, as Marx ignored small craftsmen and other remnants of the old petty bourgeoisie, but they are coming increasingly to dominate the social spectrum, at the one end absorbing the unskilled worker into their ranks, and at the other absorbing the old-style capitalist. It is, indeed, largely for reasons which should commend themselves to Marx that these changes in the class composition of society have come about, that is, because of the changes in technology, the structure of industry and trade, and the rising productivity. The existence and growth of these new middle classes, outside the Marxist framework, is of course fatal to the polarization thesis. That Marx should not have foreseen the new social structure is understandable; he can hardly be blamed for not anticipating in 1848 the full social consequences of modern technology and the joint stock company. It is less understandable in present-day Marxists, who persist in applying the old framework of analysis to a society that has long been rapidly outgrowing it.

To this argument Marxists retort that this huge and growing middle class, which in the main works on a wage or salary, is not capitalist and does not think as a capitalist class. In one way that is true. Members of the new middle classes are not capitalists in that they do not normally own the factories (and even if ownership of shares is dispersed this does not normally carry with it effective control of industry): but it is not true that therefore they are militant proletarians. They are not proletarians nor do they think of themselves as such, and no amount of Marxist propaganda seems able to convert them. Then, too, since even the most highly paid executive is not usually owner of a substantial part of the enterprise he directs, he is also job-conscious and easily weaned from any allegiance to property or capitalism as it was thought of in the early nineteenth century, when a man owned and operated his own business and no nonsense about it. The relation between the forms of economic organization and the attitudes of people seems to be this: as industry becomes increasingly dominated by large-scale corporate enterprise, as business becomes more interdependent and less competitive and independent, both production and man's psychology are in a sense 'socialized.' [6] In other words, business, especially if on a large scale, is coming to be judged pragmatically by the test of public welfare instead of by an appeal to property rights on the one hand, or class consciousness on the other.

III

It is at this point that Marx's economic theory comes into its own. His economic theory is the only systematic part of his whole work, the theory of history and the rest being found for the most part

6. J. Schumpeter, *Capitalism, Socialism, and Democracy*, London, 1943, pp. 156ff.

scattered through numerous writings. Very little will be said here on the technicalities of Marx's economics, but enough must be said to relate it to his thesis of the class struggle. Marx as an economist has one advantage over many orthodox theorists in that, like earlier economists such as Adam Smith, he was not content with piece-meal theories, but set out with the grand design of exploring the economy as a whole and its development through time. It was an analysis of historical sweep, not of a static situation.

Yet despite this broad approach Marx's economic theory must on the whole be regarded as purely instrumental. It is not, properly speaking, economic theory at all, but a social philosophy written in economic terms. The whole of the economic analysis was meant to show the inevitability of the decline of capitalism, to prove the truth of the Marxist social philosophy. In much the same way classical economic theory was traditionally employed for different partisan purposes, to rationalize the behavior of private-property owners and to defend a laissez-faire theory of government.

The operative concept which Marx used was that of surplus value, which purported to show how the capitalists as a class, driven by competition and regardless of their intentions, must inevitably exploit the workers. Surplus value in turn was derived from the labor theory of value plus the doctrine of subsistence wages, and its ancestry is through David Ricardo and Adam Smith, back at least as far as John Locke.[7]

Now it is easy to refute Marx's theories of value and surplus value if they are taken to mean merely a theory of exchange values or prices. Most economic theorists, when they condescend to notice Marx at all, assume that he meant to explain exchange value; and having set up this straw man proceed to knock him down with a few casual shots.[8]

---

7. Marxists differ on precisely what was Marx's greatest contribution to economic and social theory. Engels (*Selected Works*, 1942, I, pp. 10–15) regarded the class-struggle theory of history and the surplus-value theory as the two great truths of Marxism; but at Marx's graveside he substituted for surplus value the fact that production is the foundation of society (ibid. p. 16).

8. The classic refutation of Marx's explanation of prices is that of E. von Böhm-Bawerk: *Karl Marx and the Close of His System*, new edition, edited by Paul M. Sweezy, New York, 1949.

Yet Marx is not so easily disposed of, since he was not usually thinking in terms of exchange value. The question of the modern economist is: how do prices come to be what they are? It is a strictly limited inquiry and achieves an air of science often at the risk of losing touch with reality. The question Marx seems to ask, most of the time, is: how are prices different from real costs? Failure to notice the different questions asked largely explains why Marx and the modern economist appear always to be talking at cross purposes.

In approaching the answer as he did from the side of supply, Marx was not so much ignoring market demand — which is the usual criticism against him — as taking it for granted for any given period. He was all the time trying to get behind market prices to a bed-rock of real costs or objective values in production. In a sense his theory dealt with what ought to be, rather than with what is, and is thus akin to a theory of natural rights. It is even more like the older idea of natural value, based upon labor time, so that if price exceeds the natural value in terms of labor time there is someone (the capitalist) who appropriates the surplus, and this process Marx called 'exploitation.' The distinction he drew is like that made by Oscar Wilde: 'A cynic is one who knows the price of everything and the value of nothing.

Marx tried to keep close to reality not only by dealing with real costs but also by dealing with use-values. By useful, Marx meant what the ordinary man means; he scarcely noticed such examples as meteorites, Rembrandts, and other rareties, but persisted in holding to the sane view that production is for use, or at any rate ought to be.

At this point it is easy to see why there is confusion in the volumes of *Capital*. Marx talked of value in at least three senses: (a) his more esoteric meaning of real costs or natural value — which led naturally to his concept of 'socially necessary labor time'; (b) use value; and (c) exchange value or prices. Often his concept of surplus value was different from that given above (the excess of price over natural value), and was defined entirely with reference to price. When it is so defined, price equals natural value, and surplus value then becomes the difference between the price received by the capitalist and the subsistence wage actually paid to the worker.

In spite of his hatred of capitalism, Marx did not fail to recognize its historically creative role. The eulogy to capitalism in the pages of the *Communist Manifesto* has hardly been bettered in any language as a description of the marvelous productivity of modern technology and its revolutionizing effect upon nearly every aspect of life. What repelled Marx, as it did other sensitive consciences in the nineteenth century, was the immediate human cost, especially the brutal treatment of human beings as a mere factor of production, their labor bought and sold like any commodity in the market. That is why Marx was good at ferreting out the facts about the seamy side of capitalism, and why *Capital* will always remain a classic of economic history, and such a terrible indictment of early industrialism.

Socialism is older than Marx, and most of the social critics of the nineteenth century were openly moral in their judgments. What Marx did was to turn the tables on the classical economists. Behind a façade of science they had but thinly veiled their approval of the system they studied, while Marx covered his moral *disapproval* in the same scientific guise. Although not admitting it, Marx in fact brought morality back into political economy, from which it had long been excluded.[9]

His economic analysis tried to demonstrate the results of the frantic effort to maintain the rate of profit. Adam Smith seems to have entertained the idea that profits would fall with increasing investment in capital equipment. On Marx's argument, too, the rate of profit should fall as machines displaced labor, since surplus value could be extracted only from labor. Marx argued that new machinery enabled the individual capitalist to undersell his competitors, and hence all capitalists installed machinery if they wanted to stay in business. Marx was forced to maintain that the capitalist, in order to keep up his rate of profit, would seek to appropriate more and more surplus value — that is, increase the rate of exploitation — and so push the proletariat deeper into the mire of impoverishment. Granted the belief in surplus value, the idea of increasing exploitation and impoverishment naturally followed.

Although aware most of the time of the increased productivity that resulted from the growing use of machinery, Marx could not

9. As noted, for example, in Jack Lindsay, op. cit. p. 196.

bring himself to believe that the workers would share in the lightening of human toil or in the other benefits of mass production.

> . . . no improvement of machinery, no application of science
> to production, no contrivances of communication, no new
> colonies, no emigration, no opening of markets, no free trade,
> nor all these things put together, will do away with the miseries
> of the industrious masses . . .[10]

The process of grinding the workers down more severely could take place in several ways. On the one hand, he thought that the petty bourgeoisie and the middle class would be steadily forced into the ranks of the proletariat. On the other, that the workers would be exploited more intensively, their standard of living and health would suffer by the lengthening of the working day, the decrease of wages, and 'the speed-up.' The increasing numbers of unemployed, whom Marx called 'the industrial reserve army,' would also put on pressure to bring wages down. Marx offered no proof that the number of unemployed would grow. It was a purely gratuitous assumption, from outside the body of his economic theory, but lending an apparent support to it.

IV

The idea of increasing impoverishment, so common in Marxism, has several troublesome points.

First, there is the implication that at some preceding time the workers were better off. Marx did not analyze this possibility.

Second, the poverty could not go below subsistence level. As Engels wrote:

> The price of labour is equal to its cost of production . . . [to]
> the quantity of means of subsistence necessary to enable the
> worker to continue working and to prevent the working class
> from dying out.[11]

Third, it is sometimes disputed whether Marx really did mean that the proletariat would become worse off in an absolute sense,

10. *Inaugural Address, Selected Works,* 1942, II, p. 437.
11. *Principles of Communism,* new translation by Paul M. Sweezy, New York, 1952, p. 7.

that is, whether living standards would actually decline with the aging of capitalism, or whether he meant it in a relative sense only. A reading of Marx shows plainly enough that he did mean it in an absolute sense, that he substantially accepted Lassalle's 'iron law of wages' as true of capitalism but believed it would not be true of the post-capitalist or communist era.

He sometimes had qualms, however, about the 'iron law of wages' and recognized that subsistence always has a traditional and social content and is never absolute. Engels expressed this idea clearly:

> A fair day's wage, under normal conditions, is the sum required to procure to the labourer the means of existence necessary, *according to the standard of life of his station and country,* to keep himself in working order and to propagate his race. (My italics.) [12]

Subsistence wages may thus vary from one country to another, so that a worker in China may be hired for less than one in England. Yet Marxism always returned to the view that trade-union action or legislation could never do more than push wages up *temporarily;* in the longer run they would fall to the minimum physical limit. Engels believed that if workers ever came to own their own homes, and thus save on rent, wages would be reduced by the amount of rent saved.[13]

At first, then, Marxism holds to the extreme position that subsistence merely refers to the physiological limit, but at other moments there is a partial retreat from it. This pattern of stating an extreme and untenable case and then partially retreating is common in Marx's thought. But the retreats are only temporary: Marx always came back to his original position for the simple reason that his whole case rests upon it.

V

Today, only the most fanatical Marxist would argue that an absolute decline in real wages has occurred. Statistics of a narrow

12. *The British Labour Movement, Handbook,* p. 198; *Selected Correspondence,* p. 335; *Selected Works,* 1942, II, p. 574.
13. Marx, *Selected Works,* 1942, I, pp. 332ff. Engels, *The Housing Question, Handbook,* p. 346; and *Selected Works,* 1951, II, pp. 370ff.

sort, such as wage indices and cost-of-living indices, certainly do not confirm the proposition. We know, for example, that in England real wages have doubled since about 1870, as the Industrial Revolution really began to 'pay off' for the workers. A number of estimates have been made of the rate at which productivity has been rising in industrial countries during the last century. One of these is that the gain in output per man hour has averaged almost 2 per cent a year for the U.S. economy. Two per cent is also the commonly estimated rate at which real per capita income has grown and may presumably be expected to grow, after due allowance is made for population increase, and so on.[14]

A reference to other data, such as the increased leisure through the shortening of the working day, week and year, and the steady extension of state-provided services, merely bears out what common experience and any veteran trade unionist will confirm: the rise in the real income and standards of living of the worker in all industrialized countries. It would, moreover, be remarkable if living standards fell in face of the continuing rise in production in a system whose fundamental basis is mass production and mass consumption.

Some people did undeniably suffer with the onset of the Industrial Revolution, in particular those whose skills were suddenly displaced by machine methods of production, such as the hand-weaver and the hand-spinner. To judge whether the early days of the Industrial Revolution were really so much worse on the whole than the century before would require a long excursion into social and economic history which would take us too far afield. What has often been forgotten by sensitive souls distressed at the social evils of the 'bleak age' is how grim, unhealthy, and laborious the lot of the worker and peasant was before industrialization. Much has also been made of the loss of skill and pride which the introduction of machinery entailed for small groups of craftsmen, without any consideration of certain offsetting factors such as the spread of education, new skills, mechanical ability, and leisure, for the vast

14. J. F. Dewhurst and associates, *America's Needs and Resources,* New York, 1947, p. 23. Real hourly wages rose more than sixfold in the United States between 1840 and 1950. Real per capita income in 1947 was one and a half times that in 1929. *Statistical Abstract,* 1947, pp. 293ff. R. A Lester, *Labour and Industrial Relations,* New York, 1951, p. 54.

majority. This point is worth mentioning, because, driven back
from the argument for an absolute decline in living standards, the
Marxist sometimes tends to argue, like many Romantics, for a
kind of 'spiritual degradation' which is said to grow ever worse in
an industrial age. Marx himself, however, could hardly use such
an argument against urbanization and industrialism with any consistency, since he welcomed the industrial age and believed that
one of the virtues of capitalism was that it had 'rescued a considerable part of the population from the idiocy of rural life.' [15]

If a case of 'spiritual degradation' may be brought against the
Industrial Revolution, it was not so much loss of skills as a breakdown of the old 'culture patterns' with the growth of industry and
urban living: in short the same kind of thing that happens today
when cities and industry grow up rapidly in a formerly rural environment.[16]

The alternative defense of Marx's case, as put forward, for
instance, by Plekhanov, is to say that it is true in a *relative* sense
only, that although the poor are improving their lot, the rich are
getting richer and at a more rapid rate. The implications of this,
which may not be favorable for the class struggle, are conveniently
ignored. For example, will a proletarian class with a rising standard
of living become revolutionary?

The statistical evidence to confirm or refute the relative worsening of the workers' condition is not conclusive. The size of the cake
(total production) is growing, and there is no proof that labor's
slice is becoming a smaller fraction. Living standards show a
marked absolute rise even on the worst assumption that labor gets
a constant proportion of a steadily growing total. Labor's share may
even be growing somewhat; there is some uncertainty on the point,
which we can hardly clear up because of the absence of proper
statistics in earlier periods; but which we may be able to settle
from now on as the statistical data become more reliable and comprehensive. The likelihood at the moment is that after taxation is
taken into account, the rich are on the whole becoming less rich.
But what is more important, as pointed out earlier, the proportion

15. *Communist Manifesto.*
16. Cf. E. Mayo, *The Human Problems of an Industrial Civilization,* New
York, 1933.

of unskilled workers is diminishing, and the former proletariat becomes more and more a part of the large new petty-bourgeois and middle class, so that the proportion of the national income going to *salaried* workers increases notably. It is only verbal juggling to call the new salariat either proletarian or capitalist, although to call them one or the other is typical of Marxist reasoning, by which everything is put on a rigidly *either or* basis, without room for third choices or compromises.

Whether the decline of living standards was meant in an absolute or a relative sense, Marx has been proved wrong by the march of events. The retort of the modern Marxist is to say that some factors have been omitted, such as unemployment and wars, and that they must all be taken into account since they are all products of capitalism. They have not in fact been omitted; unemployment and wars are taken into account in such statistical series as we have. Some things have, it is true, been omitted from the indices, but they tell against, not for, the Marxist case: the leisure, the spread of education, the lengthening of the span of life, and the many tax-provided amenities.

The only other sense in which Marx's prediction could be true is to say that the workers are not as well off as they ought to be; that is, that production is not as high as it could be under a system other than capitalism. Such is, for example, the argument of J. D. Bernal: 'What is produced has to be measured against what might have been produced.' [17] There may be a *prima facie* case in favor of the charge that production is not always at a maximum when one considers idle resources in times of depression, and restrictive practices on the part of corporate 'monopolies' and trade unions. There is also a *prima facie* case against it when one considers the costs of rapid obsolescence and social instability if every scientific invention is immediately put to use. The facts, as distinct from *a priori* arguments, show that technical progress goes on rapidly and total production continues to rise, despite all the Marxist nonsense about 'fetters' on the forces of production.

The real strength and the immediate cogency of the Marxist argument rests upon trade depression, when total production is unquestionably cut back. Whether total production over the long

17. In *Philosophy for the Future*, p. 407.

run, taking the good times with the bad over the last century, could have been higher under any alternative economic arrangements is naturally impossible to prove, and certainly to measure its extent is impossible. What is true, however, is that we are as well off as we are because our forefathers were poor; that is to say, had they consumed more, instead of making the enormous capital investments that were made, we should today be very much poorer. But whether or not production of consumer goods has been always as high as it could be, is not relevant to anything Marx meant. He clearly had in mind a process of deepening and more widely spreading poverty, and the falsehood of that prediction is what damages his case.

If impoverishment *were* increasing, it is surely strange to suppose that the proletariat would then be the stuff of which successful revolutions are made. Revolutions are rarely if ever made by poverty-stricken classes who are becoming more poverty-stricken, any more than really poor 'have-not' nations declare wars against powerful industrial states. Misery may love company, but poverty easily leads to political apathy, and is as likely to divide as to strengthen a working class — as trade unions know only too well when they see their membership decline in hard times.[18] As the rise of capitalism itself shows, a confident, strong, and advancing class is much more likely to get its way than is a slowly declining class. This is the lesson visible in the civil wars in seventeenth-century England and in the French Revolution. Any hope of an inevitable revolution based on growing and finally unendurable poverty may therefore be dismissed as fantasy.

Historical case studies go to show that revolutions are produced by something more than poverty. They demand an awareness of one's lot and ideas of reform, or at least the conviction that things are bad but could be better. They require organization and leadership, and, even more important, a revolutionary situation, typically found in the social disorganization following a defeat in war. Then, if the government is weak and corrupt, has lost confidence in its right and ability to rule, and (usually) if some foreign aid is forth-

18. The political apathy of the poor Saskatchewan farmers during the 1930's is documented in S. M. Lipset, *Agrarian Socialism*, New York, 1940. Only with returning prosperity did the poorer farmers become politically active.

coming, or if the masses can be inflamed by nationalism or some other fighting faith, a revolution has a reasonable prospect of success. The revolutions in China and Indonesia since the Second World War are of this kind. Revolutions, like most social phenomena, can be analyzed and accounted for, and some of the Marxist concepts may help us to explain them: but not this particular concept of increasing impoverishment.

Since the doctrine of increasing impoverishment is not true the communist in the Western world finds himself in something of a dilemma. If he works with trade unions and so improves the workers' lot, he thereby lessens the evils of capitalism and dims the revolutionary ardor; if he will not work for short-term objectives he has no hope of workers' support. That is to say, the more successful are union activities in raising the standard of living, the less hope is there of creating a class-conscious proletariat to bring about the communist's ultimate aim. As the workers' lot is improved they behave less and less as Marx's idealized and class-conscious proletarian is supposed to behave.

Such considerations help to explain the communist emphasis on strikes, even when they are hopeless and even over the most trivial grievances. In a sense the communist may prefer that strikes should *not* succeed in their immediate aims, their real use being to sharpen the militant class consciousness of the proletariat. For that reason no rational argument about the economic 'cost' of a strike makes any impression on the Marxist, since it is simply irrelevant. If the strike leads to riots, premature uprisings, and so on, all that is regarded as good training for 'der Tag.' Lenin recommended that trade unions should be a 'school of communism.' [19] Hence we can see why communist leaders do not always secure trade-union support. The union members generally want tangible benefits, not rash strikes that have a poor chance of success.

Nor is there any comfort in the Marxist contention that only in so far as capitalism works undisturbed, or is true to its inner nature, will impoverishment actually spread. The argument here is that Marx merely abstracted, and spoke of capitalism *per se,* as it would be if his abstraction were worked out to its logical conclu-

19. *Left Wing Communism, Handbook,* p. 859.

sion. To abstract any of the tendencies at work in society is a perfectly legitimate procedure, and one commonly followed in economic analysis. The trouble is that it merely reduces Marx's famous law of motion to a single *tendency,* one which plainly existed under early laissez-faire, but which has been counteracted by other tendencies, and has accordingly become less and less noticeable as laissez-faire has receded into the past.

VI

But the major defense relied upon to save Marx's prophecy of polarization and impoverishment is that the operation of the law has been postponed by colonialism and imperialism. Lenin developed this theory of economic imperialism, and extended it also into a theory of the causes of modern war; or to be more accurate, he popularized with Bolshevik trimmings the work of the English economist J. A. Hobson in his book *Imperialism* (1902), and that of the Austrian Marxist Rudolf Hilferding in *Finance Capital* (1910).[20]

Ostensibly what Lenin set out to do was to trace the changes that had taken place in capitalism since Marx's day. By reference to selected statistics and authors he argued that the early or competitive stage of capitalism had passed, having been replaced by trusts, cartels, monopolies; and that industry had come under the control of finance. Lenin relied on banking practice in Germany for his proof of finance capitalism, and there he found the banks in control of many industries. By contrast, the British banking system rarely engaged in long-term financing and control of industry, and so lent little support to his theory.

With the decline of competition and expansion at home the capitalist was forced into overseas activities: to find new outlets for investment in order to keep up the rate of profit, to find markets for products and sources of raw materials. Capitalists in a number of countries indulged in the same feverish scramble, and the results were imperialist rivalries and wars. This stage of 'monopoly finance

20. V. I. Lenin, *Imperialism: The Highest Stage of Capitalism,* London, 1940.

capitalism' was the 'highest' or 'dying' stage of capitalism, on the very eve of the world revolution. Lenin dated the transformation into imperialism about 1900.

Lenin obviously mixed his dates somewhat. The great days of empire building had been under the competitive conditions of the nineteenth century, and to a large extent even earlier. The building of the British and French empires, the expansion of the United States across a continent, the colonizing and opening up of South America are a few of the outstanding instances. The nineteenth century was also the century par excellence of the search for overseas markets and raw materials, and the age when the greatest overseas investments were made. This is not to deny that such investments continued after 1900. They are in fact still going on, and quite properly so, since much of the world is desperately short of capital. But it is simply false that the political policy of conquest and empire building, together with the policy of 'export of capital,' was typical only of late finance capitalism. Nor was it true, as Lenin maintained, that 'the principal spheres of investment of British capital are its colonial possessions.' [21]

Lenin's investigations showed him that the stage of competitive capitalism had not been passed until about 1900. Being thus compelled to choose a late date, he had therefore to distort the order of historical development, and to attribute earlier events to a process of industrial and financial combination which did not appear until later.

If Lenin's *Imperialism* is judged as a theory to explain why overseas trade and investment took place it is hard to see what it contributed. Marx himself had noticed the tendency to capital accumulation and overseas expansion; geographical discoveries and overseas trade were indeed among the extraneous factors which he called upon to explain the rise of capitalism. He had in fact placed the rise of capitalism at about 1600, or two hundred years before modern technology. Marxist literature had always been full of the conflict between expanding productive 'forces' and the allegedly limited markets. Emphasis on the latter point leads naturally to a kind of deficiency-of-purchasing-power theory of capitalism, and

21. *Imperialism,* p. 59. *Towards the Seizure of Power,* New York, 1932, II, p. 83.

Engels occasionally invoked something very close to this idea in an over-production theory of the trade cycle. Lenin also used it to show one of the advantages of exporting capital: by that means the home capitalist could get rid of some of his production to overseas buyers.[22] It will be recalled that C. H. Douglas, the father of Social Credit monetary theory, diagnosed the fatal flaw in the economic system as an inability to distribute enough purchasing power to consumers to enable them to 'buy back' the products of industry. This purely monetary explanation of crises is not on the whole a feature of Marxist theory.

It would be a mistake, however, to suppose that Lenin was a serious student of recent economic development, content to follow where the evidence might lead. The significance of Lenin's *Imperialism* lies in its application to the class struggle. It was meant to account for the failure of the revolution to occur in the industrialized countries. The reason he gave was simple: workers of the creditor or imperial country shared in the benefits (or 'plunder') of foreign lending, trade, and colonies. Because of that, their standard of living could rise, instead of falling as Marx had predicted. Skilled labor in particular, the 'workers' aristocracy,' was said to be living at the expense of the foreign proletariat in backward countries, and was thus 'bribed' into support of capitalism.[23]

This made an especially neat explanation of why Marxists had always beaten their heads in vain against the brick wall of the indifferent British trade unionist. But it skimmed rather lightly over a number of objections: that countries such as the Scandinavian, without empires, had also shown a high standard of living; that colonial powers such as Portugal showed a much lower standard of living; and that the bulk of the world's trade is not with colonial and 'backward' territories at all.

Above all, the Leninist theory quite ignored the fact that debtor countries, some of them colonies, showed even more rapid progress in raising their levels of production and standards of living. Perhaps it does not necessarily follow from Lenin's theory that foreign trade and investment have somehow 'impoverished' colonies and

22. Engels, *Selected Correspondence*, pp. 116, 441ff.; *Selected Works*, 1942, I, p. 461. Lenin, *Imperialism*, p. 60.
23. *Imperialism*, p. 13.

independent backward countries. Yet it is a proposition that is widely believed by communists, and they have persuaded a great many other people to believe in their version of colonial 'exploitation.' Imperialism has passed from being a rational theory into becoming a term of abuse for all overseas economic activities. Hence arises the 'salt-water fallacy': if the expansion of a country, territorial or economic, is over land, it is never thought of as imperialism.

It is quite impossible to support with evidence the general proposition that colonies and independent overseas countries have been brought closer to starvation by reason of investment and trade. The immense amount of British capital which poured into the United States, Canada, Australia, New Zealand, and the Argentine during the nineteenth century lends no support to Lenin's theory. Nor can it be supported by appealing to the experience of colonies such as Malaya, or former colonies such as Ceylon or the Philippines; or a score of other instances. 'If you are looking for real poverty, you must go to the countries whose capital imports per head of population have been low.' [24] The trouble is not that capital has been invested in, and trade fostered with, 'backward' areas but that not enough capital has been put into these areas, as much of the world now recognizes and is trying to remedy with the Point Four Program, Colombo Plan, and Colonial Development Plans.

The introduction of law and order, the suppression of the slave trade (1807), the improved transport, the elimination of famine, the improved agricultural and industrial techniques, the steps toward more education, medical and health services, all are factors to be set on the credit side; while the enormous growth of population is in itself a living witness to the increased production. The cake of production has certainly grown larger all over the world, and it is not necessarily to be imputed as a crime to investment, trade, and industry that the gains from higher production have in some areas been wiped out by the stupendous increase in the number of mouths to be fed.

Even more important than explaining away the failure of Marx's prediction has been the complete alteration of communist tactics

24. W. K. Hancock, *Wealth of Colonies*, Cambridge, 1950, pp. 11–14.

demanded by Lenin's theory: if the revolution can be stirred up in colonial and backward areas and these can be detached from the imperial powers, this in turn will force down the standard of living in the imperialist countries and so *make* Marx's forecast come true.

Traces of this line of thought can occasionally be found in Marx himself, as when he thought the proletarian uprising in England must be preceded by the independence of Ireland: 'The English working class will *never accomplish anything* before it has got rid of Ireland.' Marx and Engels gave rather divided counsel on this matter, since they also told the British Chartists that their best contribution to the emancipation of Poland would be first to overthrow the bourgeoisie in Britain. One may thus find in Marx's writings a number of references to prove two contradictory propositions — that colonial emancipation should precede, and should follow, the revolution of the industrial proletariat at home.[25]

Lenin and Stalin were, as usual, less concerned with a consistent theory than with tactical measures. In discussing movements for national independence Lenin had noted that it was the duty of the proletariat in the imperial country always to take sides with the 'oppressed' nation or colony. He also enunciated the doctrine that 'uneven economic and political development is an absolute law of capitalism,' from which the deduction was drawn that since capitalism is world-wide the chain may break (i.e. the revolution break out) at the 'weakest link.' [26] Although in disagreement with Marx's main theory of the revolution occurring first in the industrialized countries, this is a perfectly good *ex post facto* rationalization of the Russian Revolution. It is also an excellent example of how later communist leaders alter or ignore Marx's main theory to suit and justify the tactics they wish to follow.

It is certainly easier to stir up revolutions in 'backward' countries, as the events of recent years have demonstrated, particularly with the favorable conditions created in the Far East by the Second World War. For one thing the capital is usually of foreign origin, the plantation or factory is foreign-owned and often foreign-

25. *Selected Correspondence*, pp. 228, 278, 281. *Relations between the Irish and English Working Classes, Handbook*, pp. 196–7. *On India*, ibid. p. 192.
26. *Leninism*, pp. 17, 18.

managed, and the anti-capitalist appeal can easily be linked with powerful anti-foreign sentiment and with a campaign for national independence, as in Burma or Indonesia. For another thing, large-scale enterprise seems somehow more ruthless in backward countries: there is normally no large middle class, no politically powerful working class, no strong trade-union movement, little of the welfare legislation, and few of the collective services found in the more advanced industrial countries. It is in short something of a repetition of the first stages of the Industrial Revolution in England and America.

Native peoples, whether in China, Indonesia, or elsewhere, who have always taken contrasts of great wealth and acute poverty for granted, are not exposed to anything new in that line; but with its investments and its mass-produced goods, the Western world also sends its disrupting ideas of democracy, its gospel of efficiency and change, its principles of rational calculation, its technology, and the very possibilities of an end to poverty. The contrasts of inequality formerly accepted quiescently are, as it were, *realized* for the first time, and believed to be unnecessary. Economic 'exploitation' sometimes occurs (although it is not easy to measure or even define in purely economic terms), but sometimes is not always. What always takes place is a profound cultural disturbance. The old ways of life and thought are seriously upset, often with much suffering, when any indigenous culture is brought into the world economy.

VII

Lenin's theory of economic imperialism is also extended to account for modern wars. The first point to make is that, strictly speaking, it sets out to explain only wars that have taken place since 1900. Its generalization is that overseas investors and industrial combinations ('finance capital') push the governments of the Great Powers to war in order to 're-partition' the world. Now this is a matter for factual determination, and case studies have not supported the theory but have, if anything, proved the very opposite. More frequently it was the politicians and the military men who pushed the investors into dangerous adventures. A partial exception to this may have been the South African war, where financiers gave the British government a powerful push. But this hardly fits the Leninist book as a war between Great Powers.[27] Everything that enters into international relations may of course be a source of tension at one time or another. Economic matters therefore often lead to friction — there is nothing new in this observation. But the only cases where friction has led to fighting appear to have been in minor wars; for example, trade interests played a large part in the pressure of the Great Powers on China in the Boxer Revolt of 1900.

When Lenin glanced backward into history he was well aware that wars are as old as man himself. Not only could modern 'imperialism' not be blamed for them, but neither could competitive capitalism. He then shifted his ground, altered his own definitions, and called even the ancient Punic Wars 'imperialist' since they were fought for domination of the Mediterranean.[28] And thus he proceeded with his historical summary, until he had relabeled nearly all wars, aside from civil wars, as imperialist. Plainly this is little more than playing with words, and adds nothing to the well-known fact that there have been wars throughout all history, and that they have taken place for many different reasons. Men have fought for bread, land, religion, race, country, freedom, and sometimes for the personal schemes of a ruler. But never, except in rare minor instances, have they fought for the investor and the trader.

Marx himself, while he recognized the importance of overseas markets, did not fall into the Leninist confusion of arguing that the closer the world was knit together by trade and investment the more the different countries would fight. If anything, he inclined to the opposite view — which Marxists such as Kautsky afterward extended to cover the twentieth century — that with the spread of international capitalism, national differences would decline. Lenin himself had pointed out the tendency in late capitalism for national barriers to break down, and to lead to a general internationalizing 'of economic life, of politics, sciences and so forth.' Indeed, that is the only conclusion which follows from the

27. Hancock, op. cit. pp. 14–16.
28. *Imperialism*, p. 75. *Towards the Seizure of Power*, II, pp. 81, 256. *The Imperialist War*, New York, 1930, pp. 61, 68.

Marxist belief in the primacy of the economic; since if the economy is international, the politics must follow suit. But Lenin never reconciled this view with his theory of imperialist wars.

A case can be made for the Marxist belief, and the stronger it is, the more it damages Lenin's *Imperialism*. During the nineteenth century, Europe had only one or two major wars, and enjoyed longer periods of peace than perhaps ever before in history. In all that age of expansion, colonial or overseas rivalry was not the cause of any major war.

The liberals of Marx's day harbored the illusion that trade barriers would vanish and national rivalries decline, so that industry and trade would bring universal peace. The Marxist illusion was that national wars would cease, to be replaced by an international class war cutting across national boundaries, after which universal peace would ensue. But other forces, mainly political, proved too strong for the world economy, and closed nationalist economies resulted. Even Britain in the end abandoned free trade (1931). The primacy of politics is perhaps seen most clearly in the case of Japan, whose rapid industrialization was the miracle of the modern world, a process that from the beginning was state-directed.[29] The order of events was the same in many countries: instead of the economic influences carrying weak governments wherever they wished, the state for various political reasons shaped the economy and in extreme cases defied all the logic of economics by setting up trade barriers and seeking self-sufficiency.

The irrationality of the case that all modern wars are 'imperialist' or, as Lenin said, 'a continuation of class policy' is well illustrated by communist treatment of the war in 1939–45. Whatever else Nazism may have been it was primarily a political movement. It was neither invented nor directed by businessmen, although some of them short-sightedly supported it and helped it to power when it appeared to them the only way to forestall a communist government. Whatever led the Nazis to war it was not German investors or German capitalists looking for markets. Long before 1939 capital and industry, like all other elements in German life, had become tightly harnessed to Hitler's wagon. Hitler sought a polit-

29. G. C. Allen, *A Short Economic History of Modern Japan*, London, 1948.

ical end, a greater Reich; and in the pursuit of this end he went
to war. (Subconsciously, perhaps, he may have sought a purely
personal end. This is the more satisfactory explanation if he is
regarded as a psycho-pathological case, which he almost certainly
was.)

The behavior of the Communist Party toward the war, once it
had broken out, is instructive. For the first two months (September
and October of 1939) the party in Britain regarded the war as a
justified defense by the democracies against Fascist (German) aggression, a not unnatural reaction, since for years the Fascists had
been held up, and had posed, as the arch-enemy of both democracy
and communism. But following the Soviet lead the party in Britain
soon came round to see that the war was merely an 'imperialist'
venture on both sides. It maintained this position until June 1941,
when the U.S.S.R. was invaded, and from that date the nature of
the war altered again, to become once more a righteous war. (There
was also a widespread disposition among churchmen in the United
States to deny that the British, French, and Polish side conformed
to the canons of a 'just war.' Pearl Harbor was the argument that
convinced the United States, as the invasion of the U.S.S.R. convinced communists everywhere.)

The Soviet Union now declares that it was an anti-Fascist war
from the beginning, and since by definition the Soviet Union is
the only implacable enemy of Fascism, it follows that the history
of the war has had to be rewritten. Soviet historians are great patriots and fully equal to the task, and are now constructing a new
version of history to make it appear that the Soviet Union fought
and won the war almost single-handedly, with only a half-hearted
effort being made by the Western Allies.

Why has the Leninist theory of wars had such a wide acceptance
even among non-Marxists? The answer lies largely in its timing.
The theory was widely circulated in the disillusioned 1920's and
1930's, when there was a fervent desire for peace and a consequent
search for 'the cause' of war. During the same period it was also
fashionable to blame wars on the armament makers, which was an
even simpler theory than Lenin's. Communists took up this cry
with great gusto, although it was obviously never in agreement
with Lenin's theory. It is also far from plain that Lenin's theory

of imperialist wars is in harmony with the class analysis of wars
discussed earlier in this chapter.

Perhaps we know better nowadays than to attribute all wars to
one clear cause. We have learned, for instance, from the Tito-
Stalin split, that even communist countries may fall out. Perhaps
we should say especially communist countries. A powerful case can
be made that 'national' communist or socialist states are more
likely to elevate every economic friction into a diplomatic or doctrinal quarrel, and hence be more tempted to fight over it, than
states in which the political is largely separated from the economic.[30]

VIII

We may now return to our main subject. The general conclusion
is inescapable, that Lenin's clumsy theory of economic imperialism
has not been able to save Marx's prediction of a sharpening, explosive class struggle. Nor would Marx be grateful to have his confident theory explained away as a tendency that could be upset by
unforeseen factors. Marx dealt with certainties, not with possibilities or even probabilities.

There seems to be only one other conceivable basis for the
Marxist class struggle: that class consciousness could be growing,
if only as a result of a hundred years of Marxist propaganda.
Misery, after all, is partly psychological. Classes could exist sub-
jectively, with class distinctions mainly psychological, and the
definition of a proletarian might become: you are a proletarian
if you think you are, or if you feel like one.[31]

Unfortunately even this last line of defense breaks down. The
difficulty with it is not so much that the white-collar worker and
the farmer are psychologically not proletarian and class-conscious
but, more, that even the skilled or unskilled wage earner is not
proletarian in outlook: something that is the despair of modern
Marxists, as it was of Marx and Engels themselves. (In a survey
made by *Fortune* (February 1940), 80 per cent of Americans
thought of themselves as belonging to the middle class.)

30. Cf. L. Robbins, *The Economic Causes of War*, London, 1939, pp. 94ff.
31. Cole, *The Meaning of Marxism*, p. 153.

It is worth examining the Marxist concept of class more fully. Marx defined class by reference to only one standard, the ownership of the means of production. Now the first objection to this is that even economic classes may rest upon a basis other than ownership. In simple societies they are often based on status or rank; in the modern world the base may be political power or *control* of economic functions; and the last two may be combined as they are in the Soviet Union, where a class structure already appears to be emerging. Stalin, for example, spoke of 'friendly' classes in Russia; of workers, peasants, and intelligentsia (the last, which includes technicians, being added after Bolshevik suspicion of this class had worn off).[32] The Soviet system is too young yet for us even to be sure that something approaching hereditary classes will not appear.

The power to make managerial and policy decisions in the U.S.S.R. can be derived from several sources — ability, luck, trade-union position, and above all party influence. Experience in the Soviet Union also follows that elsewhere: it is usually not long before those who exercise the vital economic functions adjust the rewards in their favor. Indeed, so long as the world is poor — and it always has been and still is desperately poor — only two things are possible: a social structure that justifies some inequalities, or brutal equality of poverty for all.

The second difficulty is this. Classes are formed, in Marx's view, because individuals have the same economic interest, in this case ownership or the lack of it. Yet, as noted in Chapter 2, if men's motives are determined by self-interest (as Engels inclined to think sometimes) there is no reason to expect joint action as a class, to which the interest of the individual must often be subordinated.

Marx usually saw the absurdity of personal determinism, except in explaining the actions of his enemies, toward whom he was less charitable. Instead he often accepted the other view of a common class interest of the proletariat, for which all should loyally work. He thus recognized that people are capable of working for other than their personal interest. But if they can transcend personal economic interest in a class, they can do likewise in a nation, a party, a church, or other grouping, as we know quite well by experience. The dispute with Marx is, then, whether class is the

32. *Leninism,* pp. 381, 458, 476.

strongest of the loyalties, and the appeal to the facts — for instance, of behavior at election time and during war — shows that only rarely is this so. Class interest, being then neither determined nor usually freely chosen as the paramount loyalty, forms an insecure basis for a theory of history.

Marx himself went out of his way to show that class origin or status did not determine class allegiance. He pointed out in the Manifesto that selected members of the bourgeoisie may be enlightened enough to see the laws of social change, and seeing them, may deliberately choose to side with the proletariat.

> Just as, therefore, at an earlier period, a section of the nobility went over to the bourgeoisie, so now a portion of the bourgeoisie goes over to the proletariat, and in particular, a portion of the bourgeois ideologists, who have raised themselves to the level of comprehending theoretically the historical movement as a whole.[33]

Nor is this merely Marx's indirect way of explaining why such good bourgeois specimens as himself and Engels were to be found on the side of the workers. His observation may be extended: most of the fathers of socialism — Owen, Fourier, Saint Simon, the Christian Socialists, the Fabians — were either rich bourgeoisie or middle-class professionals, and the same is true of nearly all the founders of communism; while among Communist Parties everywhere today it is the intellectuals who provide the leadership and ideas and in some cases a considerable proportion of the membership as well.

A demonstration of freely chosen allegiance is severely damaging to Marx's class-struggle theory, since even if his theory of impoverishment were true the workers would not necessarily be loyal proletarians. Further, even though the workers were somehow to think of themselves as a class, they would not on that account necessarily be good communists. As Engels put it: 'No man is naturally a socialist by virtue of his class.' There are frequent complaints in the Marx-Engels literature of the lack of revolutionary fervor among the English proletariat when England in the nineteenth century so obviously had the 'objective' conditions for a

33. *Communist Manifesto.*

revolution. The complaints — which are somewhat inconsistent if, as Engels argued elsewhere, motives are of secondary significance in the class struggle, and if economic determinism is true — are expressed in such phrases as these: 'these thick-headed John Bulls'; 'inertia . . . pervades the working class in England';

> . . . the English proletariat is becoming more and more bourgeois, so that this most bourgeois of all nations is apparently aiming ultimately at the possession of a bourgeois aristocracy and a bourgeois proletariat *as well as* a bourgeoisie . . .

> . . . all revolutionary energy has faded practically entirely away from the English proletariat.[34]

Nothing is indeed harder than to persuade solid trade unionists to accept and act on the Marxist theories. Workers left to themselves, if socialist at all, are much more likely to evolve a vague and sentimental brand of socialism, always with a strong moral flavor. Marx did not go wrong in anticipating the political significance of the industrial proletariat; where he did go wrong was in assuming that the workers would become revolutionary, or act through the Communist Party.

There is often, of course, some measure of solidarity of the poor, and of the rich also, although it would not be accurate to describe it as a consciousness of economic class. Among the poor it may be a kind of 'fellowship of the disinherited'; while businessmen may similarly close ranks when their interests are threatened, even though they may not normally be class-conscious. The sociologists find many other examples of 'in-group' behavior below the conscious or rational level. The last point has a consequence for the class-struggle theory of history which is worth noting.

Marxists interpret wars and social movements in class terms, even though the participants are at the time not aware of the real nature of the struggle. A class struggle, they say, may have been fought ostensibly over religious or other ideological issues, but in Marx's words: 'We cannot judge of such a period of transformation by its own consciousness.' [35] In language less Marxist, William

34. *Selected Correspondence*, pp. 102, 115–16, 147, 213. *Selected Works*, 1942, I, pp. 458–9.
35. *Selected Works*, 1942, I, p. 356.

James pointed out we must not fall into the 'psychological fallacy' of believing that the mentality being studied is conscious of itself as the psychologist is conscious of it.

Class struggles of the past have been instinctive, or automatic, but the point is that on Marxist theory the 'right' side won anyway, that is, the 'progressive' movement of history went on. To insure the overthrow of capitalism, however, it is not enough to put our trust in the instinctive movement of the dialectic, but instead the proletariat must be made conscious of its class and of its destiny before victory can come. 'Theory becomes a material force as soon as it has gripped the masses.' 'What they [Marx and Engels] did was to give to a relatively blind and instinctive struggle the *theory* which converted it into a conscious struggle with a specific plan and purpose.' [36] In Lenin's words: 'Ideas become power when they seize hold of the masses.'

Hence communists must work overtime to enlighten the workers on the 'real' nature of the issues, and only if the proletariat is clearly aware of the underlying forces at work can the revolution really be inevitable. Sometimes, however, there is some qualification of this assertion, and it is said to be sufficient if the leaders — the self-appointed party vanguard — are in possession of the advanced theory. In Lenin's words: 'Socialism can never proceed out of the economic or social developments without the directive aid of men who have grasped the theoretical implications,' and the leaders must 'aspire to elevate spontaneity to consciousness.' [37]

These considerations reveal another of the dualisms inherent in Marx's social theory. On the one side the movements of history go on even though the participants are not conscious of what they are 'really' fighting for, or even think it is over something quite different; on the other side the proletariat, or at any rate its leaders, must have a clear grasp of the theory behind it all if the movements are to succeed. This difference between the overthrow of capitalism and the overthrow of earlier economic systems is nowhere analyzed in Marxism, although it is often asserted.

In his class-struggle thesis Marx regarded the class as all-important, the individual as nothing in his effect on history.

36. Marx, *Selected Essays,* New York, 1926, p. 26. Stalin, *Leninism,* p. 418. Jackson, op. cit. p. 23.

37. *The Iskra Period,* ii, p. 67. *Towards the Seizure of Power,* ii, p. 51.

> If I speak of individuals, it is only insofar as they are per-
> sonifications of economic categories, representatives of special
> class relations and class interests.[38]

Such a view, as with Hegel, continually leads to a playing down
of the role of the individual. Perhaps it needed some playing down
in Marx's day, and for that matter maybe it still does, in face of
the let-us-now-praise-famous-men school of history writing. Individual differences may often be ignored for certain purposes —
as when one is dealing with voters' lists, actuarial figures, population studies, or other statistical measurements. In the same way
it may be said that science is not interested in the unique event.
Nevertheless, it is the leaders who activate the social process, it is
people who follow and take part in movements as individuals, and
statistical probabilities are often upset when we deal with social
behavior. It is not surprising therefore that the typical class behavior postulated by Marx, and by other social analysts, so often
fails to materialize.

A further difficulty with Marx's conception of ownership or lack
of it as the overriding interest uniting people in a class is that
groupings may be formed on the basis of any common interest;
and this explains how harmony of economic interest, as well as
conflict, can arise. We see this demonstrated clearly when labor
and management unite to exploit the consumer by a tariff or a
policy of price maintenance, or when they join to promote restrictive immigration laws. The truth is that throughout society, as in
the family, there is both co-operation and conflict, and the co-
operation is, if anything, more important.

Just as Marx took insufficient notice of the co-operation, so he
failed to do justice to other conflicts and cleavages than those of
capital and labor: for example, those between urban and rural
dwellers, between stockholder and manager, unskilled and skilled
worker, lender and borrower; conflicts between industries, occu-
pations, regions, and countries. A clash between private interests
and between private and public interest can occur at a multitude
of points and it is mere obscurantism to assert that all such clashes
may be ignored, or subsumed under a general two-class category.
Only a dialectician is capable of such gross simplification.

38. *Capital*, I, p. 864.

The modern world is especially liable to sectional economic conflicts by virtue of its stress upon goods and services as the measure
of the standard of living. Broadly speaking, society lives by a
material and this-worldly philosophy in which money, and what
it can bring, is the common measure of success. The general level
of production rises slowly, but any one group can benefit to an
almost unlimited extent at the expense of others. A great many
of the conflicts that occur in the political and economic life of the
democracies can be explained only by reference to this clash of
sectional interests.

Two of the great categories of the modern world deserve special
mention: the first is the farming community, neither capital nor
labor in outlook but often hostile to both, a group that has been
and continues to be a weak spot in the Marxist analysis. The role
to be played by the peasantry has led to great differences within
the communist camp, including differences between Lenin and
Trotsky. Democratic socialist parties, too, have often been sorely
perplexed about how to appeal effectively for farmers' support,
and at the same time to stand upon the principle of public ownership of resources, including land.

Marxists often assert that Marx and Engels paid great attention
to 'the peasant question.' In the sense that they wrote about it now
and then, this may be true, but it is also misleading. The gist of
the peasant question to Marx was that the discontent of the peasants might be used by the communists for revolutionary purposes,
but their role was to be secondary; they were expected to find
their natural ally and *leader* in the town proletariat. Marx applied
his industrial diagnosis to farming: just as handicrafts and small
manufacturing gave way to machine mass production, so, Marx
thought, the same process would quickly eliminate the peasant
and independent farmer, and replace them by wage workers in
large-scale, heavily capitalized agricultural units. People do not
like being told they are doomed, or obsolete, so it is no wonder
Marxism usually makes little appeal to farmers. But when modern
communist parties hush up Marx and put forward plans for giving
more land to the peasants they at once touch a responsive chord.[39]

39. For a study of the relation of Marxist and Peasant Parties in Southeast
Europe see David Mitrany, *Marx against the Peasant*, London, 1951.

The other great division is the national. As Marx saw it: 'The working men have no country'; 'National differences and antagonism between peoples are daily more and more vanishing . . .' [40] It was perhaps a natural enough conclusion to draw from the course of economic development in the nineteenth century, at least in free-trade England; but since politics is not a mere 'reflection' of economics, patriotism and nationalist policies of various kinds have been greater forces in world affairs than Marx foresaw.

What has come to be known as the 'National question' occupies a prominent place in later Marxist literature. The Marxist authority is Stalin's book, *Marxism and the National and Colonial Question,* written before 1914.[41] But even with this to guide us, it is not easy to find any consistent theory.

In general, Marx expected the future to bring a nation-less as well as a classless society, nations being regarded as a 'historical category' typical only of the capitalist era. Marx had nothing but scorn for such nationalities as Czechs and Poles.

In terms of attitudes and tactics, rather than of explanatory theory, it is no easier to find consistency. Yet Marxists were compelled to take a stand for or against certain nations, if only when war broke out. On lines of economic determinism the only tenable attitude, which Marx himself usually adopted, was to support the nation whose cause in war would favor economic development and hence growth of the proletarian movement. But the general principle had to be interpreted. Did it, for instance, always point to support for the more economically advanced nation against the more backward nation? In specific cases therefore a difference of opinion often appeared in Marxist circles as to which nation represented for the time being the 'advancing historical forces.' [42]

In a similar way Lenin and Stalin regarded some of the wars for national independence in Western Europe in the eighteenth and nineteenth centuries as 'progressive,' that is, waged by the rising bourgeoisie and hence an advance over feudal rule: a necessary

40. *Communist Manifesto.*
41. English edition, Moscow, 1940.
42. On the Marxist attitude toward war see E. H. Carr, *The Bolshevik Revolution, 1917–1923,* London, 1953, III, pp. 549ff.

stage in the building of capitalism. Eastern Europe and Asia were expected to go through the same stage in the twentieth century.

Unfortunately, in the twentieth century Lenin had come out with his theory that wars between nations, being mere capitalist quarrels, were all equally to be condemned. Like Marx, he scoffed at the distinction between aggressive and defensive wars. His assumption was that all nations were bourgeois. He was therefore compelled to work out a new tactic for the proletarian movement. Accordingly he advocated resistance by the proletariat to all national-capitalist wars, and their conversion into civil wars. It was easier for the Russian Bolsheviks to take this internationalist line, because the Russian state (although not a bourgeois state) was clearly their enemy and legal political activity was circumscribed. It was harder for social democrats and communists in Western Europe to take the same attitude, since the state was not so obviously the enemy, trade unions and Marxists flourished openly, and the workers often had a stake in the country and were on the whole susceptible to patriotic appeals. The clearest example, perhaps, was Germany, where the alliance between socialism and nationalism had been forged by Lassalle and taken advantage of by Bismarck.

One problem remains however. What of a war for national independence, the struggle, say, of a colonial territory against a capitalist country with a strong proletarian movement? Marx himself was of two minds on this, and economic determinism is no guide. Lenin's prescription was, on the surface, plain: support the backward country if this will further the revolution within the capitalist nation. (The responsibility of a 'socialist' country with colonies never seems to have crossed his mind.)

In giving this advice, as in asking the proletariat to turn every war into a class war, Lenin, like most zealous Marxists, overlooked the psychological fact that proletarians are also keen patriots, and the economic fact that their interests often coincide with the national interest.

The simple truth that there is no overriding identity of interest between workers, or capitalists, of different countries militates strongly against the international class struggle. Neither class interest, in the Marxist sense, nor the internationalism of any of the great world religions has yet proved strong enough to overshadow national loyalties. The predominant strength of patriotism was widely illustrated at the outbreak of the war in 1914 when the greater part of the socialist parties in all countries fell in behind their governments, a step which Lenin heatedly and vainly condemned as 'social chauvinism.' In a later day, too, communists in Germany (heavily influenced by Moscow) tragically failed to gauge accurately the powerful and terrible appeal of nationalist sentiments in that country, and by following instead their paralyzing diagnosis of Fascism as 'the last stage of capitalism in decline,' they contributed much, especially after 1928, to the rise of National Socialism and the downfall of democracy.

It remains to be seen whether the threat of atomic destruction can perform what economic and religious forces have so far failed to accomplish, and break down national prejudices sufficiently to insure world peace.

The first great step is always the organization of the workers into an independent political party.

ENGELS.

A revolution is only possible when both these factors, the modern productive forces and the bourgeois productive forms, come in collision with one another.

MARX.

He who recognizes only *the class struggle is not yet a Marxist . . . A Marxist is one who* extends *the acceptance of the class struggle to the acceptance of the* dictatorship *of the proletariat . . . On this touchstone it is necessary to test a real understanding and acceptance of Marxism.*

LENIN.

The dictatorship itself only constitutes the transition to the abolition of all classes and to a classless society.

MARX.[1]

5

Party, Revolution, and Dictatorship of the Proletariat

I

ALTHOUGH MARX BELIEVED that the downfall of capitalism was inevitable, he did not think that the class struggle of modern times could be relied upon to achieve its ends blindly as it had done in the past. There was an essential role to be played by communists, and it is that role which is examined here.

The first question which may be asked is: should the communists

1. Engels, *Selected Correspondence,* p. 450; Marx, *Selected Correspondence,* p. 57, and *Selected Works,* 1942, II, p. 299. Lenin, *State and Revolution* (in *Towards the Seizure of Power*) New York, 1932, II, p. 176.

form their own political party? The *Communist Manifesto* gives
the impression that they should not. 'The Communists do not form
a separate party opposed to other working class parties. They have
no interests separate and apart from those of the proletariat as a
whole.' Instead they are to ally themselves with all progressive
parties: now with Social Democrats, now with Radicals, now with
the party of agrarian reform, and even with the bourgeoisie when
the latter are fighting against the older regime, and 'support every
revolutionary movement against the existing social and political
order of things.'

In whatever temporary alliance may be made, communists are
to distinguish themselves by continually emphasizing the common
class interests of the proletariat and the vital property question.
Because of their greater theoretical grasp of history they are 'the
most advanced and resolute section of the working class parties
of every country.' 'Finally, they labor everywhere for the union and
agreement of the democratic parties of all countries.'

The Communist League, for which the *Manifesto* was written,
was not a political party in the ordinary sense, but rather a propaganda and discussion agency, while the German communists at that
time were merely a wing of the larger Democratic (lower middle
class) Party. Moreover, the First International of the 1860's, in
which Marx played a large part, was also not a party but a weak
federal organization loosely united around the Marxist philosophy.
Even the Second International, founded in 1889 in Paris after
Marx's death, although formally Marxist, contained members with
a variety of social philosophies.[2]

In view of all this, where do modern communists derive their
policy of a separate communist party? The answer is from Marx
himself. If one turns from the *Manifesto* to Marx's *Address of the
Central Council to the Communist League,* written two years later,
quite specific recommendations are found. A definite program was
given for the organization of the Workers' Party (whose nucleus

2. The Third International (the Comintern), founded in 1919 under Russian
influence, was strictly communist from the start. The non-communist element
withdrew and in 1923 formed a different international. The Comintern was
abolished in 1945 amid a great fanfare of publicity. The present Cominform
established in 1947 may in many respects, however, be justly regarded as the
successor to the Comintern.

was the Communist League) in Germany, and in the detailed prescription which Marx gave on tactics, the need for a separate party
was taken for granted throughout. The question of party is also
explicit if we rely on the evidence of Engels, as given in the quota-
tion at the head of this chapter, and in the following:

> For the proletariat to be strong enough to conquer on the day
> of decision, it is necessary, and this view Marx and I have up-
> held since 1847, that it should form its own party, separated
> from all others and opposed to them, a class conscious, class
> party.[3]

There are many such comments in the writings of Marx and
Engels.

The question of whether or not there should be a communist
party is more apparent than real, and arises from Marx's single-
minded point of view. He was of the opinion that there would, and
perhaps could, be only one genuine party of the proletariat, whatever its name; and that the only possible philosophy it could hold
was that of communism. Any other parties bidding for the allegiance of the workers, such as the French Socialists, he regarded as
not genuine workers' parties at all but assorted groupings with
assorted views, who at their best were petty bourgeois and preoccupied with what Lenin later called 'constitutional nonsense.'
One may conclude therefore that Marxism has always implied a
separate political party, and that in this respect modern communist parties are in the true Marxist tradition.

At the same time there is a considerable difference between the
nature of the party as it was conceived by Marx and Engels and as
later developed by Lenin. Marx seems to have had in mind a mass
party, officered by communist intellectuals who would provide the
advanced theory and the leadership, yet with the rank and file
sharing actively in the discussion and the decisions; a party, in
brief, rather like the type of political party usually found in the
democracies.

About 1900, when he was in exile and writing for the paper
Iskra (The Spark), Lenin sought to draw lessons from the failure of
the Marxists to achieve power in any country. He thereupon formu-

3. *Selected Works*, 1942, II, p. 28.

lated a new policy and his reasoning, set forth in his pamphlet
What Is To Be Done?, ran thus: with the advance of capitalism, discontent would grow, but the proletariat would not automatically
become class-conscious and revolutionary. They would, he thought,
if left to themselves tend to become bourgeois or at best merely
'trade-union conscious.' The peasantry, too, were hopelessly petty
bourgeois in outlook, and both classes must therefore have class
consciousness brought to them, *'from without,'* by party intellectuals.

Marx and Engels would have had no quarrel with this, for they
held much the same sentiments, but Lenin went even farther. The
communist party must be small, 'narrow,' 'unified,' 'a professional
organization of revolutionists,' to *direct* and *dominate* the proletariat; not a party democratically controlled by the workers, but
instead one that controlled the workers. Membership was to be
confined to those who played an *active* part in the organization. A
close watch must be maintained over doctrine, and those who
dissented even on minor points of tactics must be expelled. The
old Marxist slogan that 'the emancipation of the workers must be
the task of the working class itself' was now given a somewhat
different meaning, and the working class was to march toward revolution directed by an organization whose closest parallel is the
military. Soon the party was in fact being described as 'the military
staff of the proletariat.' 'It is the conversion of the authority of ideas
into the authority of power, the subordination of the lower Party
bodies to the higher Party bodies.' [4] In a word, the party is now
monolithic.

We ought, of course, to remember the context of Lenin's advocacy of this kind of party. He was writing a tactical policy to meet
the special conditions in Russia, where it was impossible for an
open Marxist party to operate. A mass-organization party, in opposition, is not possible under any despotism. His prescription is best
thought of as one suitable for an underground movement. Hence,
too, his stipulation that all the secret side of the work should be
concentrated into the hands of 'a dozen experienced revolutionists,' supported by a limited amount of open work in the trade

4. Lenin, *The Iskra Period*, pp. 185ff. Stalin, *Foundations of Leninism,
Handbook*, p. 843.

unions. It was not so much, at first, a theory of a party suited to all times and places — although it became that later when his ideas hardened into orthodoxy — as the shaping of an instrument to make a revolution inside Russia.

Yet, even after making all due allowance, one sees that Lenin's new theory of the party was a great break within the Marxist tradition. It is a clue to the understanding of many other of his adaptations. Marxism, like nearly all revolutionary or protest movements, had included a genuinely liberal and humanitarian strain, which Lenin now rejected. Along with this went an abandonment of the belief in reason and the powers of persuasion. There was to be no waiting until a combination of circumstances and propaganda won over an increasing and finally irresistible number of workers to communist views. Not only was it hopeless to expect the bourgeoisie to change — Marx also thought this — but now Lenin gave up the proletariat, too, as hopeless. The workers were regarded as too stupid to see where their own real interests lay, and hence the revolution must be engineered for them by the party. The indispensable function of the workers was to act as followers. They need not be consulted, still less would they determine policy, for was not the elite party after all acting on their behalf, with full understanding of the real interests and historic destiny of the proletariat? The same attitude toward the masses may be seen on every hand, among impatient fanatics who believe themselves to be the chosen instruments of fate, called upon to build a new world.

By 1903 Lenin's ideas on the party and on other matters had become official, and it was over the Leninist interpretation that the Russian Social Democratic (Marxist) Party split into Bolshevik (majority) and Menshevik (minority) factions. Trotsky, Martov, and, later on, Plekhanov and many others differed sharply, preferring to build a party organized on more democratic lines, and so went over to the Mensheviks. For most of the time thereafter, until 1917, the Mensheviks were actually in a majority within the Social Democratic Party.

When put to the test in Russia in 1917, Lenin's Bolsheviks (renamed the Communist Party) succeeded in obtaining and holding power. Once they controlled the state, the Bolsheviks imposed their ideas of the nature of the party by force. Success is a powerful argument, and the Communist Party model has accordingly been copied elsewhere. The theory of the centralized exclusive party in every country, joined in membership in the Third (Communist) International where the Russian Party always dominated, also explains why the Moscow line is always followed abroad, so that joint action with other parties, when it has occasionally been taken, has always been too little and too late to prevent the victory of right-wing dictatorships. The refusal of the communists to join with other working-class parties in the early 1930's did much to pave the way for the Nazi victory in Germany. Yet other parties ought to have no delusions if they should happen to be supported by a communist party. Marx's advice to the Communist League in the 1850's had been little more than to work with other parties to make temporary use of them, and then to destroy them. Lenin repeated the same advice almost *ad nauseam*. As the postwar history of Eastern Europe shows, too, other parties co-operate with the Communist Party in the sure prospect of absorption or suppression. In the Soviet Union the party is in full control of all the institutions in the country, whether political as laid down in the constitution, or economic such as the trade unions. The party, and more especially the inner circle of its central committee, the Presidium, is the nerve center of everything, and it was as Secretary-General of the party rather than as leader of the State that Stalin was able to exercise his tremendous influence. It is through the party that the ambitious Russian must, and in fact can, hope to rise to a high position. The party more than anything else welds together the diverse nationalities of the federated republics. And with the passing of time the party appears to permit less and less 'democracy,' i.e. discussion of policy, within its ranks. Decisions are made more and more by the top, and then rigidly enforced with all the instruments of control at the disposal of a totalitarian state.

Stalin thus went even farther than Lenin intended. However much he believed in strict party rule, Lenin did allow an element of free discussion in the top echelons of the party, while Stalin moved away even from that. There must be no 'factions'; 'the Party is strengthened by purging itself of opportunist elements.' But it is merely the logical and tragic conclusion of Lenin's decision in 1902, a decision for a course of action which Lenin deluded himself would be only temporary, because required only by the special Russian circumstances.[5]

II

In the *Communist Manifesto* Marx had something to say on the immediate program as well as on the ultimate aims of communists. The immediate program, he noted, would differ in different countries, but 'in the most advanced countries the following will be pretty generally applicable':

1. Abolition of property in land and application of all rents of land to public purposes.
2. A heavy progressive or graduated income tax.
3. Abolition of all right of inheritance.
4. Confiscation of the property of all emigrants and rebels.
5. Centralization of credit in the hands of the state, by means of a national bank with state capital and an exclusive monopoly.
6. Centralization of means of communication and transport in the hands of the state.
7. Extension of factories and instruments of production owned by the state; the bringing into cultivation of waste lands, and the improvement of the soil generally in accordance with a common plan.
8. Equal obligation of all to work. Establishment of industrial armies, especially for agriculture.
9. Combination of agriculture and manufacturing industries; gradual abolition of all the distinction between town and country, by a more equable distribution of population over the country.
10. Free education for all children in public schools. Abolition of children's factory labor in its present form. Combination of education with industrial production, et cetera.

The list is a kind of party platform, setting forth the practical political reforms for which the communists of Marx's day should

5. *Foundations of Leninism, Handbook,* pp. 852–3. B. Russell, *Roads to Freedom,* London, 1935, p. 108.

agitate.[6] Some of them, for instance the second and tenth, are now accepted commonplaces; others, such as the fifth and sixth, are substantially accepted, while the democracies have gone far toward adopting most of the remainder.

Resembling as it did a party platform, the *Manifesto* could be expected to show a certain circumspection in dealing with topical issues on which there might be genuine differences of opinion among proletarians of different countries. Doubtless for that reason Marx and Engels said nothing in the *Manifesto* on such controversies as the demands of the Chartists, or the subject of free trade versus protection. In their other writings they did comment on these matters, and for the most part seem to have adopted the usual conventional views, advocating free trade for an industrialized country (England) and protection for less developed countries such as Ireland or the United States.

Of more importance, however, is that Marx saw no possibility of conflict between the short-run program and the ultimate revolutionary objective; and Plekhanov after him also argued that they both have their place and are not opposed. Yet they do conflict, and as a result communists are always confronted with an embarrassing situation. The more successful the short-run program, the less revolutionary the workers become; so that nowhere is revolutionary communism less appealing than in the wealthy industrialized countries where so much of the program has been attained. Once more we come back to the fact that Marx was not really convinced that any substantial reforms could be achieved under capitalism, or that if they were achieved they would alter the *essential nature* of capitalism and make it tolerable. Marxists usually talk in the language of Aristotelian 'essences' and hence are rarely convinced by an appeal to experience.

III

The nature and role of the party in the class struggle derive their meaning only from Marx's theory of revolution. When Marx spoke

6. The demands of the Central Committee of the Communist League (1850) for Germany included: a republican form of government, adult franchise at twenty-one, the payment of M.P.'s, universal arming of the people, the free administration of justice, and limitation of the right of inheritance. *Selected Works*, 1942, II, pp. 17–19.

of revolution he was of course thinking of what might be called 'socially significant' revolutions. Others, such as the palace revolutions of the South American type, Marx would dismiss as without significance, and Stalin in turn called them 'toy rebellions.'

The first point to note is Marx's attitude toward the use of violence. Unlike the Nihilists, he did not idealize violence as such, although the use of force is often mentioned in Marxist literature, and Marx himself set the tone with his dictum that 'force is the midwife of every old society pregnant with a new one.' Marx and Engels were rather more exuberant believers in violence in their younger days, but later tended to regard it as a necessary evil. Marx may personally have preferred that capitalism should be superseded peacefully, but he showed no signs of believing that this was possible, except once or twice in rather casual references to England, Holland, and the United States. He believed that a resort to violence by the proletariat would be necessary for two reasons.

In the first and original Marxist case, the veiled civil war which he regarded as endemic in capitalism must give way to an open war, with the proletariat as the aggressor. This belief made a certain amount of sense in 1848, since in face of the autocratic governments of Europe there was in fact no way open for the proletariat to gain power except by violent means. With the broadening down of the franchise to include the proletariat, however, the communists would be able to thrive on legal methods, as Engels, Plekhanov, and later Marxists noted. Yet faced with the prospect of a legal proletarian victory by ballot in the democracies, the entrenched bourgeoisie, so Marxists believed, would not hesitate to use force and hence could be met and overcome only by force.

The second case is therefore a more subtle Marxist position and was adopted in view of the patently non-revolutionary attitude of the proletariat. The proletariat might form a government by peaceful voting, but once they tried in all seriousness to dislodge the bourgeoisie from economic power and from control of the organs of state, a counter-revolution would ensue — with the bourgeoisie as aggressor — and in self-defense the proletarian government would be compelled to take up arms to consolidate the revolution. In either case, open warfare, or what Engels called a 'democratic revolution by force,' was inevitable and, however reluctantly, the proletariat would be compelled to fight.

Marxists make great play with the slogan that no ruling class in history has ever given up its power without a struggle. The historical generalization is partly true, partly a trick statement. Common experience bears out that any privileged class or group will tend to universalize its privileges, to resist change, and is unlikely willingly to give up its privileges or position. But the real question is whether the unwilling surrender of privilege, especially control of the government, can be effected only by civil war. A detailed examination of historical transfers of power and privileges cannot be made here. It is in any case largely beside the point, because unless peaceful and constitutional provision for a change of government is provided — which was seldom true except in recent history — no other way than that of forcible change is possible. In addition, unless history repeats itself — which is a thesis impossible to establish — what has happened in the past can give no certain rule for the future, although it may give a degree of plausibility.

The question is also too sharply put. What is a ruling class? In Marxist theory, history has seen only a few specimens, the ruling classes of slavery, feudalism, capitalism. Obviously the transition from one to the other of these historical epochs (even granting what is not true for most of the world, a sequence of these three steps) was a long, slow business, in which many influences, including wars, played a part. There was certainly no dramatic overthrow of one system and its replacement by another, in the way in which Marx foretold the end of capitalism.

If a ruling class is defined more broadly and realistically, history will, as usual, be found to speak with several voices. For instance, it required a revolution to shake off the rule of Britain from the American colonies, and Ireland, too, had to make a display of force in a later day; but in the cases of Canada, New Zealand, Australia, India, Pakistan, and Burma, the transfer of sovereignty proceeded peacefully and the same is true of the separation of Norway from Sweden, and of Iceland from Denmark. The white population in South Africa may also be regarded as a ruling class, which, however, if it keeps on with its present policies, is hardly likely to be persuaded to share its power with the non-whites by anything short of civil war.

In the case of the transfer of political power from the landed interests to the bourgeoisie in Britain, there is some uncertainty in

Marxist circles. It seems to be agreed by historians, and was often noted by Marx, that the first Reform Act of 1832 effectually ended the monopoly of the landed aristocracy as the ruling class. Now the relevant point about the Reform Act is that the landed interests did not resort to civil war, but reluctantly gave way in the end rather than fight, so that it must be considered as a peaceful shift of power from a ruling class. There was never, of course, any complete 'transfer of power' from one class to another. It may perhaps be called a *sharing* of power, since the influence of the landed aristocracy continued far into the nineteenth century, and for that matter is felt to some extent even today.

Since this judgment could hardly be approved by Marxists, they tend to deny that a transfer took place in 1832, and prefer to look back upon the civil-war period of the 1640's as marking the real and forcible overthrow of the landed class; an event of which the participants in the political struggle of 1832 were singularly unaware. Engels tried to have it both ways, stating that the civil war was a bourgeois victory, but that a fresh struggle was needed in the 1830's. He called the 1688 Revolution a 'class compromise,' by which 'the political spoils went to land owners, and economic power to the bourgeoisie . . .' Marx thought sometimes that the landed oligarchy was still in control of England in 1869.[7] We need not enter upon the fruitless controversy, since the historical process was essentially a long one in which the civil war, the Glorious Revolution of 1688, the Reform Act, and many other events were merely stages and not sharp corners or 'leaps,' of which indeed there are very few in history.

Marxism is also divided over the victory of German capitalism. Some Marxists say it occurred in the seventeenth century, but Marx thought that Germany was still feudal in 1850, the year in which he expected a bourgeois revolution. He admitted that the bourgeois revolution failed. Since another did not take place, are we to conclude either (a) that Germany is still feudal, or (b) that it became bourgeois without a class war?

Historical analogies aside, what concerns us most today, as it did

---

7. *Selected Works*, 1942, I, pp. 406, 409. *Selected Correspondence*, pp. 88, 279. Cf. also Marx on *The English Revolution*, in *Selected Essays*, op. cit., and Durbin, op. cit. pp. 193ff.

Marx, is the theory of the necessity of violence for the overthrow of capitalism. Now, it is unlikely in the extreme that the votes of the industrial proletariat alone could win an electoral victory for communism. For one thing there are not enough of them, and they are steadily becoming a smaller proportion of the employed in all industrialized countries, so that the votes of the salariat and new middle classes are also necessary. But these latter voters are not attracted by the prospect of a violent revolution, and it is difficult enough, as most labor parties know to their sorrow, to get them to vote even for democratic socialism. In the absence of a complete breakdown of the economic system, for which again there is no precedent or evidence, surely the opposite of Marx's thesis is nearer the truth: that capitalism *in the democracies* can be transformed *only* by peaceful methods. But where capitalism exists in non-democratic countries, the Marxist or any other forcible solution may well be more realistic.

IV

The great question that must now be asked of Marx is: when did he think the revolution would break out, that is, at what stage and under what conditions of capitalism? There is one main theory in Marx on this point, with traces of a second which has been further developed by later communists. First, let us take the main theory. Here the answer is beyond dispute: the revolution will come only when the 'objective possibilities' are present, when capitalism is ripe, when the productive forces have outgrown the existing property relations. The dialectical processes of history can never be telescoped or by-passed. Marx was quite definite:

> No social order can ever disappear before all the productive forces for which there is room in it have been developed; and new higher relations of production never appear before the material conditions of their existence have matured in the womb of the old society itself.

> [Society] can neither overleap the natural phases of evolution, nor shuffle them out of the world by decrees. But this much at least it can do; it can shorten and lessen the birth-pangs . . .

> A country in which industrial development is more advanced than in others, simply presents those others with a picture of their own future.

And Engels:

> Revolutions are not made intentionally and arbitrarily, but everywhere and always they have been the necessary consequences of conditions which were wholly independent of the will and direction of individual parties and entire classes.[8]

All this, and much more in the same vein, is quite clear in Marx and Engels: the economic revolution must precede the political; one system must play out its historic role before another can succeed it. Revolutions of this kind cannot be made to order, but when the conditions are fulfilled, the revolution is inevitable; when the egg is ready to hatch the shell will be broken: 'the economic revolution must be followed by a political one, for the latter is only the expression of the former.' The *coup de grâce* would be given, Marx thought, during a trade crisis or perhaps during a war. Asked by an American labor delegate to the Soviet Union when the revolution would occur, Stalin was much more cagey, and replied that 'such a revolution can unfold itself only under certain favourable economic and political conditions.'[9]

There is no need to dwell on this, for, as we have seen, capitalism has not developed along the lines envisaged by Marx: the will to revolution is therefore not present in the Western democracies and in any case the nature of modern weapons of warfare has made almost obsolete the old conception of violent proletarian revolution with its barricades and popular uprisings. Given the appropriate economic, social, and other conditions, no doubt a *coup d'état* may be engineered by communists, or by any other unscrupulous party, or a revolution may occur on the Russian model, but we need no Marx to tell this. Even more important, as shown by the examples of Germany, Austria, and Hungary after the 1914–18 war, there is no guarantee whatever that seizure of power will result in

8. Marx, *Selected Works*, 1942, I, p. 357; *Capital*, I, pp. 863, 864; Engels, *Principles of Communism*, p. 13.

9. *Selected Works*, 1942, I, p. 80.

a lasting proletarian victory. (Premature seizure of power is known
in Marxist language as 'Blanquism' after Louis Blanqui, a revolutionary who for a few hours was head of a provisional government
in Paris toward the end of the Franco-Prussian war.)

The obvious and correct Marxist reply to this must be that such
revolutions were premature because capitalism in these countries
was then immature. As Marx wrote in an early essay:

> If, therefore, the proletariat should overthrow the political
> rule of the bourgeoisie its victory would only be temporary,
> so long as the material conditions which would render neces-
> sary the abolition of the bourgeois mode of production . . .
> had not yet been created in the course of historical develop-
> ment.[10]

Unfortunately for Marxism this not only would account for the
failure of the Hungarian and other post-1918 ventures but would
rule out, *a fortiori,* the Russian Revolution itself.

It is then useless to stage a premature revolution, nor can a revolution be just willed into existence: fifteen, twenty, fifty years of
wars and class-conscious training may have to come first. A rather
different but interesting question arises in regard to the communist tactics that should be employed in pre-capitalist or underdeveloped countries. Again, Marx's main theory is clear: 'They [the
workers] can and must take part in the middle class revolution, as
a condition preliminary to the Labor revolution.' [11] That is why
he believed the proletariat in England, as in the Chartist movement, should work with the free traders and the Anti-Corn Law
League. Similarly the proletariat was right to support the bourgeois
revolution in France in 1789. Marx thought that once the powerful,
industrialized areas such as Western Europe and North America
had gone through the revolution, they would dominate and set the
pace for the rest of the world. In the meantime, then, on Marx's
argument communists ought to do their best to further the cause
of capitalism in all backward areas of the world, since capitalism
is a necessary stage before the revolution. There is something
attractive about the picture of an alliance of capitalists and com-

10. *Selected Essays,* p. 137.
11. Ibid. p. 161. *Selected Correspondence,* p. 92.

munists setting out, for different reasons, to industrialize the undeveloped countries, but it is quite fanciful. When put to the test of
action, as in Russia in 1917, communists soon threw over their support of the bourgeois Kerensky regime, under which capitalism
would have been developed to a riper stage, and set up instead their
full-fledged dictatorship of the proletariat. Nor do the Russians today show much enthusiasm for the United Nations Technical Assistance Program.

Apologists of the Soviet Union tend to put forward two contradictory defenses of the Russian revolution. To harmonize the
revolution with Marx's main theory they try to prove that Russia
was really a highly industrialized country in 1917, with the roots of
capitalism going back for centuries. But they also point to the
backwardness of Russia in 1917, in contrast with the present industrialization, in order to show the great achievements of the
Soviet regime. There were in fact some three to four million urban
workers in Russia in 1917, and although largely unorganized they,
like the peasants, who formed 80 per cent of the population, were
ripe for revolution because of the extraordinary conditions prevailing in that year (see p. 150).

About Marx's main theory of the conditions under which the
revolution would occur there can be no mistake. Yet the revolution
has not in fact taken place in any largely industrialized country,
but on the contrary has taken place only in Russia and other comparatively less industrialized countries. Since Marx's main theory
will not serve, communists must find some other explanation of
this apparently embarrassing turn of events.

The later communist theory bases itself on Marx's *ad hoc* pamphlet to which reference was made earlier, the 1850 *Address of the
Central Council to the Communist League.* In 1850 he was firmly
convinced that revolution was just around the corner in Germany,
and the *Address* was written to give tactical advice to the communists in Germany concerning the part they were to play in
the forthcoming bourgeois revolution.

The advice Marx gave to the communists was that they should
work with the Democratic Party (which Marx diagnosed as a petty-
bourgeois group) so long as they both faced a common enemy,
but once the enemy was vanquished and the petty bourgeoisie

showed signs of resting on their laurels, the communists should press on toward proletarian victory. To this end, they must set up their own organizations, encourage instances of popular revenge, employ conspiratorial methods, form revolutionary workers' governments, organize an independent militia from the armed proletariat, resist disarmament if necessary by force, and 'make the revolution permanent . . . until the proletariat has conquered state power.' By 'permanent' Marx in this context meant *continuing,* in the sense that the communists should press on, far beyond the bourgeois, constitutional reforms, which would satisfy the Democratic Party. In substance, Marx was advising the communists to seize power as soon as they could. They would be compelled to seize power or to submit to suppression, for obviously no government could tolerate for long an armed, rioting conspiracy. What they should do after seizing power in a pre-capitalist country Marx did not say.

The tactics recommended by Marx — including secrecy, arming, and duplicate governments — were clearly meant to apply only when a revolution was imminent. It is no less clear that the prescription to press on, in a semi-feudal country, from the bourgeois to a 'proletarian' revolution, is in flat contradiction to Marx's main thesis of the priority of economic development. His economic determinism and his sweeping social theory are all forgotten and Marx acts entirely as a political adviser, a man anxious to see his following form a government. (He also believed that the Germanic tribes had gone directly to feudalism, without the intervening stage of slavery — which of course makes nonsense of any dialectic of history.)

Marx himself came around afterward to abandon the 1850 view, and in his later years, although he gave an evasive answer to anxious Russian questioners, he remained doubtful whether Russia could be unique, and by-pass the full capitalist stage. He did not wish to go back on his main theory or yet to disappoint his Russian admirers. His noncommittal reply, framed after careful consideration, ran thus:

If the Russian revolution becomes the signal for a proletarian revolution in the west, so that both complement each other, the present Russian common ownership of land may serve as the starting point for a communist development.[12]

Nor did Plekhanov think it was possible to short-circuit any stage of development. The 1850 *Address* might be entirely written off as a historical curiosity, an example of Marx's youth or eagerness for revolution running away with his better judgment, were it not for the fact that it was elevated by Lenin, who called it a 'magnificent and valuable mistake,' to the level of official Bolshevik doctrine. Lenin subscribed to every detail of the advice contained in the *Address,* on the weak ground that Marx 'never subsequently took back what he said then about tactics.' [13]

By 1905, both Trotsky and Lenin had worked out the ideas of 'continuing revolution' and the 1850 tactics in relation to Russia, and their arguments were later used to justify the plan of going straight from Czarism to socialism. In doing this Lenin had a good deal to build upon, for the idea of missing the intervening capitalist stage, although jeered at by Engels in 1852, became a strong tradition among the Populists (rural revolutionaries) of Russia in the late nineteenth century. Alexander Herzen, for instance, an influential Russian radical, had rejected the Marxist analysis, and had argued that where the capitalist class was weak, and the peasantry strong, 'socialism' could be much more easily introduced.

The Mensheviks took the more strictly Marxist line, which Lenin heartily abused as the heresy of 'economism,' that not until the bourgeois democratic revolution had run its course would the stage be set for the proletariat. In the interim, they thought, Marxists should sit in the Russian Duma as the opposition. Such a belief tends to paralyze action and to make any party that holds it reluctant to force the pace of events. In addition it was hard doctrine for Lenin and other aging revolutionaries, whom years of exile and frustration had rendered so eager for livelier action and for the reality of political power. They had become, as Engels had said of himself and Marx in 1848, 'spoilt for the role of preachers in the wilderness . . .' Lenin used a further *ad hoc* argument: to act merely as an opposition might discredit socialism with the masses,

12. *Selected Works,* 1942, I, p. 192; but cf. *Selected Correspondence,* p. 353.
13. *Selected Works,* 1942, II, pp. 23, 28.

would alarm the bourgeoisie and frighten them into reaction, since the Russian bourgeoisie was not 'revolutionary' as was the bourgeoisie in other countries. This may have been good tactical sense, but it was something outside the Marxist recommendations, and is another good example of how Lenin interpreted Marx for his own purposes. As always, Lenin was interested in the practical usefulness of his ideas, not in their consistency with Marx's main theory.

Lenin was in the great tradition of the Russian revolutionaries in his profound distrust of legal activity to further the ends of the party. Marx had been disgusted and disillusioned by the Frankfurt Assembly in 1848 and thenceforth had little faith in parliamentary democracy. Lenin absorbed Marx's skepticism of parliaments and added to it a lifelong bitterness regarding the cowardice of liberals. He believed that parliamentary action had achieved nothing for the workers in Russia, while who could tell how many years of delay would elapse before its slow process brought the Bolsheviks to the top? Lenin therefore opposed liberalism and bourgeois democracy as stoutly as he fought Czarism.

Extremism usually calls forth an opposite extremism, and the distrust of moderate reform and legal activity was a natural growth from the soil of Czarist Russia. How to make a revolution, not how to promote reform, had been the chief problem of nearly all Russian political thought. Russian revolutionaries of several persuasions had employed terrorism and assassination as normal political weapons. To do them justice, Marxists in general have not given terrorism such wholesale approval (Plekhanov and Lenin both condemned Narodnik assassins) but have favored its use only as part of the final revolutionary onslaught. Its use at other times Lenin regarded as 'inopportune' or 'inexpedient.' [14]

Lacking any historical precedent, Lenin applied the formula for the continuous revolution, as outlined in the 1850 *Address* of Marx, with remarkable fidelity. He could follow Marx's prescription because events in Russia in 1917 were very like the situation which Marx had wrongly believed to exist in Germany in 1848. The Bolshevik Party first joined forces with the parties of the bourgeoisie, the petty bourgeoisie, and the peasantry — all allies against

14. *The Iskra Period*, I, p. 111.

the common enemy of the Czarist regime. Although on principle Lenin hated 'alliances, understandings and blocs with social reformist liberalism which . . . only blunt the consciousness of the masses,' he often welcomed alliances and compromises if they served his temporary purposes.

Lenin had for many years led the Bolsheviks from exile, and was in Switzerland when the Russian pot boiled over in the spring of 1917. He arrived in Russia in mid-April, a month after the Czar's abdication. The bourgeois-democratic regime which had followed, with its grandiose talk of parliamentary government, and of extensive land reform, may have satisfied some of the enemies of Czarism but was merely a beginning for Lenin and his Bolsheviks (and for some of the other parties as well). The provisional government was pledged to carry on the war against Germany, a tremendous handicap to the popularity and efficiency of any government in the circumstances, while in addition it was beset by famine, inflation, and war defeats, and harassed on every side by a number of revolutionary parties.

The union of different classes, 'always the necessary condition of any revolution,' cannot last long, as Engels once pointed out. Lenin turned first against the bourgeois government: it was, he said, 'a military dictatorship,' and after July had become 'counter-revolutionary.' By November, the Kerensky government was overthrown by an alliance of peasantry and proletariat, with the Bolsheviks in the dominant role, in spite of the fact that most of the peasantry supported the Social Revolutionaries, and the more stable portion of the proletariat supported the Mensheviks. The trade unions had on the whole been dominated by the Mensheviks and remained aloof from Lenin until *after* the November revolution. The Constituent Assembly which met in January of 1918, and in which the Bolsheviks had secured only a minority of seats, was dissolved by Lenin, and that was the end of the feeble attempts at parliamentary government in Russia. Thenceforth the Bolsheviks were supreme in the cities, although the elimination of opponents dragged on for some time, and a fearful civil war had to be fought before the party was firmly entrenched throughout the country.

The process by which the Bolsheviks gained ascendancy is not hard to understand. Lenin was a forceful and gifted leader and tactician. (Trotsky was in many respects even more talented, as linguist, writer, orator, and military strategist, but was less practical on the whole, and far less specialized and single-minded than either Lenin or Stalin. He had disliked the aridity and rigidity of Marxism in his early days, and had not hesitated to break with Lenin. He returned to Russia in 1917, joined with Lenin, and as commissar of war did a great deal to save the revolution for the Bolsheviks.)

Lenin knew what he wanted and how to get it, and was not hampered by any scruples. He had a carefully prepared program of demanding more and more from the government and promising more and more to the people, and of dispensing with his temporary allies as soon as he could. He led a tight and disciplined party organization, and after September he controlled the dual government of 'Soviets' or workers' committees behind the scenes, in factories, cities, towns, and villages. He was, above everything else, aided by the circumstances of the time: the defeats and confusion of war, the shattering economic collapse, the discontent of the peasants, the mutinies in the armed forces. 'The war has in three years dragged us [in Russia] thirty years ahead,' Lenin wrote.[15] Add to this the weakness and divisions in the opposition parties, including the vacillation of the Mensheviks and the failure of the Social Revolutionary party of the peasants, and one can almost say that the autumn Bolshevik revolution, like the first revolution in the spring, was made *for* Lenin. His astute appeal of 'Peace, Land, and Bread' was irresistible.

A similar underlying pattern of tactics emerges from the post-1945 history of southeastern Europe, the main difference being that in Russia a revolutionary situation existed, and the party arrived in sole power in a matter of months, while in the Balkans the process was extended over a few years, under the shadow of Soviet military might. It is still perhaps too early to say whether the party will achieve a similar tight control in China after exploiting nationalist feeling and the support of the peasantry, but we should not be surprised if it does. None of these historical processes makes sense in the light of Marx's general analysis of capitalism, but they

15. *Towards the Seizure of Power*, I, p. 131.

are all explainable to the letter on the basis of the *Address* of 1850 with its theory of uninterrupted or permanent revolution.

There is no reason at all, on Marx's main theory, to expect anything more than a premature seizing of power in a non-industrialized country. Lenin and Stalin have merely remarked on the 'zigzags of history,' and appealed to the doctrine of 'uneven development' to show that the conditions for revolution may be in *any* country, even in backward areas, because the 'national and colonial question is a component part of the general international proletarian revolution.' [16]

It is not to Marx, then, but to Lenin and Stalin that we must go for the rationalization of the Bolshevik success, and they could find plenty of *obiter dicta* in Marx to justify almost any course of action. The justification of Bolshevik methods lies not so much in the inevitable operation of the dialectic, the forces of production conflicting with property relations; nor even in the proletarian class struggle; but is much more a question of opportunism, shrewd tactics and timing, and the control of men and events. The only successful communist revolutions in their own right, without serious outside aid, have been in such countries as Russia and China and have been made by relying on the peasantry, the largest class in these countries. (Alternatively, if party tactics had followed the Leninist example a number of seizures of power in Europe could perhaps have been durable after 1918.)

What we are dealing with is the age-old political problem of how to seize and retain power. Leninist and modern communist theory on this point is nothing more than a Machiavellian prescription for handling the problem with special and ruthless efficiency. 'What a part,' Marx once wrote, 'stupidity plays in revolutions and how they are exploited by scoundrels.' Engels pointed out that 'insurrection is an art quite as much as war or any other,' and approved Danton's sentiment that audacity above all is the thing. Engels and Lenin both read Clausewitz and recommended him to party workers because of the similarities between military and political strategy. Lenin went to the heart of the matter when he wrote: 'Let us

16. *Marxism and the National and Colonial Question; Towards the Seizure of Power*, II, pp. 93, 94; *Selected Correspondence*, p. 207. E. H. Carr, *The Bolshevik Revolution, 1917–1923*, London, 1950, I, pp. 410ff.

not forget that the question of power is the fundamental question of every revolution.' [17]

Current communist theory on the questions of party and revolution, as on everything else, can be understood only if we remember that it has been shaped almost entirely with reference to conditions in Russia. Lenin desperately wanted to make the Bolshevik revolution, and he refused to be handicapped by more orthodox Marxism, which taught the priority of economic development. Russia can 'leap across bourgeois democracy.' He did not ask: is the stage set for the exit of capitalism? — but, how can we seize power and build a kind of 'state capitalism' which can later be converted into socialism? His words were: 'We are out to rebuild the world'; and Stalin after him said: 'There are no fortresses which Bolsheviks cannot capture.' Lenin believed, rightly enough, that a 'revolutionary situation' existed in Russia, but that the revolution would not come of itself: a government must be 'helped to fall,' and 'history will not forgive us if we do not assume power now.' [18] There would be time enough afterward, he thought, to socialize and industrialize the country.

The same flexibility of tactics was characteristic of Stalin's consolidation of the revolution, and is the reason why he could call his method 'creative' as compared with that of 'dogmatic' Marxists such as the early Mensheviks. Today 'Bolshevism can serve as a model of tactics for all.' [19]

V

One other query on the communist revolution must be raised: was it to be international in scope? In Marx's writings the answer is clearly yes. Although 'the proletariat of each country must of course first of all settle matters with its own bourgeoisie,' yet since capitalism is world-wide in scope, the uprising in one capitalist country would be the signal for revolt elsewhere. Engels, too: 'the communist revolution will be not merely a national phenomenon

17. Marx, *Selected Correspondence*, pp. 100, 144; Engels, *Selected Works*, 1942, II, pp. 117, 135–6; Lenin, *Towards the Seizure of Power*, I, p. 43.

18. *Leninism*, p. 791; *Handbook*, p. 202.

19. *Towards the Seizure of Power*, I, p. 222. *The Imperialist War*, pp. 279ff. *Leninism*, p. 14.

but must take place simultaneously in all civilized countries, that is to say, at least in England, America, France, and Germany.' [20]

The early successful Bolsheviks thought the same; and Trotsky continued to believe that the spread of the revolution to the industrialized West was the main thing, and that this in turn would give a better chance of consolidation in Russia. The argument with which Lenin and Trotsky met the objections of Western Marxists to their 1917 revolution was that the Russian affair would be merely the spark to ignite Western Europe. When the scales seemed heavily weighted against them in early 1918, Lenin said: '. . . without a German revolution we are doomed.' He had been fearful in September 1917 of a separate English-German peace, at the expense of Russia and the revolution. As late as 1920 he thought the revolution might collapse in Russia if it were not supported by outside revolutions. Yet whether a revolution occurred elsewhere or not, Lenin had no intention of giving up power in Russia.

At that time he also believed the two types of system, the communist and capitalist, would not co-exist for long in the same world. 'International imperialism . . . could not under any circumstances, on any conditions, live side by side with the Soviet Republic . . .' 'In the end one or the other will triumph — a funeral requiem will be sung over the Soviet Republic or over world capitalism.' [21] Western intervention in the civil war, though half-hearted and ineffectual, lent some justification to this belief, but no justification was needed for what was essentially a fanatical conviction derived from his general theory of the international class struggle.

Until now, at any rate, he has been wrong on all counts. The tide of revolution ebbed in Western Europe and none followed the Russian example, while on the other hand the Bolshevik regime did not collapse inside Russia itself, and the Soviet Union has continued to live in the same world with capitalist states.

In the 1920's Leninist-Stalinist thinking shifted appreciably. Whereas Lenin had argued earlier that although the revolution can happen first in any one country, it cannot be 'final' until

20. *Communist Manifesto;* Engels, *Principles of Communism,* p. 16.
21. E.g., *The Iskra Period,* II, p. 23; *Lenin, Selected Works,* Moscow, 1951, II, Part 1, pp. 422, 429.

taken up by several advanced countries; Stalin argued that a 'Socialist' society may be built in Russia, but can never be completely successful, because of the danger of intervention from abroad and of counter-revolution at home.[22] For a long time, therefore, the Soviet policy was to concentrate on industrialization and socialism inside Russia, and to gain time and to arm for the expected attack, without serious expectation that communist parties abroad would be successful. Hence the invention of the slogan that 'Socialism is not for export.' It is sometimes argued that the policy of 'Socialism within one country' is the policy from which stems all other Stalinist modifications of Marx.[23]

It was partly a difference of opinion over this issue, as well as a difference in temperament, which led to Trotsky's break with Stalin. The difference between the two points of view must not, however, be exaggerated; it is largely a matter of emphasis. Russia's role was in any case to be 'the citadel of world revolution,' but on one view the world revolution had priority, while on the other it must never go so far as to endanger the 'citadel.' World revolution and export of communism was thus not altogether given up by Stalin, nor is it certain that Trotsky (or Lenin) would have sacrificed the Russian experiment in favor of world revolution, had he stood in Stalin's shoes. In the long run the main difference between Stalin and Trotsky may have been that Stalin remained in power, while Trotsky lost the fight and in 1927 was forced into exile (and was later assassinated in Mexico).

At this point the revival of Russian patriotism may be mentioned. Until about the mid-1930's patriotism had not been particularly emphasized in the Soviet Union — after all Marx and Lenin had been great internationalists — and it was not until the outbreak of the 'Great Patriotic War' in 1941 that the campaign got into full swing. Ancient heroes were then resurrected and held up for admiration, while frank appeals were made to history and to traditional feelings of patriotism. Communist rule tended to be identified with Russian patriotism, through pride in having the first successful communist revolution. It was even argued that the Russian language is replacing Latin and French as an interna-

22. *Leninism*, pp. 20ff.
23. R. N. Carew Hunt, op. cit. p. 170.

tional language.[24] Yet for a time care was exercised in pointing out Russian achievements so as not to offend the sensibilities of the many other nationalities making up the Soviet Union.

The fact that the U.S.S.R. contains many nationalities has agitated Soviet leaders from the time of the revolution onward. Lenin was against Great Russian chauvinism, and was willing in the case of Finland to allow secession as a necessary price for the revolution. Later, however, he insisted on unification of the Soviet Union, and the right of secession by the constituent Soviet republics was conceded *provided it was not exercised;* and that is exactly the right of secession 'enjoyed' by the several republics today as a result of the Stalin constitution of 1936.[25]

During the war, too, the party ranks were widened to include large numbers of army personnel, and there was a tendency to play down the international aspects of Marxism-Leninism. A certain slackness in enforcing the party doctrine also became apparent but was reversed after the war, by party purging and a revival of doctrinal teaching. A former Indian communist, M. N. Roy, who used to be in the inner circle of the Comintern, has written a disillusioned book in which he argues that Stalin forgot the international revolution in the Marxist sense, turned instead to neo-nationalism, and hence through Soviet power became a threat to world peace. Stalin is labeled 'the red Napoleon.' [26] But such an end result is not surprising. Once patriotism is tapped as an emotional source of support for the regime, the policy of 'Socialism in one country' easily passes over into a kind of National Socialism.

The emphasis on patriotism is quite understandable in the party leaders, especially if they felt doubts about the loyalty of the people. The reconciliation of the nationalist aims of the Soviet Union with the aims of international communism has, for the most part, been at the expense of the latter; and has often made things rather awkward for communist parties abroad, since it has

24. J. Towster, *Political Power in the U.S.S.R., 1917–1947,* New York, 1948, p. 100. J. S. Curtis and A. Inkeles, 'Marxism in the U.S.S.R. The Recent Revival,' *Political Science Quarterly,* September 1946. Cf. also *Annals of the American Academy of Political and Social Science,* May 1949.

25. Lenin, *Towards the Seizure of Power,* II, pp. 93, 192. Stalin, *Report on the Constitution, Leninism,* pp. 398ff.

26. M. N. Roy, *The Russian Revolution,* Calcutta, 1949.

meant subordinating them everywhere to the dictates of Soviet foreign policy. It was all very well for Marx to say that the working man has no country, but the Communist International has in fact given him one: 'the U.S.S.R. is the only fatherland of the international proletariat . . .' [27] Communists outside the Soviet Union, however, are sometimes inclined to put the interests of their own country first, and the result not unnaturally has been a strong tendency to 'Titoism' among communists in a number of countries.

VI

Marxist theory has it that after the revolution there will follow the stage known as 'the dictatorship of the proletariat.' The phrase was used only a few times by Marx and Engels but, thanks mostly to Lenin, became one of the commonest in later Marxist literature. In order to be understood, it must be related to Marxist political philosophy.

The Marxist theory of the state is incompletely worked out, and like so many other parts of Marxism is marred by inconsistencies. The fullest expression of the theory (or theories) is found in Engels' confused and wildly speculative book, *The Origin of the Family, Private Property and the State*. At first mankind is said to have passed through a stage of primitive communism. Engels was never quite sure whether a 'state' existed in this primitive society. At times he denies it, at others he mentions a simple state, which serves such common interests as 'adjudication of disputes' and the maintenance of public order and water supplies. Somehow — we are never told how — the state later becomes 'parasitic,' upon all classes, even though serving the useful purpose of keeping all classes in check.

Generally, however, the 'parasitic' and above-class state plays little part in Marxist theory. For the most part the state is simply defined as an instrument of ruling-class oppression, and the state is identified with the ruling class. To speak of the state as meaning only the ruling class is an old usage, and is found in many writers before Marx — for instance, in Machiavelli.

27. *The Programme of the Communist International, Handbook*, p. 1022.

Marxism gives no satisfactory explanation, by the dialectic or otherwise, how primitive communism broke down into the cruel class society of later history. Engels contented himself with the speculation that the state arose with the invention of private property, division of labor, and specialization, which, resulting in greater productivity and a surplus of food, made it possible for an idle and exploiting class to live off the labor of another. Again, one notices how possibility or opportunity is assumed to be the same as a determining cause.

In any event, in Marxist theory the state is said to rest on force, and every state, once established, embodies the authority and interest of a ruling class. The origin of law is the same: it is merely the expression of class interest, the will of the dominant class, its purpose being the protection of private property. Since the state is by definition a class state, the very existence of a state is taken as proof that classes exist. 'Political power, properly so called, is merely the organized power of one class oppressing the other.' 'Force, that is state power, is also economic power.' The characteristic instruments of the state are a standing army and the police, and the state is somehow regarded both as standing *above* society, and as 'the tools of the exploiters.'

The origins of law and the state are lost in the mists of time, and are much disputed. The dispute will not be taken up here, although it may be noted that Morgan's work, upon which Engels' theory was based, has been much discredited by later sociologists. Marxists are fond of illustrations drawn from early primitive societies. One reason for this is that since so little is known about pre-history there is plenty of room for speculation. But one cannot prove anything about the modern world from hypothetical stages of pre-history. It is not the origins of the state which concern us, or which are relevant to Marxism, but rather the Marxist criticism of the contemporary state.

The so-called democratic state is said to be merely the latest example of class rule, and is just as bad as its predecessors (though somewhat more subtle in its methods), since 'the executive of the modern state is but a committee for managing the common affairs of the whole bourgeoisie.' [28] It follows from Marxist premises that

28. *Communist Manifesto; Selected Works,* 1942, I, p. 388.

the proletariat upon coming to power would naturally and necessarily also constitute a class government. Since one class must always rule in any state, the only question is: which class? The
immediate difference, Marx thought, would be merely that the
more numerous class would then rule over the few, the dictatorship of the bourgeoisie being replaced by the dictatorship of the
proletariat. There is no doubt that both Marx and Engels expected
the dictatorship of the proletariat to have a real democratic content, at least for the great majority, the workers (an opinion also
held by Lenin, at least until 1917). They thought that the dictatorship would be less oppressive than the bourgeois state because
there would be no 'exploitation,' there would be an end 'to the
State as State'; it would be 'a half-state,' 'not a state in the proper
sense of the word.' [29]

For the first time, as Marx saw it, universal suffrage and frequent
elections would give the worker the substance of political freedom
equal to that of the bourgeoisie. It was not an unrealistic argument
in the 1850's, since the workers did not then have the vote anywhere, and may be said to have become fully enfranchised in Britain only with the introduction of the secret ballot in 1872. Engels
pointed to the Paris Commune of 1871 as a demonstration model
of the dictatorship of the proletariat, which Lenin also was fond
of noting; but it would be very difficult indeed to find many points
of resemblance between the short-lived Paris Commune and the
government set up by the Bolsheviks in Russia. Proletarian rule
would be the 'bourgeois state . . . without the bourgeoisie!'; it
would *establish a democratic constitution*' . . . 'a democratic republic.' [30] One thing it did not mean to Marx, or to Lenin in his
early days, was the dictatorship of the party *over* the proletariat
and the rest of society. The attachment of Marx and Engels to
democracy is evident enough in their writings. But it was to democracy *after the revolution,* and not in the era of capitalism.

Such is Marx's main theory, as it emerges from the bulk of his
analysis. On the other hand, if his 1850 *Address* is taken literally
for the case when the revolution is made in a backward country,

---

29. *Towards the Seizure of Power,* II, pp. 186ff. Engels, *Handbook,* p. 295;
Lenin, Selected Works, 1951, II, Part 1, p. 57.
30. Engels, *Principles of Communism,* p. 14. *Selected Works,* II, p. 460.

where the industrial proletariat is in a small minority, then clearly a modification must also be made in the theory of the dictatorship of the proletariat. The Russians have accordingly made this modification, as they have altered the concept of the party. Lenin developed it, and Stalin carefully and explicitly approved it.

In its essentials, the theory of the dictatorship of the proletariat as presently expounded by Leninism-Stalinism for a non-industrialized country is the apologia for the rule of a small minority, the proletariat, which in turn is ruled by the party. In the first instance, when the proletariat is co-operating with the peasantry and other allies, the dictatorship of the proletariat is the name given to the joint class alliance against the bourgeoisie. From July 1917 Lenin had used the slogan, 'the dictatorship of the proletariat and the poor peasantry,' as an effective weapon against the provisional government. But even in this temporary class alliance, as Stalin put it, the 'guiding force is the proletariat.' As time goes on, the communist party becomes the 'instrument of the dictatorship of the proletariat.' In short, dictatorship of the party is inevitable whenever the tactics of communist revolution are applied to underdeveloped countries; and this doctrine was officially adopted by the Comintern in 1920. In a nutshell: seize power, no matter how backward the country, and force through industrialization regardless of the wishes of the population.

If the proletariat came to power in an industrialized but *non-democratic* country, a single-party rule is also likely to result, and might be defended fairly enough on realistic grounds as a temporary defensive measure to prevent a counter-revolution. In any non-democratic country, a revolutionary party could of course come into power only by intrigue, a *coup d'état,* or perhaps a civil war; since the ordinary constitutional means of achieving power would, by definition, be absent. (A third possibility is for a party to come into power constitutionally, through election, and then set up a dictatorship, as Hitler did.)

The dictatorship of the proletariat is thus identified with dictatorship of the party and forms an essential part of the present-day communist theory. Some, such as Sorel, arguing that the class struggle was the only essential feature of Marxism, have rejected Marx's emphasis on political action and concentrated entirely on direct action by means of the general strike. Both Marx and Lenin, however, were severely critical of such notions. Marx carefully pointed out that he was not the first to discover the class struggle, but that he proved 'the class struggle necessarily leads to the [temporary] dictatorship of the proletariat,' while Lenin made the acceptance of the dictatorship the basic test of Marxism.

If we bear in mind the Leninist theory of party dictatorship, it is quite naïve for people in the Western world to be surprised and hurt that political allies have been removed from power in the Balkans or Poland or Czechoslovakia, and the sole dictatorship of the communist party installed, since that indeed is the only possible method of operation contemplated by Leninist-Stalinist theory.

VII

How long was the dictatorship of the proletariat to last? The question cannot be answered without considering the purpose of the dictatorship. In Marx and Engels it was clearly meant only as a transitional phase, its object being to make the conversion from private to public ownership, and to ensure that the bourgeoisie does not stage a counter-revolution. Once this change is made, 'the abolition of classes' will have taken place. The purpose of the temporary dictatorship thus appears logical enough on Marx's theory, given his assumptions about the bourgeois state.

It was also natural for Marx to envisage this period as a troubled one throughout the world, as an epoch of 'prolonged struggles.' After all, the extension of the franchise in 1832 in Britain, while not actually leading to violence, had been too near it for comfort. And, as Spain has shown us more recently, the danger of a counter-revolution can be real enough. Yet a dictatorship of the proletariat has never been installed when socialists have come to power in the democracies. Their labor parties have been moderate, the confidence of capitalists has not been so shattered as to leave the economic system floundering in chaos, and it is hard to rally support for a counter-attack when the dispossessed owners are given reasonable compensation. (Marx and Engels once or twice mentioned the possibility of compensation for landowners, but the point is a small one, since later Marxists, following the Russian example, have rejected all idea of compensation.)

Marx was vague on the duration of the dictatorship of the proletariat, but certainly the Russians have once more gone beyond anything Marx had in mind. Lenin mentioned 'the entire historic period which separates capitalism from the "classless society" ' — not a very precise estimate — and the Russians announce that this may last for a generation, and perhaps much longer. They have also altered greatly the conception of the nature and purpose of the dictatorship, and its duration is intimately bound up with the nature and purpose.

Its nature today, as we have seen, is that of a strict party dictatorship. All revolutionary governments tend to be despotic. The few Bolshevik acts of generosity after the revolution were in fact ill repaid and disillusioning; and it was natural that the Bolshevik dictatorship, beset by foreign enemies and civil war, should become strict, even ruthless, when fighting for its life. A historical explanation of the early despotism is one thing, however, and the theoretical justification for its continuance is another. The dictatorship has been justified on several grounds.

There is first the need to eliminate the bourgeois as a class, i.e. to dispossess them from ownership of the means of production. The dictatorship in this phase becomes '. . . the use of violence by the proletariat against the bourgeoisie, rule which is unrestricted by any laws,' 'the fiercest and most merciless war.' Lenin went on to add that this was necessary, since — strangely enough — '. . . the resistance [of the bourgeoisie] is increased *tenfold* after its overthrow . . .' [31] (Sometimes he says 'hundredfold,' and even 'thousandfold.')

Since the Bolsheviks came to power in a relatively undeveloped country, there is secondly the need to promote industrialization. This had not been recognized as a problem by the original Marxists, because they had assumed that the proletariat would come to power in a fully industrialized country. The Bolsheviks could thus find only general guidance in the works of Marx and Engels when

31. Lenin, *Left Wing Communism,* London, 1920, pp. 10ff. *Proletarian Revolution and Renegade Kautsky,* London, 1918.

they set out to do for the Soviet Union what had been done by capitalists elsewhere.

A particularly troublesome problem was how to organize agriculture. The difference between agriculture and industry, and hence whether different methods of organization should be applied, has always perplexed Marxists. Engels, for example, believed that expropriation would not be best for the small peasants, but that they should instead be shown by example and 'social aid' the advantages of co-operative ownership and production, and they would then fall into line.

But there is also a strong strain of thought in Marxism, noticeable first in the *Communist Manifesto*, which had advocated 'abolition of all the distinction between town and country.' Engels had written: 'Civilization has left us a number of large cities, as an inheritance, which it will take much time and trouble to abolish. But they must and will be done away with, however much time and trouble it may take.' [32] Industrial production was to be dispersed throughout the country, in what we should today call 'garden cities,' while at the same time agriculture would be treated almost exactly like industry, its basis to be a kind of factory production. Marx knew little and cared less about life on the land, and thought mainly in terms of a rural proletariat. Lenin, too, tried to show that the independent peasant and farmer were doomed, because of the steady enlargement of the scale of farm operation and the concentration of ownership and investment in land.

But in any case, if extensive industrialism was to be pushed through rapidly in Russia, factory workers had to be found, and they could only be found on the land; while a larger surplus of farm produce had also to be obtained to feed the new industrial workers. It required only these practical considerations, added to the Marxist contempt for peasant life, to evolve the Stalinist policy of state and collective farming which was pushed through swiftly and cruelly in the Five Year Plans; and the more recent policy of industrial patterns of organization in agriculture.

Because the dictatorship has sometimes been justified on the ground that it is necessary only until the proletariat makes up the

32. *Selected Works*, 1942, I, p. 48; *Anti-Duhring*, Chicago, 1907, p. 203.

majority of the population, and until all danger of a counter-revolution has passed, some observers have been tempted to foretell a relaxation of the dictatorship within the Soviet Union. The Soviet Union moreover, as a result of more than a generation of expropriation and conditioning, contains no bourgeois class in any Marxist sense, so that the regime could hardly be in danger from a nonexistent bourgeoisie if it were to relax its fantastically rigid grip on the people.

But this easy optimism misses the point of present-day Soviet communism. The Russians have not only ignored the elements of democracy in the transitional stage, as put forth by Marx, and by the early Bolsheviks themselves; they have not only gone on to invoke the argument for industrialization; *but they have also gone on to rename their present system 'democracy.'* Marxism promised the workers real democracy once the revolution had come, and so the Soviet leaders are compelled to identify their regime with Marxist dreams. To identify reality with our ideals is a type of behavior common enough in daily living and in history. Woodrow Wilson defended the imperfect Versailles Treaty on the ground that it did in fact incorporate every tittle of his own higher principles. Married folk often profess to be ideally wed although they know well that their marriages are nothing like the ideals of married love which they formerly held.

The Soviet system is known as proletarian democracy: '. . . the highest type of democracy in class society.' Democracy is used in several senses in the Marxist vocabulary, but the two more usual meanings are 'bourgeois' democracy, which is bad, and 'proletarian' or 'people's' democracy, which is good. Both senses, however, refer to class societies. Proletarian democracy means 'subordination of the minority to the majority,' but since the Soviet Union long ago eliminated its minority capitalist class, Stalinist theory is somewhat vague on the identity of the class minority which is 'subordinated.' Proletarian democracy also means the dictatorship of the proletariat, but again Soviet theory is less than clear about what class is subjected to dictatorship.

Proletarian 'democracy' takes the form of single-party rule, since the party is described as a 'higher form' of class organization of the proletariat than other kinds of organization such as trade unions, co-operatives, or the state itself; and in the party there must be 'iron discipline.' For that reason the much-discussed Soviet Constitution of 1936 cannot be translated into Western terms; and any discussion of democracy between communists and Western democrats will only bog down in confusion unless the different usages of the word are clearly recognized.

Lenin once wrote: 'the will of a class is at times best realized by a dictator who sometimes will accomplish more by himself and is frequently more needed.' Stalin has said that Lenin never hesitated to set himself against the party majority, since he knew best 'the correct policy.' It is only a short step from that position to the argument that a government on behalf of the proletariat, serving their 'real' interests, can hardly be called 'dictatorship' at all. If it were not so tragic for Russia and the world, it would be amusing to note in Stalin's writings the hair-splitting and double talk, the reinterpretation of Marx and Lenin, intended to show that the party does not *really* exercise a dictatorship in the U.S.S.R.

The Soviet theory of democracy is one of the oldest forms of justification for absolute rule, resting entirely upon the fallacious and abominable assumption that the self-appointed experts know what is best for people and how to promote it. Stalin used to say that his slogan was 'convince then coerce.' But no one can tell whether conviction is genuine without the freedom to disagree, to listen to opposing arguments. All the evidence points to the fact that Soviet rule is one of coercion regardless of conviction on the part of the ruled. The peasants, for example, wanted land, not collectivization, despite the most persistent campaigns to persuade them; yet the party program was forced through in face of stubborn peasant resistance.

VIII

The dictatorship of the proletariat is closely related to another famous Marxist phrase, 'the withering away of the state.' The phrase is partly equivocation, a matter of Marxist semantics: the bourgeois state by definition is an instrument of class coercion, and after the revolution, when the bourgeois class is dispossessed, then, *ipso facto,* the state in this sense has disappeared. There is also, in this usage, a suggestion of the Aristotelian idea of essences, the state being realized only in its pure form or essence, which in this case is class rule. Trotsky argued in the same fashion that trade unions would not be needed under communism, since trade unions are by definition class weapons against private employers. Engels proposed to 'replace the word "state" everywhere by the word *Gemeinwesen* [community].' [33] Marx had a good deal to say about the state in his *Critique of the Gotha Programme,* and Lenin and Stalin attached 'exceptionally great importance' to the views there expressed. At first sight it is somewhat surprising that this quibbling and hasty letter, written out of deep feelings of animosity against the leaders and program of the German Social Democratic Party, should have been taken so seriously. It appeals to latter-day communists, however, because, like the *Address* of 1850, it may easily be used to justify the methods which the Bolsheviks employed in Russia.

Yet apart from the matter of definition, Marx was clear not merely that the revolution would transfer the existing bourgeois state machinery to the proletariat, but that the machinery itself — parliament, the army, the police, law courts, and the civil service — should be 'smashed' or 'broken up.' By this he did not mean that the machinery of the state could be eliminated immediately after the revolution, but that it should be democratized, or manned by faithful proletarians who would carry out the will of the proletarian government. When Marx wrote, the state apparatus was mainly as he described it, on a class basis (aristocracy plus bourgeoisie) in Prussia, France, and even England. His very class-struggle theory led him to believe that the state would grow more and more repressive. One can understand his fear that if the proletariat achieved parliamentary power, by the ballot, the rest of the government machinery, in particular the army, the courts, and the administration, would be able to distort or actually defy the will of the majority. Something very like this did indeed occur in Spain in our own day. One of the first acts of Hitler and Mussolini, as of the communists, was to purge the state machinery of opposition, to 'smash' it in the Marxist sense.

Probably all states throughout history have had some functions

33. *Selected Correspondence,* p. 337.

such as maintaining peace and order, which have benefitted all classes, as Engels occasionally noted without realizing the implications. The capitalist democracies since Marx's time have gone far in extending the non-class functions of the state. Not a legislative session passes in any of the democracies which does not put on the statute books some new act extending welfare services to one group or another, or controlling some sector of the economy in the public interest. The democracies have also gone far in democratizing the machinery of government, notably through the competitive examination and the career open to talents, and the admission of the working class to political power.

No one would wish to rest on present achievements, to deny that inequalities of opportunity for government service still exist, or to admit that all branches of the administration are staffed wholly on the merit principle. Nevertheless, the process has gone far enough to make it unnecessary for a democratic socialist government, on taking office, to undertake any drastic purge of the existing state machinery. Friends of the Labour government in Britain have sometimes argued that the government did suffer because of lack of enthusiasm for its policies among administrators; and it is certainly true that the hereditary House of Lords attempted to obstruct the Labour government in 1947 as it had done the Liberal government of Lloyd George and Asquith in 1909. Obstruction of political policy by unsympathetic and sluggish civil servants has been seen in many countries. But all this is a far cry from the threat of counter-revolution.

Marx meant more than a democratizing of the existing government. He also meant that the 'proletarian state,' the short dictatorship stage, would itself 'wither away' to become the classless society. Did he further mean that society would then require no legislature, executive, or judiciary; no army or police; and nothing of the huge administrative machine so typical of modern democracies? There are indeed strong evidences for this belief in Marx, in Engels, and even more in Lenin. Logically, it follows from the concept of the state as only an instrument of class rule that when the classless society is achieved there would be no ruling class to exploit and no class to be exploited.

This belief of Marx's, however absurd it may be, may be traced to several sources in his thinking. There was first of all the influence of his contacts with Bakunin and the philosophical anarch-ists, all of whom were possessed of a deep aversion to all authority. Secondly, and largely derived from Proudhon, there was in Marx a strain of guild socialism, as when he wrote, 'where the organizing activity begins . . . there socialism casts away the political hull.' Engels wrote in the same vein: 'In proportion as anarchy in social production vanishes, the political authority of the state also dies away.' [34] Thirdly, there was Marx's simple determinist view that law and the state are merely elements in the superstructure of a class society. Closely related to this was his conviction that private property is somehow the root of all evil, with the corollary that the proletariat, a property-less class, is an injured and hence also a uniquely virtuous class. Such a naïve view of the peculiar virtues of the proletariat is certainly not confirmed by either priests or mag-istrates. Marx's proletarians were idealizations; they would not abuse their power in the interim period of the dictatorship, while in the classless society no one would hold power. As Marx saw it, the future belonged to the proletariat; no other class could be the historical successors to the bourgeoisie.

Given this type of thinking, it follows that with the abolition of private property in the means of production, the proletarian vir-tues would come into their own and dominate the new society. To put it more accurately, on strict Marxist lines the new property relations would *create* the new morality and there would be a kind of automatic transformation of the human species; a dialecti-cal 'leap' to a new and higher morality.

The fourth source was perhaps the most important: his gross exaggeration of the productive possibilities of modern technology. Here Marx is in good company. A great many laymen and sci-entists believe with J. D. Bernal that 'physical science can now solve completely the material problems of human existence — with one to three hours of work a day.' [35] Marx believed that once the productive forces were no longer hampered by private owner-ship, the classless society could soon usher in the age of plenty. In a short time the harsh maxims of 'to each according to his work,' and 'he who does not work, neither shall he eat' would be

---

34. *Selected Essays*, p. 133; *Selected Works*, I, pp. 173, 188.
35. Bernal, *Frustration of Science*, p. 69.

replaced by the more pleasant principle of 'to each according to his need'; and in that coming elysium the coercive and controlling state would be superfluous. The classless society is wholly predicated upon an age of abundance, attainable in the near future, when 'poverty and scarcity will be unknown.'

Lenin held much the same beliefs, at least until 1917, and fortunately they are clearly set forth in his book, *State and Revolution,* so there can be no doubt about them. They are among the most unrealistic and superficial of political theories ever written; but since the Russian leaders assert that they intend to implement them at some uncertain future date, it is worth looking at them.

Lenin believed that even the interim stage of proletarian class rule would need a much simpler state apparatus than the hated bourgeois state. It would be 'almost without "machinery," without any special apparatus, by the simple organization of the armed masses.' The police function, he thought, would eventually disappear, since the police were merely an instrument of class rule to suppress the proletariat. A few wicked individuals might linger on, and would have to be controlled in their excesses, but 'this will be done by the armed people itself, as simply and as readily as any crowd of civilized people, even in modern bourgeois society, parts a pair of combatants or does not allow a woman to be outraged.' ('The fiercest and most merciless war' — mentioned on p. 161 — was to be a short period, immediately after the revolution, during which the bourgeoisie were being eliminated as a class.)

As for all the manifold economic and financial functions which must be carried on in any society, these would practically run themselves.

> Capitalist culture has *created* large-scale production, factories, railways, the postal service, telephones, etc., and *on this basis* the great majority of functions of the old 'State power' have become so simplified and can be reduced to such simple operations of registration, filing and checking that they will be quite within the reach of every literate person, and it will be possible to perform them for 'workingmen's wages' . . .

The functions of control and accounting, which he conceded to be necessary for some time, are 'within the reach of anybody who can read and write and knows the first few rules of arithmetic.' Nor would there be any trouble with technicians, 'the scientifically educated staff of engineers, agronomists, and so on. These gentlemen work today, obeying the capitalists; they will work even better tomorrow, obeying the armed workers.' After all, 'the armed workers are men of practical life, not sentimental intellectuals, and they will scarcely allow anyone to trifle with them.' As for judges: '. . . anybody can act as a judge basing himself on the revolutionary sense of justice of the toiling classes.' Lenin also thought that all officials, without exception, should be elected and subject to recall 'at any time.' [36]

The concessions here made to the need for management and organization were merely for the intervening and transitional stage. In time morals will be improved, perhaps by force of habit, so that even individual 'excesses will inevitably begin to "wither away." We do not know how quickly and in what succession but we know that they will wither away.' The object of the intervening stage is thus to prepare men for the perfect state of society, in which all laws, discipline, and government will become unnecessary.

In economic affairs, it would in time be possible to dispense with wages and a money economy — as in William Morris' utopian *News from Nowhere* — and 'unpaid work for the common good becomes the general phenomenon.' People 'will voluntarily work according to their ability . . . all will take a turn in management, and will soon become accustomed to the idea of no managers at all.' There will be no distinction between mental and physical labor, or between town and country. Like Rousseau, Marx and Lenin seemed unaware that private and group interests could conflict with one another or with the public welfare. Engels described the prospect thus:

When all capital, all production, all exchange have been brought together in the hands of the nation, private property will disappear of its own accord, money will become super-

36. *State and Revolution*, pp. 184ff., 221, 229, 230, 244. See also 'Lenin's Theory of the State,' in E. H. Carr, *The Bolshevik Revolution*, I, pp. 233ff. The recall provision in the Soviet Constitution of 1936 was highly praised by Stalin: 'This is a wonderful law, comrades.' *Lenin, Selected Works*, 1951, I, Part 1, p. 60; II, Part 2, p. 166.

fluous, and production will so expand and man so change that society will be able to slough off whatever of its old economic habits may remain . . . Education will enable young people quickly to familiarize themselves with the whole system of production and to pass from one branch of production to another in response to the needs of society or their own inclinations.[37]

Comment is almost superfluous, but if any is needed it is best found in the experience of the Bolsheviks themselves. The childlike notions of Engels and Lenin were to some extent tried out in the early days after the Russian revolution. For a short period, known as 'War Communism,' a combination of grave economic conditions and Bolshevik theory led to an experiment with an economy of 'moneyless accounting,' which was very exciting while it lasted, until the resulting chaos and almost complete running down of the economic machine forced even the most ardent revolutionaries to come to terms with common sense. Accordingly money and trade were again recognized as necessary, the party took over control of the state, and the state of much industry, while in many sectors a large measure of private enterprise was restored in the famous New Economic Policy of Lenin (1921). When by 1928 the economy was running again with reasonable efficiency, Stalin thought the time had come to abolish private enterprise, whereupon the first Five Year Plan was inaugurated.

In the early Bolshevik days, too, the idea was prevalent that law, even the criminal code, would not be necessary for very long; an idea that found some expression in the Soviet Constitution of 1918, and which persisted until the 1930's, when Stalin came out strongly against it. Nevertheless, it may be wrong to suppose that the dream of 'full communism,' of the final classless communist society of plenty, has entirely faded. It is still common enough in Marxist literature, and within the U.S.S.R. may serve a real psychological purpose by directing the attention of the people beyond their present hardships to a brighter future. The point is, however, that the dream of the stateless society *has* been postponed for realization in a distant future; and Soviet theory must there-

37. *Principles of Communism*, pp. 15, 17; Cf. *On Authority. Selected Works*, 1951, I, pp. 575ff.

fore give an explanation why so little apparent progress toward it is being made.

The official explanation, as mentioned earlier, is that the interim stage of 'socialism' can come in one country, but that the final stage of full communism must wait upon the coming of the revolution in the rest of the world, or at least in the most advanced states. This is all very well, as far as it goes, but of course it avoids the question: why is the interim stage so vastly different from that anticipated by Marx and Lenin? And to that question the usual answer is: the U.S.S.R. is not an island isolated from the rest of the world, but is encircled by a 'system of states' hostile and threatening. Hence it is necessary to preserve all the usual state apparatus: of government, law, and the constitution, of secret police and armed forces, so long as the Soviet Union is threatened from abroad. There is no way of telling how much the leaders themselves believe that the Soviet Union is the potential victim of foreign attack, or how much the threat of foreign danger is used as an excuse to justify the existing order in the U.S.S.R. But if the Soviet *people* really believe it, as they presumably do, since they have been told often enough, we can understand how easy it must be for the Kremlin to secure genuine and widespread approval of its regime.

For one reason or another, then, the dictatorship of the proletariat continues, and 'stateless administration' — whatever that expression may mean — cannot arrive until (a) all or most of the world is communist and (b) what Stalin called 'absolute abundance' has been attained.

Sometimes the Russians assert that the problem of the withering away of the state is entirely theoretical and of no present interest. More often they argue that the proletarian state is a state with a difference, the difference being that it is not a *class* state, that Soviet law is not class law but 'norms of behavior.' The apparent contradiction between the original expectations of Marx and Lenin and the existing situation in Russia was 'explained' by Stalin:

> We are in favour of the state withering away and at the same
> time we stand for the strengthening of the dictatorship of the

proletariat, which represents the most powerful and mighty authority of all forms of state which have existed up to the present day. The highest possible development of the power of the state: that is the Marxist formula. Is it contradictory? Yes, it is contradictory. But this contradiction is a living thing, and completely reflects Marxist dialectics.[38]

As recently as 1951 he argued that the nearer the Soviet Union comes to communism, the stronger the state must be.

If this is not mere double talk, it means that the state machinery will grow more and more powerful and totalitarian before it begins to 'wither'; that is, things will get much worse in the Soviet Union before they can get better. As to how the withering process is to take place, we are given the dialectical paradox: 'It is precisely along the path of the consolidation and higher development of the proletarian state that the withering away of the state takes place.' Even the party will 'wither away' in time: 'When classes disappear and the dictatorship of the proletariat dies out, the party will also die out.' [39]

IX

Perhaps the most just, and certainly the basic, criticism of the Marxist-Leninist theory of the state's withering away and of the classless society is made by calling attention to its incredibly naïve and Utopian outlook. The future is to bring a condition of complete anarchy, without any government at all, by the voluntary abdication of the proletarian dictatorship. Or, since the vision of Marx and Lenin is a confused one, perhaps a better name for their classless society is 'organized anarchy.'

Politically the vision rests upon the assumption that government by its very nature is repressive and forcible; and this in turn is based upon the anarchist fallacy that every element of force is bad. The only difference between Marx and the anarchists was that Marx approved of temporary force, the dictatorship of the proletariat, which was a unique expression of authority: the force to end all force.

38. *Selected Works,* 1942, I, p. 184, note by Stalin.
39. Stalin, *Foundations of Leninism, Handbook,* p. 851.

Economically, the vision rests upon the assumption of an automatic, self-regulating economic machine. Only rarely does one find in the Marxist literature casual references to the need for authority or economic planning in the classless society, when 'the government of persons is replaced by the administration of things and the direction of the processes of production.' Marx displayed singularly little recognition of the economic problem of choice and alternatives, and made no useful suggestion about how it may be solved, as it must be, so long as man lives with unlimited wants in a world of limited resources. Other economists also, both before and after Marx, have not thought of the economic problem in those Robbinsian terms. Adam Smith, for instance, was concerned only with increasing the scarce means, the wealth of nations, and not with the problem of allocation.

Not only did Marx, like Lenin after him, fail to take note of the problem of allocation of resources, of the balancing of alternatives, but he also labored under the false impression that control of production and the making of economic decisions were extremely simple, and that all economic processes would somehow almost run themselves once capitalism was overthrown. This is due mainly, as mentioned, to his gross exaggeration of the possibilities of modern technology to usher in the world of plenty once the exploiting class had been liquidated.

All Marxist literature is full of the same simple faith. Marx and Engels therefore abused Malthus and his population theory with great gusto: 'the contemptible Malthus,' 'the *fundamental meanness* of his outlook,' 'a libel on the human race,' 'this repulsive blasphemy against man and nature.' Lysenko has echoed the same sentiments: 'the mad-brained reactionary Malthusian scheme on population.' [40]

The theory of Malthus had, as a matter of sober fact, been widely used in the nineteenth century to stifle humanitarian impulses and to block social reforms, and this so annoyed Marx that he seems never to have realized what Malthus was driving at. Engels once or twice conceded a certain truth in the Malthusian

40. *Selected Correspondence*, pp. 20, 198; *Death of a Science in Russia*, p. 100. Ronald L. Meek (ed.), *Marx and Engels on Malthus*, London, 1953, pp. 60, 115-53.

population-subsistence ratio, but argued that there was no need
to worry about it until the vacant lands of the earth were plowed
up. Should communist society ever be 'obliged to regulate the
production of human beings,' it will do so, and 'it is for the people in the communist society themselves to decide . . .' [41]

In much the same way Marx and Engels showed the greatest
contempt for the law of diminishing returns (by which followers
of Malthus later supported his theory) and held it to be sufficiently
refuted by the progress of science. Lenin went to great pains to
refute the same law, and the Soviet authorities similarly misunder-
stand it, and assert that 'practical refutation' is given by the
mechanization of agriculture in the Soviet Union.[42]

Contemporary Western Marxists are inclined to regard Malthusianism today as merely an ideological weapon used by the bourgeoisie in the fight against the social revolution:

> If the social struggles of the early nineteenth century were
> essentially summed up in the controversies between Malthus
> and Ricardo, those of our own times are perhaps not unfairly
> summed up in that between Malthusians and Marxists.

Keynesian theory is regarded as a somewhat more sophisticated
extension of Malthusianism, serving the same 'reactionary' purposes.[43]

The original views of the successful Russian revolutionaries
were, as previously noted, extremely elementary on the subjects
of trade, industry, the civil service, and the immediate possibilities of public ownership. Their crude and unrealistic theory was
in fact a considerable handicap, and goes far to explain why it
took so many years after the revolution to restore the Russian
economy. Lenin and his party learned slowly and by the bitter
and costly lessons of experience.

The civil war, although it set back economic reconstruction,
was in one sense the event that saved the Russian revolution. The

41. Meek, op. cit. p. 109.
42. *Selected Correspondence*, pp. 31, 170, 201; Lenin, *The Agrarian Question
and the Critics of Marx, The Iskra Period*, I, pp. 185ff. Engels thought there
would be no housing shortage if owners of big houses were expropriated, and
the poor moved in. *The Housing Question, Handbook*, p. 344.
43. Meek, op. cit. p. 47.

Bolsheviks could appear as the champions of the social revolution in the eyes of the poor peasants and workers, both of whom were bound to react strongly against any attempt to restore the old order. Armies led by the old Czarist officers, supported by landlords, were enemies against whom Bolsheviks and peasants could unite. The war also forced the Bolsheviks to lay aside their more unrealistic theories, to forge and use instruments of government — a professional army and an administrative bureaucracy — which they had formerly despised. Above all, during the war the party was tempered and improved, and a secret political police (the Cheka) was founded and perfected.

Whereas in 1917 Lenin had talked of allowing 'complete freedom to the creative faculties of the masses,' by 1921 he was deploring the 'low culture' and ignorance of the Russian workers and peasants, the fecklessness and inexperience of the intellectuals. Perhaps gold might be used in the future for 'building public lavatories in the streets,' but in the meantime it must be mined and sold at the highest prices to buy goods from abroad.[44] The need for a managerial and technical class became desperate, and he decided that even 'bourgeois' experts must be retained; while wage differentials and severe factory discipline were firmly established and systematized. Following some remarks of Engels, Lenin redefined 'equality of wages' to mean the *abolition of classes,* a definition that left plenty of room for justifying large disparities of income, rank, and privileges.

Nowadays the Russians seem to realize — although they have been loath to admit it publicly — all the elaborate implications, in terms of technology, incentives, bureaucracy, and law, that are demanded by the planned economy, whether production is for use or for profit. The Stakhanovite or piece-work system in mines and factories is one sign of the new realism. Another is the forced-labor camps which are integrated into the economic plans: camps that are probably much worse than the Lena goldfields of Czarist Russia, which had been notorious for their massacres and conditions of semi-slavery. Public law and the criminal code have grown rapidly, and penalties have become more severe in order to cope with the mounting number of offenses against details of the

44. *Lenin, Selected Works,* 1951, II, Part 2, p. 608.

planned economy and against public property. As we have seen, too, the temporary nature of the elaborate dictatorship is now less emphasized, and the extraneous factor of capitalist encircle-ment is more often called upon to reinforce the argument for a strong state.

We find in Marx no word on the elaborate arrangements that are needed if industry is to be conducted 'democratically'; or on the conflicts that will always be present between individual and sectional interests and the public interest. Nor is there in his writings any conception of the extensive social controls and laws that are required to insure the civil liberties and the freedom of personality which Marx so much desired for the workers; or any conception of the place of voluntary and other group organiza-tions in mediating between the individual and the state. Prob-lems of politics and economics vanish altogether once capitalism is abolished. Human behavior can, we hope, be improved in the course of time, but it is unwise to the point of foolishness to ex-pect any great transformation because of a change from private to public ownership. The experience of the Soviet Union has not shown us anything new in this regard, despite all the absurd talk about the new 'Soviet man' with his 'norms of behavior.' It has merely underlined the old lesson to be learned from every tyrant: that if the tyranny is complete and ruthless enough any nation can be forced into conformity to the ruler's wishes.

Marx also had nothing to say on the commercial policy or for-eign relations between communist and non-communist countries, an omission no doubt due to his belief that such a relationship would be only temporary, since the revolution was to be expected more or less simultaneously in the capitalist countries. Lenin and Stalin were forced to repair the omission. In the 1920's, and espe-cially with the banishment of Trotsky, and the concentration on building communism within Russia, Stalin tended to favor the doctrine of 'peaceful co-existence.' This policy was taken a step further, toward more active co-operation with the democracies after 1932, as Stalin became aware of the threat from the Nazis. And so Soviet policy shifted to the support of collective security and the League of Nations until Munich showed, or seemed to show, Stalin that the West could not be relied upon, and he entered the pact of non-aggression with Hitler in order to provide more 'breathing space' in which to prepare for the expected war.

Today the policy seems to be that commercial and other relations may be entered into on a basis of *ad hoc* negotiations, but since the world revolution is sooner or later bound to come, all arrangements are meant merely to bridge the gap of time until the revolution is world-wide. Meantime the U.S.S.R. aims at maximum self-sufficiency, and prefers to trade only with its satellites. Occasionally foreign-trade agreements may be sought, when the Soviet Union feels in need of materials, or has surpluses, or when trade may be used as an instrument of foreign policy.

Marx was preoccupied with the dangers of economic power in the hands of the bourgeoisie, so preoccupied that he gave no thought to the dangers of combined political and economic power in the communist state, or to the social organization of the class-less society. It is a pity, however, that he did not lift his gaze beyond the revolution and make some attempt to analyze his more distant goals. He merely assumed that the new property relations of public ownership would almost automatically produce the ideal society; that given the procedures of the Marxist laws of history the content would take care of itself.

Again, the nature of the economic problem under a planned economy has only recently entered prominently into the realm of socialist discussion. All socialists have historically been concerned with the evils of capitalism, and have usually done less than justice to the role of the market and the social function of profit in co-ordinating economic activities. Marxists have been even less realistic and have tended to disparage economics as a 'bourgeois' science, its principles holding true only of the capitalist economy, and economists being — in Marx's phrase — 'scientific representatives of the bourgeois class.'

There are many signs that the Soviet attitude toward economic studies has changed. We are told, for example, that the 'law of value,' formerly thought to have no place in 'socialist economics,' applies also — though 'transformed' — in the Soviet Union. Stalin's pamphlet of 1952, *Economic Problems of Socialism in the U.S.S.R.*, asserted bluntly that the laws of economics are valid in the U.S.S.R. as elsewhere. Soviet economists have been, as it were, restored to respectability and now discuss among themselves the technical problems of savings, investment, priorities, and so on. These problems are, moreover, not confined to the Soviet Union but are becoming urgent in the rest of the world also as the role of the free market is steadily being reduced. The question of supplements or substitutes for the more or less free pricing mechanism is one of the most technical and pressing of economic questions. But it is not one on which Marxism throws any light.

There is no basis in jurisprudence, sociology, economics, or mere common sense for the extraordinary Marxist doctrine regarding the withering of the state. We know from the experience of every controlled and planned economy that the very opposite of the Marxist theory is true: that there is bound to be a great proliferation of law and bureaucracy once private enterprise and the market mechanism are replaced by an economic plan. To say this is not to pass judgment on the merits of economic planning, which are often many and substantial, providing that planning is flexible and not pushed to an extreme. But even if the merits are admitted, simplicity and an absence of state machinery are not among them.

> *In nature . . . there are only blind unconscious*
> *agencies acting upon one another and out of whose*
> *interplay the general law comes into operation . . .*
> *In the history of society, on the other hand, the ac-*
> *tors are all endowed with consciousness . . . But*
> *this distinction, important as it is for historical in-*
> *vestigation, particularly of single epochs and events,*
> *cannot alter the fact that the course of history is*
> *governed by inner general laws . . . and it is only*
> *a matter of discovering these laws.*   ENGELS.[1]

> *One intellectual excitement has, however, been de-*
> *nied me. Men wiser and more learned than I have*
> *discerned in history a plot, a rhythm, a predeter-*
> *mined pattern. These harmonies are concealed*
> *from me.*   H. A. L. FISHER.[2]

6

Marxism as a Philosophy of History

I

MARX'S ECONOMIC INTERPRETATION of history may be judged in two
ways. One way is to subject it to analytical scrutiny and relate it to
the evidence of historical and statistical research (a task that was
attempted in Chapters 3 and 4). It may also be judged on more
broadly philosophical grounds. When looked at in this way, Marxism becomes an instance of the species known as 'philosophy of
history.' This fashionable phrase does not refer to a method of
writing or studying history (methodology), but to something much
wider, which may be called the 'meaning' of history, or the attempt
to understand and give 'significance' to the course of events.

1. *Selected Works*, 1942, I, p. 457.
2. *History of Europe*, London, 1935, I, Preface.

The search for a meaning in history is an ancient pastime. From Plato onward men have tried to agree on the 'fable of history.' The plain man clearly holds a philosophy of history, even if it is only a few ancient saws or the lessons in patriotism which he absorbs from his school books and his environment. Never more than now were men frantically examining the records of the past to find the laws upon which they can base a faith to live by. Many people, like Marx, make this search with their faith already cut and dried, and it is not surprising that they then emerge from the archives with a set of selected or even manufactured facts to guarantee the truth of their interpretations of history. Even so, it is a search that has often employed the most sensitive and subtle minds, and one may well hesitate to add to the ocean of ink that has been spilled on philosophies of history in general.

One great stumbling block faces us at the outset: can *any* philosophy of history be tested by an appeal to the evidence of historical events? The answer is not easy to give, but on the whole it appears that the record of events is not such as to establish the truth of any philosophy. Most of the basic philosophic and theological questions are of the type that neutral and scientific inquiry cannot answer. What is the purpose of life? Is there a meaning behind history? Such questions are not answerable by the natural or social sciences, and this warning must be kept in mind in any rational or scientific analysis of Marx's laws of history.

The idea that the course of history, like the physical universe, is subject to laws lying behind the seemingly fortuitous events is one that has fascinated many learned people in all ages. Marx never doubted that such laws exist, and that they are knowable. He claimed indeed to have discovered them, to have laid bare the pattern of law that actually exists beneath the surface, to have 'made the processes of history conscious.' The question of historical laws is intimately woven into the Marxist meaning of history, for to Marx the laws were the guarantee that history would bring the revolution and afterward the classless society. The Marxist science of history was meant to prove the truth of the Marxist philosophy of history. As Stalin expressed it:

. . . the science of the history of society, despite all the complexity of the phenomena of social life, can become as precise a science as, let us say, biology, and capable of making use of the laws of development of society for practical purposes . . . Hence socialism is converted from a dream of a better future for humanity into a science.[3]

We may now put the question to Marx. Has he, by calling attention to economic influences, done more than give us a useful clue to understanding how social change often occurs? Has he in fact revealed any law by which history ineluctably develops? The facts of industrial development since Marx's day have not conformed to Marx's expectations, since neither the sharpening class struggle nor the increasing improvishment has come about. This does not noticeably worry the Marxist, because he rests his case upon an ultimate act of faith which, like most faiths, is elastic enough to cover all contingencies. The dialectic of history, like all ambitious historical interpretations, can thus hardly be refuted by experience; on the contrary, experience must be adjusted to the theory — which is always an easy task for an ingenious believer. Marx himself believed, as any thorough-going Hegelian does, that there is a pattern of logical and dialectical necessity in history. The Marxist construction is not so much a series of deductions from a few fixed premises (which it is often taken to be) as a kind of *Gestalt* or pattern imposed upon society and history. To assume such a fixed and necessary pattern in history is metaphysical in the worst sense of that word, and puts the shaping of events forever beyond the reach of man, even collectively, and even in the classless society.

Here, as elsewhere, Marx occasionally broke through the fog of the dialectic. Once, in later life, when he was behaving like an economic historian and not like a dialectician, he protested against a 'historico-philosophical theory of the *marche générale* imposed by fate upon every people.' [4] But this lapse into clarity was only temporary, and did nothing to alter his conviction of the truth of *his own* inevitable law of history.

3. *Leninism*, p. 416.
4. *Selected Correspondence*, p. 354.

II

There are several weighty reasons why Marx the dialectician was wrong, some of them telling with equal force against all ambitions laws of history. The first great error, underlying the assumption of any law of history, is to assume that there is only one history revealed to us. History (that is, the narrative) is not a tale of events that have happened once and for all, a record of limited and available facts which all must accept. To begin with, there are many gaps in our records, so that it is always easier to derive so-called laws where the historical record is scanty. Perhaps for that reason it has been said that 'ignorance is the first requisite of the historian,' and for the same reason, too, the scientific historians such as Vico, Montesquieu, Machiavelli, and Marx have been led astray by the limited historical evidence available to them. Many civilizations have come and gone of which we possess only the most fragmentary knowledge. There is little doubt, too, that only Marx's ignorance of the ancient and medieval worlds enabled him to make his wide generalizations about them.

Then again, such information of the past as we do possess is heavily weighted in certain directions. Only some types of material were put on record, for example, legal codes and the chronicles of kings, and even this documentary evidence is often meager and written to prove a point. The records of archaeology are of a certain durable kind — pots and tombs and arrowheads — so that in reconstructing an early civilization, reliance is put on evidence weighted in favor of the material and practical. But a civilization is much more than its artifacts.

Finally, and even more important, is the fact that the only history we can be aware of is history as we read or select it. At times the information is absent, while at others the facts are too numerous for all of them to be taken into account. Selection is always personal, and 'facts' are not the same to all. Since all historical events are unique, so far as we know, choosing those that are significant or relevant is always difficult and is invariably carried out in the light of a prior theory or principle of selection. Even the historian who goes to history out of disinterested curiosity cannot begin to order his material unless he first has a question to put.

Yet such a view is not sheer skepticism and is not to say that history is whatever we say it is. Many if not most scientific events are also, in a sense, unique. Yet in history, as in science, generalization is possible and, indeed, necessary if we are to explain anything. The evidence must be scrutinized with care, and above all assessed with intellectual integrity. There is both good and bad written history, aside altogether from literary style, and even though it may be written from different points of view it is not all merely agreeable fiction. We are entitled to demand of the historian that he should state his bias and make plain what question he puts to the historical record. If different questions are put different answers will be obtained, and so there is often a gulf between an agreed account of what happened and its interpretation. In short, the only answers we can get from history are those our questions are designed to elicit, the only meaning we shall find is the meaning we ourselves put into history. Our question, or meaning, then becomes the principle of selection which determines what things 'matter,' and how they are interpreted. Marx, like all interpreters of history, was incurably teleological (although he would never have admitted it) when he wrote the story of history and gave it a plot and a climax.

In his recent book, *The Free Society,* J. Middleton Murry describes his search of history to find something which would give meaning to his existence, which would enable him to integrate his life by showing him where his main duty lay. For a while he was overwhelmed by Marx's vision of history and wrote his early book, *The Necessity of Communism,* to justify and spread the good tidings. With the passing of the years he lost his enthusiasm, and from a Marxist became a true liberal, realizing that present history can have a meaning to man only in a free society. We can give it a meaning, good or bad, by choosing an end and promoting it. But no account of the past can possibly tell us what we *ought* to do, or what *will* happen. To think otherwise is very much like saying that history is unfolding according to a divine plan, of which we arrogantly claim to have private knowledge. Any such clue to history by means of which we can know the course and destiny of man on earth is something to be discerned by the eye of faith and is not deducible from a study of economic or any other history.

The ends men have chosen, the questions they have asked, the meanings they have read into history are legion. To some, history is the rise and spread of Christianity, tending toward a goal that is variously defined; to Hegel history was the dialectical progression toward freedom in the deified state; to Voltaire it was the growth of human reason; to others it may be the growth of conscience, or of the 'liberal idea,' or the progress of philosophy, or an ever-closer approximation to the truth, or the improvement of man's technology and his command over nature. Often history has been merely an account of power politics, or the record of 'the crimes, follies, and misfortunes of mankind,' or what Carlyle called 'a distillation of rumour.' If social conditions are really bad, men may take refuge in a timeless world outside history altogether — this is a notable feature of Oriental mysticism. The Western world has in the main been saved from this, largely because of the keen sense of history in Judaism, which in turn was incorporated into Christianity. Mass mysticism and withdrawal are always tempting, however, in a period of social disintegration, such as the present, or when the verdict of history seems to be going against our cause. St. Augustine's *City of God* may, from one standpoint, be justly regarded as a classic example of escapist literature, pointing the way to a retreat from a world in ruins.

Since there is and can be no one exclusive meaning, the search for a simple formula, a single pattern of law, is futile. There are in short as many histories, as many 'red threads,' as there are interests or beliefs or philosophies. The cyclical theories of the Greeks, the organic analogies of Spengler, the challenges and responses of Toynbee are not publicly verifiable interpretations of all history, but merely suggestive abstractions reflecting the tastes of their inventors or of their times. Marx, too, seeking to justify his pattern of the historic class struggle ending in the classless society, was engaged in a metaphysical and non-rational quest. Man is responsible for what happens, not destiny or chance or any economic or social forces, or any other factor external to man himself. The future therefore also depends on ourselves and is not written in the stars or the dialectic. We must learn, as adults, to live with the fact that we do not and cannot know the course of the future.

Marx may retort that his law of history is merely a probability, a generalization based upon a large number of cases. When treated in this way Marxism becomes a working hypothesis which may be tested by the evidence. But it is not a tenable reply for Marx, for two reasons (as noted at greater length in Chapter 7). First, Marx used only three cases — slavery, feudalism, capitalism — of which the first two were examined with so little care that they hardly serve to support any kind of generalization. The foundation of the whole law is in fact the one case of capitalism, and hence there is no induction about it; and even this one case, as we have seen in the preceding chapters, has not conformed to the law. Second, Marx was not setting out a cautious statement of probability, a working hypothesis, an extrapolation of social trends prefaced by *ceteris paribus*. He cast the horoscope of capitalism, making no allowance for other trends, and admitting no possibility that the future could take a course other than that which he outlined. The error behind Marx's dialectic law of history may be summed up by saying that he was merely universalizing his private plans for capitalism.

An essential part of Marx's theory, it will be recalled, is that ideologies are a 'reflection' of the economic foundation; that they are merely part of an economically determined superstructure. If this is true, then the second great objection which may be raised is that what Marx had to say was relevant only to nineteenth-century conditions, especially those prevailing at the time he lived and wrote, but is not applicable either to past economic systems or to the future. Marx saw this clearly enough in the case of the bourgeoisie of his day, and Engels, too, noted the same thing when he blamed the bourgeoisie for identifying generalizations from their own class point of view with the eternal laws of nature.[5] Yet what is said about the bourgeoisie is equally true of Marxists. Plekhanov came near to admitting this when he said that Marxist theory could have come into being only when determined by the evolution of capitalist methods of production. Max Beer wrote: 'Marxism is quite a natural growth of the revolutionary soil of the

5. Ibid. p. 512.

first half of the 19th Century'; and J. B. S. Haldane writes today: 'Marxism is the best and truest philosophy that could have been provided under the social conditions of the mid-19th Century.' [6]

The essential truth of this common criticism of Marxism still holds: if Marxism is right, the Marxist theory itself is economically determined and it is an open question whether another theory will not be thrown up out of another foundation. This does not altogether dispose of the broad generalization at the basis of Marx's system, that is, that economic forces are immensely important in history — a truism which can hardly be denied — but it is a fatal objection to the more specific parts of the Marxist ideology and to any determinate predictions. Like all determinist theories Marxism is trapped in its own logic, although Marxists appear to think their theory is exempt from determinism. The conclusion is inescapable: that Marxism is true only as an abstraction of one of the tendencies at work in the capitalist society of the mid-nineteenth century. Or as Marx himself put it: the theory expresses 'in general terms, actual relations springing from an existing class struggle, from a historical movement going on under our very eyes.' [7] That was in 1848. It makes a good rationalization in support of what Marx wanted for the proletariat in the future, and may be a useful guide to the historian or sociologist, but it is a long way from this to a massive interpretation of all history.

The third great objection to Marx's conception of history is his explanation of the course of history by reference to a single factor, the basic proposition of which, as Engels emphasized in his speech at Marx's graveside, is that mankind must eat before it can do anything else. Now this is vulnerable on two counts: first, one can explain history just as well by reference to any other single desire of man, such as his sexual instinct, or his will to power. We have even been offered a 'syphilitic interpretation' of history. Second, all single-factor explanations of history are open to suspicion, whether the factor is found in man or in nature. If it is found in nature there is the insuperable difficulty of explaining away the different cultures that have flourished in the same geographi-

6. Plekhanov, *Fundamental Problems of Marxism*, p. 95; M. Beer, *Life of Marx*, p. 71. Haldane, *Marxist Philosophy and the Sciences*, p. 17.

7. *Communist Manifesto*.

cal environment. If the factor is found in man the obstacle is no less. From the dawn of recorded history man has had the same biological nature as he has now, but reference to this constant factor will not explain why the same basic 'urges' have taken such different forms in the many civilizations. No doubt it is true that the economic foundation has conditioned, or influenced, other social changes; but it is equally true that other changes and factors have conditioned the economic. The rise of industrialism, for example, has taken significantly different forms in England, the United States, and Japan. Marx and Engels are both on record as noting that the results may differ because of differing circumstances, and the action of man himself. As a student of economic history, Marx wrote: 'Thus events strikingly analogous but taking place in different historic surroundings led to totally different results'; and Engels: 'Everything which sets men in motion must go through their minds; but what form it will take in the mind will depend very much upon the circumstances.' [8] But this modest and sensible attitude is rarely found in Marxist literature, and is quite out of keeping with Marx's implacable laws of history.

There is even serious doubt whether it is possible to isolate the influence of one factor throughout all history. Are not historical causes so complex and interacting that it is in fact impossible to say that most great historical events had a single cause? This seems particularly true when we are trying to analyze the rise or fall of a civilization, and especially when we bear in mind the shortages of historical information on earlier civilizations. Many things contributed to the rise and fall of the Roman Empire; a long series of steps led up to capitalism, some of them peaceful and some of them not. To take one alleged overriding influence, and by using it to impose an order upon the complexities of historical change with all their contingencies and imponderables, is only to achieve simplicity by violating the facts. We may as well confess it: we do not know how some factors, even relatively straightforward factors such as the physical environment or the role of leadership, have affected history at different times.

Oscar Wilde was not merely coining an epigram when he said that truth is seldom pure and never simple. An imposed simplifica-

8. *Selected Works*, I, p. 459.

tion may often be useful, even necessary: but *which* order or unity is chosen and imposed on the facts will depend on the purpose in hand, and so will have only a special or particular validity. That is one of the reasons why history is always being rewritten. New histories are written as new philosophies and points of view are adopted, so that every age turns to history for its own purposes. To use Croce's famous aphorism: all history is contemporary history. Hence, too, national histories differ greatly in their accounts of the same events. What Marx did was to insist that his personal order had a universal, almost an absolute validity.

III

The fourth objection is closely allied and arises from Marx's assumption that history has moved 'upward,' whether in a straight line or, as the Marxist would prefer to put it, in a spiral by a series of dialectical leaps. One trouble with this is Marx's bland assumption that there is something called universal history of which it is possible to trace the lineage. Toynbee avoided this mistake neatly enough, although he showed some doubt about how many civilizations he should count; that is to say, he dealt with specimens which he was unable to identify when he saw them. Marx, like Hegel before him, was concerned only with European history, and his references to other civilizations, whether in the contemporary East or in the ancient world, were seldom more than perfunctory. Most philosophies of history have grossly neglected the non-Western world. These many civilizations were not, and cannot be, brought into one stream which may be traced from its source through all its meanderings, until it ends in European industrialism.[9] A variation of this criticism arises from the use of the dialectical method: Since history has no *terminus ad quem* and no *terminus a quo,* any period may be taken as thesis or antithesis, depending on what one wants to prove. The dialectic in history is open to all the objections raised in Chapter 2 against the dialectic in logic.

9. Lenin's view was that world history since 1848 is clearly divided into three periods: (1) from the 1848 revolution to the Paris Commune of 1871, (2) from 1871 to the Russian Revolution of 1905, and (3) the period since then. *Selected Works,* 1942, I, p. 70.

Another difficulty lies in the idea of historical progress. Before a discussion of progress can be carried on intelligently, some acceptable criterion must be laid down, and this is not at all easy to do. It is also hard to define what is meant by progress in a biological or evolutionary sense. A common definition is this: some biological changes — in adaptation, reproduction, and so on — are restrictive; that is, they are dead ends, and prevent any further changes or adaptations being made. If the environment should then change, the lack of adaptability may mean extinction for a species. Some changes, on the other hand, permit scope for still further changes, and these may be called progressive, since they are flexible and *leave the future open.* (A dinosaur would not, I think, have accepted this criterion of biological progress.) On the analogy of the biological argument we could call an increase of knowledge or mastery over nature progressive, since they increase the adaptability of man or the possibilities open to him. But possibility is not inevitability, so that the result still depends on what we do with our possibilities.

Although hardly any standard of historical progress which we choose to take would be beyond dispute, nevertheless a plausible case can be made out for progress as measured in certain terms commonly accepted in the Western world. If we could agree on some objective standard, such as productivity per capita, then progress could be measured with fair ease. Indeed the Marxist standard of progress, as well as the standard by which he evaluated different cultures, was just that: efficiency in producing goods and services. Hence he could speak of later societies, since they were more productive, as being in advance of their predecessors. Not everyone however would agree that the society with the highest output of goods per capita is necessarily the best.

Sometimes the Marxist standard has been described as freedom for mankind, which in turn involves three factors: (1) increased productivity, (2) collective action, and (3) human development. The first two may be measured, but the third is of course subject to a number of interpretations. Marx himself once gave a more humorous test of progress:

> Anybody who knows anything of history knows that great social changes are impossible without the feminine ferment.

> Social progress can be measured exactly by the social position
> of the fair sex (the ugly ones included).[10]

We could perhaps take the extension of man's scientific knowledge as progress, and if that is our standard mankind has clearly
traveled upward in the last few hundred years. Never before has
mankind had the scientific and technological basis for civilization
which modern man possesses. Moreover, as superstition and
ignorance with respect to nature have given way to knowledge,
we have been able to use that knowledge to cure disease and ease
pain, decrease poverty, diffuse education and the arts, lengthen
the span of life, and to support a vastly increased world population. This was the standard of 'verifiable progress' which Walter
Bagehot put forward in the last century, and it is perhaps the most
plausible.[11] Some, perhaps all, of these things would be called
good in themselves, even by the moral philosopher; but if not, at
the very least they have made it more possible for man to lead
a good life by widening his opportunities and removing handicaps.

Our knowledge of nature and, to some extent, of man's social
behavior has enabled us more and more to take our personal and
collective destiny in hand, and consciously to plan it in many
directions. This enlargement of our freedom, by enabling us to
substitute choice and intelligence for drift, seems to be a step
forward, since it enables us to build more rationally. All this, however, is clearly a liberal view of progress, which was on the whole
common to Hegel, Marx, and a great majority of nineteenth-
century writers. Increases in productivity, knowledge, and freedom of choice would no doubt be dismissed by many high-minded
people who would take only an improvement in morals as a sign of
progress. In fact, jeers at the idea of progress are very common
nowadays. But even with reference to moral standards a plausible,
though not of course conclusive, case can be made out for progress.
Over a portion of the world at least, life has grown more tolerant,
manners are gentler and more kind, laws less harsh, cruelty to men

10. *Selected Correspondence*, p. 255. Engels once gave an explanation of
progress on other than the usual Marxist grounds: 'historical progress as a
whole was dependent [in the past] on the activity of a small privileged
minority.' *Selected Works*, 1942, I, p. 12.

11. W. Bagehot, *Physics and Politics*, London, 1912, pp. 208–9.

and animals has lessened, 'witches' are no longer burned; the standard of public honesty has been raised; we subscribe to the idea that happiness is for the many, not only for the few; and so on. A reading of the social history of ancient Rome, of the Middle Ages in England, or of the frontier life of the American West, makes out a strong case for progress along these lines. There is of course an obverse side to the medal (Buchenwald, the Soviet labor camps, and so on) and one must never forget that all knowledge may be used for good or evil purposes; but it is hard to believe that any person in the Western world would, after reflecting on the contrast, really prefer life in an earlier age if he had to take his chances then as an ordinary person, without special privileges.

But whether this view of progress, or some other, is held does not greatly matter here. Even if it be granted that man has progressed (by any standard at all) in some parts of the world over the period of recorded history, there is surely no evidence that this has been uniform; and there is no law of history that guarantees progress, or guarantees it in a linear or any other regular sequence. Whatever we believe to constitute progress, we can see decline as well as growth, retrogression as well as progress in history. It is easy to see that the civilizations of the Levant had their ups and downs, that Rome also fluctuated; and it would be hard to show that the Dark Ages were an improvement upon Rome at its best, or the Nazi Reich an advance upon the Weimar Republic. History has seen its ebbs as well as its flows, whatever we take as a tidemark, and of this Marx's upward-spiraling dialectic takes no account. Many civilizations have come and gone, and there has been no upward continuity by which one civilization has always begun at the peak reached by its predecessor. For all we know our most prized achievements may be wiped out almost overnight, and our Western civilization become one with Nineveh and Tyre; there is a fair prospect of such a fate in the near future. Yet if history does not prove a steady progress neither does it confirm pessimism. It is we who read our own hopes and fears into history.

The course of history (if we must use that ambiguous phrase) has been influenced by many factors among which the economic have doubtless had their part and an important one. Climate, geography, natural disasters, diseases, great leaders, ideas, even chance, or the length of Cleopatra's nose — all these and many more influences have made events what they have been. The appearance on the world stage at a particular time of Marx himself or of Hitler or Lenin may in a sense be regarded as an accident. Yet it seems foolish to assert that the course of events in Europe and Russia would have been precisely the same had these men not lived when they did.

Engels took the view that when the time was ripe for it the idea *had* to be discovered, and the related view that the great man miraculously appears whenever the circumstances demand him:

> . . . that if a Napoleon had been lacking, another would have filled the place, is proved by the fact that the man has always been found as soon as he became necessary.[12]

This is clearly untenable, for all that circumstances can create is the opportunity for someone to come to the fore. And what of the times when the idea and the man did not appear? And who is to judge when the man has been necessary? Many have echoed Wordsworth's cry: 'Milton! thou shoulds't be living at this hour,' but they have cried in vain. Where, one may ask, was the genius to unite the Greek city states, to save the Roman Empire from collapse, to forestall the rise of Hitler, Mussolini, or Franco, to prevent Stalin's travesty of Marx's more humane dreams, to lead Britain out of the depression of the 1930's, or to bring together in accord the squabbling victors of 1945?

Marx had a part of the truth in stressing the play of technology and economic forces in history. It is an important part of the truth, and in our personal lives we all readily see that there is an economic aspect to almost everything we do. Certainly there have been conflicts of many kinds in history, among them class conflicts; and doubtless at any one time, there were and are economic limits, and limits set by nature, within which man's choice must operate. But when allowance has been made for the economic and all external factors, it remains true that the most important element in man's history is man himself — his hopes, his beliefs, his purposes.

It was partly because he overemphasized the limits and under-

12. *Selected Correspondence*, p. 518; Cf. Plekhanov, *The Role of the Individual in History*, London, 1941.

estimated the extent of choice that Marx proved less accurate at prediction than he thought he would be. It was because he read his own presumed meaning into history, and then borrowed Hegel's dialectical law to support it, that he was able to view history as a single track inevitably leading upward. But it nonetheless was a pure assumption, a hope, not a proven thesis.

IV

Engels once wrote that 'with Hegel philosophy comes to an end,' meaning thereby that Hegel's Absolute Idea would become self-realized with the establishment of the German State. There remained nothing more for the Hegelian dialectic to do, or at any rate nothing that could be foreseen. The Moving Finger, having writ, would then stop writing.

What, we may ask, is to happen to the dialectical process in Marx's classless society? The answer is silence, except for the cryptic hint that it will proceed on a 'higher plane.' Soviet spokesmen have now and then suggested forms which the dialectic takes in Russia. The chief of these is 'criticism and self-criticism,' which is said to be 'a new dialectical law.' [13] In practice this seems to mean that higher organs of the party are free to criticize the lower, and the lower may indulge in strictly limited criticism of practical details, but the general policies, being decided by higher formations, must on no account be questioned. Or it has been put as the 'struggle between the old and the new' — which seems to amount to the fact that the old is always wrong, on the ground that any opposition to the regime can only be remnants of bourgeois ideology lingering on in the consciousness. (One of the objectives of the second Russian Five Year Plan was 'the elimination of capitalist survivals from the Soviet popular consciousness.' [14] Quite obviously these are nothing more than half-hearted attempts to rescue the Marxist dialectic from the same kind of stalemate in which Hegel's dialectic had ended.

Regardless of what new forms it may take, the dialectic can

13. A. A. Zhdanov, cited in J. D. Bernal, *Marx and Science,* London, 1952, p. 54.

14. S. Kovalyov, *Ideological Conflicts in Soviet Russia,* Washington, 1948, p. 1.

clearly operate no longer through the class struggle based on ownership of the means of production. But whatever we may have been taught by the authors of *1066 and All That,* history does not come to a 'Full Stop' with any 'Good Thing,' even if it be the classless society. Marx's idea was that capitalism constitutes 'the closing chapter of the *pre-historic* stage of human society' and that only with the establishment of the classless society can 'real' history begin.

Marx's point here was that the past has been ruled by necessity and has not been deliberately willed by man. Society has been at the mercy of powerful natural and economic forces which man has not understood and often not even recognized.

> The forces operating in society work exactly like the forces operating in nature: blindly, violently, destructively, so long as we do not understand them and fail to take them into account.

> For what each individual wills is obstructed by everyone else, and what emerges is something that no one willed. Thus past history proceeds in the manner of a natural process and is also essentially subject to the same laws of movement.[15]

Social and economic forces, seemingly as mysterious and omnipotent as the forces of nature, have been accepted in a spirit of resignation, in much the same way as some pious people are said to accept all the vicissitudes of life as the inscrutable ways of Allah or of Providence.

This brings us to the fifth error in the Marxist theory of history — the great confusion of the laws or uniformities of nature with 'laws' or tendencies in society. Over and over again the identity of the two are asserted in Marxism: regardless of man's will there is the same necessity in history as in nature. Men in the mass are mere instruments of fate carried along by the 'blind forces of society.' The analogy between physical nature and society can be very misleading. If a biological analogy is drawn, it may, for example, lead to a social Darwinist outlook, toward which Walter Bagehot inclined, and with which Marx himself sometimes flirted. He once wrote:

15. *Selected Works,* 1942, I, pp. 180, 382.

> Darwin's book is very important and serves me as the basis in natural science for the class struggle in history.[16]

But generally he refused to view human history as merely another case of natural selection and the survival of the fittest, so that he did not end up as a social Darwinist. As a result he avoided many silly and dangerous mistakes. Engels was of the opinion that Darwin had transferred the social-economic struggle to nature; whence it was tranferred back again to society to prove the 'eternal natural laws of society' [i.e. of laissez-faire].[17] When one recalls the writings of Herbert Spencer and other arch-individualists of the nineteenth century, it becomes easier to sympathize with Engels' resentment.

If analogies are drawn between physics and society there may, at a superficial level, be some small truth in them. For instance, the resultant of a number of forces in mechanics bears some resemblance to a compromise of interests in politics. The 'broker's' job of political parties in a democracy is usually taken to be a hammering out of a compromise among a diversity of conflicting interests. But Marx meant something more than that. He also meant that there has been no over-all planning of history and society. This, too, is so trite that it is hardly worth taking issue with. His more important meaning seems to have been that all wills somehow neutralize each other, so that nobody gets his own way. Apart from the fact that this contradicts Marx's main thesis that a ruling class always gets its way, it is also wrong on other counts. Because there is no master plan for everything it does not follow that some things are not planned. Buildings and cities are erected and managed, wars are planned and won, social and economic policies are formulated and carried through, such as care of the aged, compulsory education, and foreign-exchange control. And so we might go on, drawing examples from very many areas of life. In short, we can and do plan many sectors of society when there is agreement on what should be done, and how to do it.

There are of course many things that are not deliberately planned. It is a truism, for example, that in a competitive market the price of a commodity is not set by any one person but is, as we

16. *Selected Correspondence*, pp. 125–6.
17. *Dialectics of Nature*, p. 208.

loosely say, determined by the forces of supply and demand. Similarly the total production of any commodity just happens to reach a certain figure in any one year, as a total of all the piecemeal decisions made by a multitude of producers. Or an invention such as the automobile is introduced with profound social effects that no one planned or perhaps even wanted, upon the mobility of labor, the tourist trade, road building, sex morality, the family, and so forth. Professor Ogburn, of the University of Chicago, has diligently listed some 150 social effects following from the invention of the automobile, 150 from radio, 61 from x-ray, and 23 from rayon. To take an instance from Marx's *Capital*, when the wool trade became profitable the Highlands were turned into sheep farms, thousands of the former inhabitants being evicted to make room for the sheep.

We often speak of events as though they took place independently of the will of man. We say that prices rise and fall, or that trade routes shift their course, and sometimes we note the waning and waxing of prosperity in the trade cycle with almost the same feeling of helplessness as that with which we contemplate the stars rolling around in their orbits. No one planned the British Empire, or the birth rate or total population of any country (although such things are becoming matters of public policy nowadays). In the same way we often speak of the entire history of the Western world for the past two hundred years as having been shaped by an entity called science or technology, and we call this changing of the face of the earth by the stock phrase, the Industrial Revolution.

It is in some such sense as this that Marx's theory implies that the course of history is not willed. The changes in the modes of production and property relations take place 'spontaneously, unconsciously, and independently of the will of men,' and as a result of the repercussions which these set up men come to live differently. Man is borne along as on a tide, and until Marx came on the scene could not even see the direction in which he was drifting. Even now, if Marx is to be believed, man cannot alter his direction, but with all his efforts can only slightly advance or retard his rate of drift.

The rule of necessity is most obviously and superficially true of

an economic system of complete laissez-faire. The classical economists, noting that economic life was not in fact a chaos, tended to
fall back upon a revised version of natural law to explain the order
and harmony that prevailed. Each individual, by promoting his
own interest, would also promote the public welfare, and government intervention could only alter the natural harmony for the
worse.

There may be no 'invisible hand,' in Adam Smith's sense, yet
it may not be altogether correct to say that a laissez-faire society is
entirely unplanned. (The point is theoretical only, since laissez-
faire, if it ever existed, is quite remote from the facts of economic
life today.) For one thing there is consumers' sovereignty, so that
although each consumer accepts prices as given, yet consumers as
a whole do determine the output of goods and services. For another, if one can imagine laissez-faire as being deliberately chosen,
it would be not so much the rule of necessity as a choice that society should be ruled by wealth. At the very least, deliberate inac-
tion is as real a policy as any other: it is a policy of approval of the
status quo.

All the detailed results of laissez-faire would, no doubt, not be
chosen, such as the earlier social consequences of a free labor market in terms of women and children coal miners, or the distressing
effects of a trade slump upon the unemployed. But the same truth,
that the detailed results are not chosen, applies to the unforeseen
and perhaps unwanted consequences of any social policy whose
main principle *is* deliberately chosen. In the latter case, as with
a choice for the free market, it is precisely because the results are
disliked when they materialize that a further choice is made; and
in both cases the resort is to political action or some other form of
social remedy. We decide, for example, that in the public interest
the school-leaving age shall be raised, and as a result of the policy
there are unforeseen repercussions upon industry and public finance. We can either deliberately allow these to take their course
or we may institute further action to take care of the repercussions.

We may go a little further. Any economic plan, to judge from
wartime experience, always turns up results that differ from the
original intention. The most that can be hoped for, even with the
kind of disciplinary control exercised in the U.S.S.R., is that in a

rough and ready way the major objectives of economic planning will be achieved. To say nothing of the fact that intentions may vary with time and experience, there are many factors that cause the best-laid plans to 'gang agley': human factors, such as inertia, error, irrationality, shifts in consumer tastes, and labor disputes; factors such as the weather, shortage of materials, the actions of other countries, and so forth. Even if the plan is judged successful, what has been proved? Merely that one sector of life can be subject to a definite policy if we wish it. The same lesson can be learned from the multitude of policies already carried through in every democracy.

Marx believed that past history had been subject to necessity because its laws had not been understood. A fair reply would appear to be that since Marx laid bare the importance of the economic foundation and revealed the laws of motion of society, it is now possible for man consciously to make use of this knowledge, just as an understanding of the laws of nature enables us to bend them to our use. Engels lent force to this point when he noted, referring to the forces operating in society:

> But when once we have recognized them and understood how they work, their direction and their effects, the gradual subjection of them to our will and the use of them for the attainment of our aims depends entirely upon ourselves. And this is quite especially true of the mighty productive forces of the present day.[18]

In other words, there seems to be no particular reason why man should not begin here and now consciously to plan and shape his own history. Marx, however, postponed the operation of free choice and conscious control until after the revolution. Under capitalism, he thought, it is futile to talk of collective planning for society; only in the classless society will man be free from the thralldom of blind economic forces; only then shall we see 'humanity's leap from the realm of necessity into the realm of freedom.'

To the non-Marxist, the first great difficulty with this is in seeing how the change from private to public ownership absolves mankind, at one stroke, from the rule of economic forces. If the

18. *Selected Works,* 1942, I, pp. 180–81.

economic is all-determining, it must be so under any system whatever.

Now it is true that Marx and Engels are frequently on record as admitting that the economic might be modified by interaction, and this (as we have noted in Chapter 3) is one of the contradictions never resolved in Marxist theory. But such admission of interaction is fatal to any law of necessity, and gives no support to Marx's main thesis, justifying neither necessity nor freedom in the classless society. As always, Marx solved the problem by summoning the magic of the dialectic; but if the argument in Chapter 2 is sound, the dialectic can work no magic, and the non-dialectician is left to make the best he can of the discontinuity, not to say illogicality, of the famous 'leap' into freedom.

A second criticism of Marx's primacy of the economic arises from the experience of communist countries, especially the Soviet Union. If anything is clear it is that the Russians with their Five Year Plans are deliberately building the kind of society they (that is, their leaders) want; in no sense are they passively waiting upon economic conditions. But the difference in this respect, great as it is, is only one of degree between the Soviet Union and the capitalist countries. Even in the most capitalist of countries, let us say the United States of America, there is widespread interaction of politics upon the economic. Every piece of collective action freely arrived at and freely worked out, whether by private organizations or by the state, enlarges the area of voluntary decision and by that very fact reduces the sphere to which autonomy and necessity apply. We had better, by God, accept the universe — as Carlyle forcibly put it — although even so we may adapt parts of it to our will; but we are not obliged, except within very wide limits, to accept the sway of social forces, and it is what we do within these limits that makes our history.

The answer of the rigid Marxist must be to fall back, as Marx did, upon a denial that any substantial reform or social planning can be achieved in the capitalist democracies, and hence his denial of freedom and planning is extended today to every country that is not openly communist, even including those that have had democratic socialist governments, such as Britain. Once more we see the rigid Marxist dichotomy, which instead of taking account of the real world gives us only the nonexistent polar extremes of complete planning and laissez-faire. At this point again we come to a parting of the ways, where the evidence is dismissed by Marxists as they take refuge in their verbal stereotypes.

V

In view of the fact that Marxism makes so much of iron laws both in nature and society, it is pertinent to ask in what sense is man 'free' in the Marxist version of history? The answer is somewhat ambiguous, and so must be broken down into its parts. First, there is the Hegelian paradox that freedom is the recognition of necessity, as in the familiar saying that 'stone walls do not a prison make.' We must, that is, recognize the pattern of history, and if we do this consciously we are free, since willing obedience to a recognized law of necessity ('necessity transfigured') is the definition of freedom in Hegel.

There is of course a perfectly common-sense truth to this, in that restraints or limits, if voluntarily accepted, do not make us feel that we are slaves. Yet Marx and Hegel go far beyond that position, and ask us to bow to a march of events beyond human control and direction. Both of them were concerned to show not only how things *did* happen but also how they are *bound to* happen.

As I have tried to show, there is in fact no such objective pattern of the movement of events in history to which we must 'freely' adjust ourselves. It is an entirely false and fatalistic analogy that is drawn for us by Hegel and Marx, between adjusting ourselves to history and to the forces of nature. This meaning of freedom is therefore spurious and must be rejected whether it comes to us in Hegelian idealism or in Marxist economic terms.

Secondly, the Hegelian meaning in practice involved submission to authority. One submits not only to 'forces' in society (such as price movements) but also and often to specific authorities, usually to persons, with the sanctions of law or other power behind them. Thus in the Hegelian system the submission recommended was to whatever authority represented for the time being the logically necessary stage of history — which to Hegel meant submission to

the Prussian State. Then somehow, by some miraculous and ob-
fuscating piece of verbal juggling, a man becomes more free by
submission than by following his own judgment. Just as with
Rousseau, whose General Will was always right and wiser than
the individual, it is only a short step to saying that one may be
'forced to be free,' which in practice means 'forced to obey.'

Thirdly, there may also be in the Hegelian-Marxist meaning
a more subtle scholastic flavor, a hint of the same kind of freedom
which is said to be enjoyed by angels and saints who 'necessarily
but freely choose the good.' Now this may be valid for angels and
saints, although it would be a proposition difficult to establish
by evidence, but when it is applied instead to human beings it can
become dangerous doctrine. If it becomes the doctrine that men
are free to accept what the party or state or any other authority
teaches but are not free to reject it, according to their own weigh-
ing of the evidence, then the scholastic and Hegelian paradox
becomes a monstrous bondage which free man everywhere must
resist so long as they claim title to humanity.

These meanings of freedom in Hegel and Marx are not acceptable to a democrat. On examination they turn out to be either a
semantic befuddling of the nature of freedom, or a sophisticated
defense of authority, or both. There is only one trivial sense in
which the Marxist definition of freedom is unobjectionable: before we can use nature we must first understand her laws; to control we must submit to nature's ways; and to this may be added
that only if we have reliable information about social phenomena
can we together live the kind of lives we want, or carry out successfully the social, political, and economic measures at which we
aim. Perhaps it is only some such simple meaning that Marx had
in mind when he asserted that the classless society would be for
humanity 'the realm of freedom.' Certainly Marx believed that it
was impossible to carry out economic planning under private
ownership. He also believed that man was free in his leisure time,
and hence that the shortening of the working day was a prerequi-
site to freedom for the worker. A corollary of this is that, since
wealth gives a greater freedom of choice and action, so a rise in
the general standard of living will, other things being equal, en-
large the area of choice. Hobson's choice, between starvation and

obedience to authority, will be removed. But these notions are commonplace, and owe nothing to Marxism.

The proviso that other things should be equal is important, since it by no means follows that large-scale economic planning will of itself lead to freedom for the individual in the sense of freedom from constraints. The Nazi Reich was a planned state but by no stretch of the imagination could it be called a free society; while in the U.S.S.R. planning and freedom certainly do not go together. There is no need to labor the point, however, since Marxism has little enough to say on the classless society, except for a few vague generalizations, and nothing to contribute to our idea of freedom.

VI

There is one other feature of Marx's inexorable march of the dialectic in history which deserves comment: to what extent is Marxism a philosophy of fatalism? At first sight it seems utterly fatalistic, at least up to the point of the revolution. History is rolling along its predestined, dialectical groove, and it would seem illogical that we should lift a finger to help. It may be illogical even to speak of helping or hindering, since our conscious decisions scarcely matter. But although illogical it is psychologically quite understandable, and psychology is more important than logic if one wishes to tap the springs of human action. If we make our prior value judgment, first deciding how we want history to go, then it often seems to encourage us if we also believe strongly that history is inevitably going our way. That seems to have been the case with Cromwell and the Mohammedans (as cited by Plekhanov in his writings on history), with the Calvinists, and many others. The idea that God or fate or history is on our side and that victory is certain may stimulate people to greater effort and does not always lead to fatalism. Now and then, especially in times of political reaction, Marxists tend to fall into fatalism, and to leave history to do all that is necessary. But Marx seldom fell into that attitude, and Lenin, too, always strongly condemned it whenever he found it prevalent among Russian Marxists.

A great part of the secret of Marx's appeal is that the moral and the inevitable, the desired and the necessary, are hopelessly mixed. He was temperamentally unable to leave the stars in their courses alone; he was not only a prophet but also a fighter, who drew strength from the belief that the future he so passionately desired was also coming with relentless certainty. Something like the same identification is made by modern Marxists when they speak of 'the need for inevitable change.'

Hegel tended to make an identity of the ideal with the actual reality of the Prussian State: Marx on the other hand identified the ideal with what was inevitably coming after the revolution. Hegel's was for the most part the morality of the *status quo*, the identification of might and right. Marx's theory has been called a kind of moral 'futurism': what is coming is right.[19]

Why did Marx make this confusion of the moral and the necessary? The first part of the answer is of course his Hegelianism, with its fusion of the morally, the logically, and the historically necessary. The second part is that Marx was a man of action who desperately wanted to change the world. By allying the historical law of necessary victory with the realization of his ideals he forged a powerful propaganda weapon and put heart and fight into the proletariat (or at any rate into the Marxists among them). The future they longed for was decreed in the stars and they would fight twice as hard for being cheered with the prospect of certain victory. Defeat is never disastrous if one believes in eventual victory. It is the old story of God helping those who help themselves. In that fight there must be slogans and 'myths'; the idea of the class struggle, or of the classless society, is such a sociological myth, comparable, say, to Sorel's 'general strike,' or to some of the myths and stereotypes of democracy. The idea of class *struggle* contains also enough of the elements of will and choice to make the fight a real one instead of leading to a passive waiting upon victory. Dialectical necessity is the other facet of the same myth, for it is this in Marxism which will *make* the revolution come true. The truth or falsity of the myth is thus irrelevant: it is like Shaw's definition of a miracle in *St. Joan:* 'an event which confirms or creates faith.'

19. K. R. Popper, *The Open Society and Its Enemies,* Princeton, 1950, pp. 385ff.

The third part of the answer is that Marx was, as we have seen, deeply imbued with the idea of inevitable progress, so common to the Enlightenment and to the nineteenth century; he was doubly imbued, for he owed a debt to Hegel and later also to Darwin. In addition, it was hard for him to see how anything in the future could possibly be worse than the society of his day; any change was almost bound to be an improvement over the distressing social effects of early industrialization in England.

If the Marxist system is so disastrously determinist, in so far as it abides by its own iron laws, and yet allows for freedom in so far as it is permeated by a moral idea, how is it that a philosophy so inconsistent has gained a hold over the minds and allegiance of men? The answer is hinted at in the question; it is precisely the moral element behind the determinism which is its greatest strength. Perhaps logical ambiguity is never a source of weakness to any popular philosophy.

Let us make no mistake about this. On the surface Marx made a great show of being scientific, of hating all sentimentality, preaching, and uplift propaganda. Underneath he was a more than usually sensitive nineteenth-century liberal with a passion for freedom, justice, and equality, and filled with invincible optimism for the future of man on the earth. For that reason Marxism has been called the illegitimate offspring of nineteenth-century liberalism.[20]

Like all social radicals Marx was close to being a moral idealist, although admittedly class hatred and resentment occupy a large place in his writings (together with traces of racial prejudice), and these emotions often attract Marxists more than does the desire for social justice. The moral quality of Marx himself, however, is shown not only in the correct Victorian standards of his family life and in his scorn for those who had not the same self-discipline, but also in the moral judgments which run sometimes implicitly, often explicitly, through all the vast pile of his writings, the whole of which may be justly regarded as treatises on social ethics. If anyone doubts this, let him reread the more emotional sections of the *Communist Manifesto,* or pick up *Capital* almost at random and read the footnotes. The judgment that Marxism is essentially a moral philosophy camouflaged as pseudo-science, while not usu-

20. R. N. Carew Hunt, op. cit. p. 74.

ally endorsed by Marxists, has been noted by one of them: 'Marx's originating and basic attitude is thus moral and humanistic.' [21]

Marx started with the conviction that capitalism was evil and must be destroyed. He reached a white heat of moral indignation at the hypocrisy and callousness of capitalism, the 'human self-estrangement,' the degradation of labor to the status of a commodity. His attacks on religion were to a great extent derived from the same moral judgment. The churches, when he judged them by their actions and not by their pious words, seemed on the side of the big battalions and the bourgeoisie; and religion, when adopted by the poor, distracted their attention from the shame of their earthly exploitation. The end of the classless society, too, is moral: to make possible a life of freedom and equality in which the dignity of labor is fittingly appreciated and personality can freely develop. Marx never won during his lifetime the recognition to which he believed his intellectual genius entitled him, nor was he able to achieve any position of real power in public affairs. His frustrated ambitions pushed him on, and reinforced the demands which he made, on more general moral grounds, for justice in the future. The Marxist challenge to democracy is, in the end, the challenge to build a just social order.

Marx, then, was by instinct and by his sense of injustice on the side of the angels. Hence he has been classified with the Children of Light and not with the Children of Darkness.[22] It is a pity that his Hegelian heritage and his fanatic zeal led him into dialectical dogma. It is a cosmic tragedy, because of the power which they wield, that his followers in the Soviet Union have adopted the dogma, have ignored the underlying strain of humanity in Marx, and have clamped an iron discipline of belief onto the minds of men. Yet it would perhaps be going too far to blame Marx for the Moscow orthodoxy, since no man should be held entirely responsible for what posterity makes of his thought. Marx may be said, however, to have invited fanaticism by the excessively dogmatic manner of his writing, although as he grew older he showed some signs of modifying his iron laws and softening his determinism.

21. Jack Lindsay, op. cit. p. 196.
22. R. Niebuhr, *The Children of Light and the Children of Darkness,* New York, 1944.

We know that when he contemplated the more extreme and absurd theories produced in his name, he used to say: 'All I know is that I am not a Marxist.' [23] But these theories merely put bluntly the logical extreme of his own economic dialectical determinism.

23. *Selected Correspondence*, p. 472.

The proof of the social science pudding must be in the eating; and that, of course, lies in the future, for the greater part of the pudding is not yet cooked, and the public are reluctant to taste the few morsels that are ready . . . Certainly, the social sciences have their hands full; but their achievements give grounds for hope, and experience is on their side.

B. WOOTTON.[1]

. . . there can be no 'impartial' social science in a society which is built up on the class struggle.

LENIN.[2]

7

Marxism and Scientific Method

I

MANY SOCIAL PHILOSOPHERS have called their systems of thought scientific but none has been more insistent on this title than Marx. It is the ambitious claim of Marxism to be the only real science of society that is examined in this chapter. But first it may be well to say something on scientific methods in general, and on how far they can be applied to the study of society.

There is of course more to the natural sciences than their methods: there is also a large and growing body of knowledge, much of it capable of useful application. To the man on the street it is probably the body of knowledge rather than the methods which he thinks of as science. The point to remember, however, is that this knowledge is called scientific knowledge only because it has been acquired by scientific methods, or at any rate has been tested by them. Metaphysics, theology, and literary criticism, say, what-

1. B. Wootton, *Testament for Social Science,* London, 1950, p. 190.
2. Lenin, *Selected Works,* 1942, I, p. 54.

ever their status, are not open to the same public tests of reliability that scientific methods can apply.

What, then, are the scientific methods? The usual answer is
that they consist of three steps: first, observation of the facts;
second, generalization or working hypothesis; and third, testing
of the hypothesis which, if satisfactory, promotes the theory to
the status of a scientific 'law.' This is the original or Baconian
recipe and in general it is the right one, although the steps may
not always be taken in the order given. A scientific investigation
typically starts with a question or a problem or, what amounts to
the same thing, with a theory or number of theories. The facts
may *then* be approached by observation, experiment, trial and
error, or with the tools of deduction, abstraction, and so on. In
the social sciences the problem or hypothesis nearly always comes
first and observation of data is the second step.

There is a prima facie presumption that scientific methods
may be applied to any data, including those of human behavior.
The social scientist must not assume that no regularities can be
found in his material. He must in fact begin operations with the
opposite assumption. Again, although the nature and purpose of
the scientific methods are in principle the same, no matter to
what material they are applied, in practice there are several
special difficulties in the application of scientific methods to the
study of society. These are well known and arise from the complexity and nature of the data; the very limited possibility of
experiment and 'controls;' the lack of any clear-cut tests for explanatory hypotheses (which is why conflicting social theories
prevail for such long periods of time); the ambiguity of testing
a social theory by its results; and the extraordinary obstacles in
the way of predictive tests (unless they are very short-run and
highly conditional). Some of these difficulties are found also in
some branches of natural science, but there are still others which
are unique to the social sciences, for instance: that many generalizations are true of only one time and place (i.e. are 'culture-
bound'); that merely observing human behavior is often to
change it; that the publication of the results of a study may alter
behavior. The last point has a direct application to Marxism,

since the reactions of people to his theory are among the influences determining whether or not his predictions came true.

I do not mention these sample difficulties in order to disparage scientific or empirical research. Since we make generalizations and hypotheses about social behavior every day, and cannot avoid doing so, there is certainly an obligation to make them as reliable as possible. One must admit however that the progress is very slow in the social sciences — slow, yet perceptible — and for a long time to come we should be wise not to expect that the social sciences will turn up the illuminating and general 'laws' of the natural sciences.

A word on the most difficult of all problems in the social sciences, that of 'values,' may not come amiss. Consider first the traditional statement of the problem. Natural science does not deal directly with moral values; the moral word 'ought' is not in its vocabulary. Doubtless the border between science and philosophy is a very thin one, yet when we finally come down to what are regarded as 'ultimates,' whether religious or moral, it seems to be true that science can deliver no final judgment, nor give a moral imperative. The knowledge which science yields may be used for our purposes, but the purposes are not found within the knowledge itself. Science is positive, not normative; the indicative, not the imperative mood; it deals with causes, not purposeful data. In principle, so it is usually argued, the social scientist, *qua* scientist, is in the same fix, and so long as he sticks to his last he has nothing conclusive to say on morals or on what *ought* to be done.[3] When we *have* agreed on the 'ought,' however, then it is at least partly a positive and scientific inquiry to determine the most appropriate means to be employed. The social scientist may also do a great deal of useful work in helping to separate means from ends, in showing how the different ends pursued may conflict, in assessing means as appropriate to the results (or to the intentions), in separating matters of fact from matters of value, and so on.[4]

3. D. H. Robertson, 'On Sticking to One's Last,' *Economic Journal*, December 1949, pp. 505ff.

4. *Testament for Social Science*, pp. 119ff., 134ff.

The emphasis science puts upon truth is often said to be the one serious exception to the neutrality of science toward values. The argument that science involves social values may be simply stated: science in all its branches assumes no final truth, but proceeds by doubt, discussion, and the free competition of ideas; this tolerant atmosphere and free traffic depend ultimately upon political safeguards, and therefore the scientist must stand for a free society; he cannot be neutral on such matters as civil liberties and democracy. The argument is strong, and the pity is that more scientists do not act upon it.[5] The argument is not impregnable however, because it is clearly possible for natural science to flourish in societies which enjoy little or no political freedom, as in eighteenth-century France or in the Soviet Union today.

The social scientist has a much larger and more direct stake in a free society, since the behavior of people is his field of study. He is more dependent on society and the government for putting any of his theories to the test of practice, and even for publication, since this in itself affects human behavior. In a tyrannical and still more in a totalitarian regime he is likely to find many branches of investigation closed to him by fiat, thus reducing his scope for research. He can flourish only if there is a widespread desire for truth in the social environment, so that he will not be inhibited by fear of offending established institutions. Even more than the natural scientist, therefore, he ought to be a constant and fearless champion of civil liberties. To that extent at any rate the social scientist, *qua* scientist, is definitely committed to certain 'values.'

(Two other exceptions to scientific neutrality on 'values' are sometimes cited. (a) Some people would add aesthetics, as when

---

5. For the argument that science inculcates other moral values than truth see some of the writings of Michael Polanyi, e.g. *Science, Faith, and Society*, London, 1946; *The Logic of Liberty*, London, 1951. For a longer discussion of scientific methods and the study of society see Gunnar Myrdal, *Values in Social Theory*, London, 1958; and H. B. Mayo, *Democracy and Marxism*, New York, 1955, pp. 182–201.

one speaks of a 'beautiful' theory or piece of analysis, and others go so far as to speak of science as a 'spiritual adventure.' There is something to this, but I shall not discuss it here. (b) It is also maintained that democracy is strengthened by science, not only because of its practical usefulness but also because the 'scientific attitude' is itself one of the highest values of man, and a value that is essential to democracy. On the whole this is merely another version of the argument given above, that science is committed to the truth.)

To conclude briefly: While the broad approach of scientific methods may be used in the study of society, the specialized techniques of the natural sciences are rarely transferable. The social sciences seldom give the working success, reliability, and accurate prediction found in the natural sciences, and may never give them. The generalizations which they turn up are often of a low level of generality and probability. Nevertheless, when all the difficulties are noted, our choice is never between absolute truth and no truth, between certainty and mere opinion. The choice is between guesswork and truth as reliable as the data permit; and when all is said and done, that is what the natural sciences also provide. It is, then, only by the painstaking objective and scientific methods which are appropriate that we can build up a growing store of established knowledge about man and society.

II

By setting up some standards, these notes on the application of scientific methods to the study of society make it somewhat easier to answer the question how far Marxism is scientific. Dialectical materialism may be omitted from consideration here, since it concerns philosophy or the metaphysical foundations of Marxism, and cannot be empirically tested. Fortunately, it is the Marxist social theory, or historical materialism, for which the claim of science is most insistently made, and this can be submitted to testing.

We need not repeat here any of the detailed examination of historical materialism made in earlier chapters. The main point to keep in mind is Marx's assumption, lying behind his entire body of theory, that history and society move according to a pattern of knowable law, the so-called 'laws of motion of society'; and that Marx claimed to have done nothing more than to have laid bare these laws. If Marx was right he obviously ranks as the greatest social scientist of all time. If he was not right he was a misguided and fanatical genius who has led man's thought up one more long blind alley.

Let us now apply to the Marxist theory such scientific tests as can be used. In the first place, as any reading of Marx's life will show, he had evolved the main outline of his system by 1845, while he was still a young man in his twenties, and before he embarked on his studies of economic history in the British Museum. This *a priori* method of formulating a theory in advance of the factual investigation is common enough in all science, and does not constitute a serious criticism of Marx. It is not a criticism of *any* social theory, since in the social sciences hardly any investigation starts with the facts, but uses instead the problem or question method of approach. The method is only to be deplored when selected facts are chosen merely to *illustrate* and not to test or verify the theory.

Marx might therefore justly retort that his theory was at first merely a working hypothesis, but one that was confirmed by subsequent investigations. It is in this sense perhaps that Marx and his followers hold that Marxism is a science, and indeed it is the only sense which would justify the claim of any social theory to the title of scientific law. The real question then becomes: how well does the Marxist theory fit the facts? If the earlier remarks on the difficulty of establishing or refuting any social theory by an appeal to the facts are borne in mind, it is easy to understand why some people are convinced by Marx and others are not. In the same way, even today, no one theory of the trade cycle commands unanimous agreement among economists and still less among businessmen.

If regarded, then, as a working hypothesis, Marx's theory rests upon three cases — slavery, feudalism, capitalism — a suspiciously small number to validate an ambitious law of history. (The Asiatic is sometimes mentioned, but never seriously explored, while Engels also mentioned an early and vaguely defined stage of primitive communism.) It is plain from a reading of Marx that the first two of his cases were not examined in any detail. To have so examined them would have entailed much work, as Engels noted when he said that even one historical example 'would have demanded years of tranquil study.' Marx and Engels, although widely read, had little more than a nodding acquaintance with ancient and medieval history. They both advised their followers of the need for study, and Engels once said in exasperation that

the materialist conception of history has a lot of friends nowadays, to whom it serves as an excuse for *not* studying history.[6]

Later Marxists have not on the whole gone very far to remedy the deficiency of factual proof for Marx's thesis, although it clearly should be a necessary labor of love.

The first case, that of the transition from slavery to feudalism, is treated in such a sketchy and perfunctory manner that it is hardly support for any theory. Large generalizations about history are easily made if one is not an expert on a period, if a few well-chosen facts are selected to fortify one's case, and if enthusiasm closes one's eyes to the awkward or conflicting facts.

The second case, the change from feudalism to capitalism, while highly suggestive, and examined with a little more care and factual knowledge, is yet far from conclusive and can only be left as an open verdict. On Marx's own showing there is no close parallel between the decline of feudalism and the expected decline of capitalism. In the one case (decline of feudalism) we are given a realistic picture of the bourgeois class growing in numbers, power, and confidence, feeling itself hampered by the old order, and overthrowing here and there the social and legislative barriers which stood in its way, until by the nineteenth century it had become the dominant class. In the other case (the decline of capitalism) we are given the quite different picture of a proletariat growing more numerous, it is true, but at the same time weaker and more poverty-stricken; and we are asked to believe that some-

6. Engels, *Selected Works*, 1942, I, pp. 363–4; *Selected Correspondence*, p. 472.

how this depressed class is to become revolutionary, and sufficiently strong to overthrow a powerful bourgeoisie in control of all the machinery of law and the state. Clearly, the dialectic and the class struggle are not working at all the same way in the two cases. A closer parallel to the capitalist and the proletariat of the modern world would be the lord and the serf in feudalism. Yet Marxists say that it was a new class, the bourgeoisie, and neither lord nor serf which succeeded to power. On this analogy, it should be a new class (say the managers and bureaucrats?) and not the proletariat which will succeed the capitalists and form the new dialectical synthesis.

Marx's theory, then, really comes down to the one supposedly firm case, the development of capitalism, which was examined in Chapters 4 and 5, and which was seen not to conform to Marx's analysis. Our statistical and other evidence is plainly not in keeping with the thesis of the sharpening class struggle and with the doctrine of increasing impoverishment; nor are later defenses, in particular the Leninist theory of economic imperialism, able to rescue Marx from disaster.

Great changes have come over the economic, social, and political systems of the Western world since Marx's day. The labels of capitalism and socialism have become not only useless but also confusing when used to describe the changing and mixed economy that now exists. All that matters, however, in this context, whatever label we use, is that the developments have been of a kind that do not at all fit into Marx's major prediction. The theory must then be seriously modified if it is to explain adequately the course of later events, and to modify it would be a perfectly scientific procedure. Yet instead of modifying the theory, the more the facts of later developments change, the more stubbornly do Marxists adhere to the original analysis. Instead of exploring economic history to test the hypothesis, Marxists typically waste their time trying to show that the facts are wrong and Marx was right.

Even if Marx's cases for the decline of slavery and feudalism were well supported, they would merely constitute an analogy with the decline of capitalism. But since the historical parallel does not hold, the analogy is not even a plausible one. Marxists see clearly enough the dangers of reasoning from historical analogy in Toynbee, for that after all is the only type of argument in the popular *Study of History*, yet Toynbee's list of civilization-cases is longer (something over twenty), far more impressive and scrutinized in much more detail than any of Marx's cases, with the possible exception of capitalism.

Let us grant, however, for the sake of argument, that Marx's laws of history are a plausible statement of trends or probabilities. In order that they may be a safe guide to the future all the things included in the basket of *ceteris paribus* must in fact remain equal, or at any rate must not interfere with the working out of the main trend. Our experience with social trends is that all other things never *are* equal; society is too complex, too dynamic, too much liable to all kinds of interferences outside any formula of probability; the repercussions of action are so far-reaching and unforseeable that no long-run social prediction ever made is more than an informed guess. Except by accident these ambitious guesses are almost always wrong, so that the historian and the social scientist are rarely foolish enough to indulge in unconditional predictions about the far future.

The real trouble is, of course, that to say Marx did nothing more than extrapolate a trend would satisfy neither Marx nor his followers. They deny that Marx stated only a tendency or a probability, and rest instead upon the certainty of an invariable law comparable to any in astronomy, by which Marx predicted and explained the course of history regardless of disturbing factors.

Marx's simplified version of history is therefore far from established, and except in the case of capitalism was only haphazardly applied. It is a hope and a prophecy rather than a scientific working hypothesis; an assumed pattern of dialectical necessity imposed upon history and not established by evidence open to all. Indeed, since determinism (or necessity) appears to be possible only in a deductive science, and cannot be derived inductively (as Hume noted), not only was Marx wrong, but it is logically impossible that anyone should be able to prove that history has any determinate pattern. In this respect the problem is akin to the logical difficulties involved in fortune telling. If this objection is waived as too purely logical, it still remains true that Marx has not given his pattern of law the kind of inductive support which is normally

available to support any statistical or causal regularities of behavior which are dignified by the term scientific law.

Judged, then, by the test of explaining the facts, Marx's analysis
may be assessed thus: his class-struggle thesis had a good deal of
plausibility for the Britain of one hundred years ago, and could
be regarded as a fair enough trend based on the abstraction of
certain forces at work. Unfortunately, as usual with abstractions,
the open or implied conditions have not remained constant, and
other forces and factors have seriously modified the operation of
those factors which Marx singled out. The result has been that
only by selecting favorable facts, and by ignoring or distorting the
unfavorable ones, can Marx's theory still be maintained.

It is perhaps only fair to add that Marx was extremely gifted
and that his insights into history were often useful. There is a
residue of suggestive hints and truths in his work which will always
be valuable in any realistic analysis of society. (Equally sound
insights may also be found in many of the Utopian socialists whom
Marx so much derided.) There is, however, a world of difference
between this selective adaptation of what in Marx is now generally
accepted by Western scholarship, and the uncritical position of
the Marxist. The latter, like Marx himself, is not content with a
partial truth, but is so zealous to overthrow capitalism that he
makes a suggestive analysis into a grandiose and intoxicating law
of history.

IV

The path of science is littered with the debris of obsolete theories. They have been outmoded or revised by the logic of criticism,
by fresh investigations, and by the never-ending search for conflicting facts and for more satisfactory theories. Perhaps this is too
idealistic a statement. A more cynical view is that of Max Planck,
who said that his experience taught him that new scientific truth
triumphs only because its opponents eventually die out and a new
generation grows up that is familiar with the new ideas.[7]

Although the test is not logically conclusive, it is instructive to

7. Max Planck, *Scientific Autobiography and Other Papers,* tr. by F.
Gaynor, New York, 1949, pp. 33-4.

consider the attitude of Marxists toward Marxism, and in particular that of the largest school of Marxists, those in communion with
Moscow.

Scientists have often been known to wrangle hotly, especially
over theories that are not very well established. Darwinism was
debated with a religious fervor during the nineteenth century,
and T. H. Huxley was quite willing to go to the stake in its defense. We should therefore be prepared to find a certain amount
of controversy in Marxist circles. If that were all, it would scarcely
be worth looking at the attitude of Marxists to Marxism.

But it is not all, and when we enter the world of Marxist controversy we are at once in a different atmosphere. No longer do we
hear anything of Marxism as hypothesis, of fresh evidence, of possible contradictory facts, or of modification and criticism. If the
Marxists in Germany, for instance, undertake a revision of the
original Marxism in the light of later economic history they are
reviled by the orthodox for altering one jot or tittle of the original
gospel (or of Lenin's interpretation of it); the very name 'revisionist' has become a term of abuse in the Marxist vocabulary. Similarly, Fabian socialism, all forms of social democracy, as well as
any form of communism other than the Moscow variety — and
there are several, from Trotskyism to Titoism — are all met not
with rational arguments from the evidence but with the accusa-
tions of being 'deviationist,' of 'following the incorrect line,' of
being reactionary, bourgeois, and so forth. The discussion is for
the most part in terms of slogans, quotations, emotional words,
and tributes to the genius of Lenin or Stalin. Above all there are
the abusive epithets, and the constant impugning of the motives
of opponents, so that the argument often amounts to little more
than defamation and slander. The words of Engels, in another
context, are strangely applicable to modern communists: 'they
stick on a label and then think the question disposed of.'

This is not to say that modern communism has made no changes
whatever in Marx's theory. There have indeed been a number of
changes, especially those made by Lenin as he adapted the theory
to fit his actions; but they are not made as a result of new evidence,
and whatever alterations *are* made in both theory and practice are
then also enforced so rigidly as not to permit of any dispute.

A recent case is that of Professor Varga, the well-known Russian economist, who after the Second World War boldly ventured to draw his own conclusions from a fresh analysis of the American economy. It appeared to him, as a result of his studies, that the system had more vitality than was commonly believed in communist circles, and that it might not be safe to count upon its collapse in the near future. The Russians and, for that matter, many Western economists had predicted a depression to follow the war. Varga concluded that a slump might be postponed for as long as ten years. Although his book circulated in the U.S.S.R. for a time, his analysis was later called into question and his conclusions bitterly assailed. Whatever may have been the pressure applied, he made a public recantation, confessed his 'reformist' errors, and admitted that he had been incorrect in the light of Marxist theory. Never at any time was there any suggestion by his critics that the evidence mattered, or that the party interpretation could possibly have been wrong, or that Varga's minor modification could be tolerated.[8] His critics followed the old theological and primitive argument from authority, which is so frequently used in communist countries, and which is so remote from the spirit of science. It recalls more the logic-chopping usually associated with scholasticism, and lacks entirely the caution and tentativeness of science, the appeal to the evidence, the self-correction, and encouragement of doubt. It is, in short, a reinforced dogmatism and a perfect object lesson in the danger of a speculative philosophy fanatically held by a party with power to enforce its beliefs.

Moreover, not only is the Marxist social theory maintained with the utmost repression of dissent, but in at least one branch of natural science itself it now appears that only the politically approved theory can be held with safety in Russia. The tragic case in point is of course the victory (possibly only temporary) of the Lysenko faction in the controversies on genetics. And if there can be a party line in natural science, how much more do the humanities and the social sciences lend themselves to this treatment, since on these subjects there is obviously much more room for legitimate difference of opinion. The result is that not only the social sciences but

8. Evsey D. Domar, 'The Varga Controversy,' in *American Economic Review*, March 1950, pp. 132ff.

also the whole field of culture — philosophy, linguistics, literature, music, and all the arts — are subject to the same rigorous control, dissenting and individual forms of art and expression being roundly trounced as bourgeois or decadent, in language strangely reminiscent of that used in Nazi Germany. The writer and the artist must serve the Cause and be an 'engineer of the human soul.' The Soviet censorship is notorious and efficient, and the rewriting of Bolshevik history to show present leaders in a more favorable light is a byword among the nations.[9] Trotsky's share in that history has been almost expunged; he is in process of becoming, to use George Orwell's phrase, an 'unperson.'

The postwar expression of this trend is associated with a new emphasis on Russian nationalism. Despite the fact that the original Marxism is a wholly Western and internationalist system of thought, based upon German, French, and English sources, and that Lenin himself for most of his life emphasized this, the Soviet propaganda machine is now doing its utmost to throw off all traces of Western influence. The universality of science is denied, cosmopolitanism becomes a great sin — labeled 'jingo internationalism' — and everything Russian is exalted. No doubt all nations suffer in some degree from the same disease of nationalism, so that it is always difficult to get a true picture of a country from its patriotic literature. No doubt, too, the Soviet attitude can to a great extent be explained by reference to Russian history and psychology. A good deal of the cultural nationalism looks to the outsider like an attempt to 'Russianize' ideas borrowed from the West, stemming partly from the acute national inferiority complex which always seems to plague the U.S.S.R., and partly from the determination of the authorities to root out all Western, or bourgeois, influences from the consciousness of the people.

Whatever the reasons for it may be, all ideas tend to be subordinated to the objectives of the party, and it is all a far cry from the scientific attitude. The upshot is that reputable scholarship, by scholars devoted to the truth, is impossible under the Soviet regime if at any point the research touches upon politics; and the wide, almost all-inclusive area of politics is defined by the party alone.

9. See B. Wolfe, *Three Who Made a Revolution*, New York, 1948, pp. 437ff.; and L. Trotsky's *Stalin*, New York, 1941, pp. 70, 272, 307, 373ff.

It may be worth noting how the Russians are able to derive their policy from Marx. Marx and Engels were great admirers of the science of their day, but nothing would satisfy them until they had brought science, too, within the scope of their economic determinism. Laws of nature also were said to change with social change. Darwin therefore was assumed to be simply reading back into nature the competitive struggle which he saw in society around him. Science, they said, always and only develops in response to technical needs, so that Marxist emphasis is put almost wholly on applied instead of pure science. 'If society has a technical need that helps science forward more than ten universities.' [10]

A number of awkward questions are avoided in this remark by Engels. Is science one of the 'forces of production' in the economic foundation or is it in the superstructure? Is the influence of a technical need the same as economic determination? Who is to define a need? Are needs always agreed upon, or even recognized? Has Engels done any more than repeat the dubious adage that necessity is the mother of invention?

Whatever difficulties lurk in Marxist thinking on science, clearly only a slight addition to the thought is required to arrive at the position of modern communism, which holds that truth is always partisan, that neutrality is impossible, and that the arts exist merely to serve the revolution. The test of a work of art is then found not in any 'artistic' merits but solely in its ability to stir up the masses in the way the party desires. Every artist is an official propagandist.

The Soviet attitude precludes any possibility of objective study of society, and quite naturally, therefore, the Russians look upon 'objectivism' as a crime. Marxist theory itself points in the same direction, since it teaches that social science, like everything else in society, is determined by the methods of production.

V

Two tests have now been applied to Marx's historical materialism. The first, that of explaining the processes of history and capitalism, like all such tests of a social theory can hardly be con-

10. *Selected Correspondence*, p. 517.

clusive; yet nevertheless it does tend to show that Marx's theory is only sporadically supported and can certainly not be regarded as established. The second test, to show the difference between the scientific attitude and that of Marxists to their theory, may perhaps be dismissed as irrelevant, or as a mere *argumentum ad hominem*, although, such as it is, it tells unfavorably against Marxism.

Several other tests of a scientific theory may, however, be applied. Think now of the test of practice: does the theory work when applied, so that the appropriate results are achieved by using it? This may be regarded as Marx's own test of truth, and should accordingly be vital. It will be recalled from Chapter 2 that in its theory of perception dialectical materialism falls back upon the criterion of action to judge the truth of our sense impressions: we know they are true because when acted upon they work. Whether this pragmatic test is good enough for sense perception does not matter here; what does matter is that by the test of ' working' a number of diverse social theories can be supported, and hence to that extent proved true.

For thousands of years men believed that the earth was the stationary center of a revolving universe; this belief worked well for them, and greatly comforted and flattered them. Many people believe today that nature is designed for man's purposes, that birds in their little nests agree and so set moral examples to human beings, that some 'races' of men are inferior in intelligence to others, that astrology and phrenology are sciences, that the unemployed are out of work because they are lazy, that trade depressions are caused by sun spots, and so forth. There is no end to the theories that have held and still hold sway over the minds of men. They all work for those who believe in them, in the sense that they give purpose and strength when action is based upon them, and 'explain' society and the universe. By the test of working they may be proved both true and false, so that if they are to be refuted or fully confirmed it must be by a resort to other kinds of tests. Unfortunately, they are not always of a kind that is susceptible to scientific testing.

Similarly with Marx's theory. Capitalism might conceivably come to an end by way of the class struggle, providing enough people wanted it to happen and supported such a struggle. A certain type of prophecy can be fulfilled by believing in it and working to make it come true. There is little to show that capitalism *is* going Marx's way, however, so that if judged by this test of success (so far) Marx's theory falls down rather badly.

In Russia itself the 1917 revolution occurred in defiance of Marx's main theory, and may be easily explained by ordinary historical scholarship without a resort to Marxist theory or the dialectic. Communists have likewise been able to set themselves at the head of revolutionary and nationalist movements in Asia, but in no case were these outbreaks originated and carried through as industrial proletarian movements. The Balkan countries and Poland have been taken over by communists, with the Red Army looming menacingly in the offing, and are now within the Soviet orbit as satellites. In Czechoslovakia, although the communists headed a coalition government, and the country was directly within the Soviet sphere of influence, yet a *coup d'état* had to be staged to ensure communist victory. By no stretch of the imagination can such 'revolutions' be fitted into the main framework of Marxism. In spite of the utmost efforts to make it successful, the Marxist theory has hitherto failed when it has been applied in the industrialized countries for which it was meant.

Lenin once wrote: 'To correctly meet events with definite tactics, one must understand the events correctly' — which is, on the face of it, a reasonable enough prescription.[11] Communists often assert that the possession of Marxist theory enables them to diagnose contemporary society and prescribe the 'correct' line of action. Marx held the same high opinion of his theoretical framework; yet Mehring, the devoted biographer of Marx, gives many examples of mistakes of political judgment and tactics on the part of Marx and Engels.[12] There is usually more than one Marxist interpretation of events, although of course the Soviets assert that theirs is the only 'correct' one, despite their repeated assertion that Marxism is 'not a dogma, but a guide to action.' Marxist theory not only is no safeguard against mistakes but is often actu-

11. *Towards the Seizure of Power*, 1, p. 15.
12. *Karl Marx, The Story of His Life*, pp. 85, 150ff., 163ff.

ally an encouragement to ignore much of the evidence necessary for an intelligent and reliable diagnosis.

A notable instance of the failure of the theory is provided by early Bolshevik policy in Asia. By all the canons of Marxist theory the Bolsheviks were right in centering their hopes for revolution upon the industrial proletariat of Japan. But all their efforts were in vain. Only when the Marxist theory was ignored, and attention given instead to the possibilities of colonial and peasant revolt, did communists in China and elsewhere in the Far East achieve any degree of success.

A slightly different way of viewing successful practice as the test of a theory was given by Hegel when he remarked that 'world history is a court of judgment'; to which Marx added that 'history is the judge; its executioner, the proletariat.' [13] With this in mind, Lenin found it easy to look upon himself as the agent of history. If, in Marx's name, the party seizes and retains power, then Marx was right; but if the party fails to hold power (as in Hungary in 1919) Marx was still right. This is neither science nor logic but revolutionary special pleading.

To this kind of survival-of-the-fittest theory the objection goes deep. Who can say what will come to pass in the end, and when the 'end' is? How long must we wait for history to pass its judgment? During the eight years before 1941 the Nazis were quite justified in claiming that their theory was astonishingly successful; General Franco's political philosophy appears so far to work, after a fashion; the communist theories are working over a large part of the earth. But this does not prove that time may not yet consign them all to the rubbish heap, along with the demon theory of insanity, the myth of Nordic superiority, and a host of other pieces of intellectual rubbish. Marxism, like any other creed, may possibly be held by future generations. We cannot tell how stupid or how intelligent our descendants may be. Subsequent history may just conceivably be forced into the mold Marx cast for it, but it will not thereby prove the truth of any Marxist law of history. It will merely show that Marxists were sufficiently numerous and powerful to shape events to their wishes; and whatever truth this

13. *Selected Correspondence*, p. 91.

may illustrate is almost diametrically opposed to Marxism, which is a theory of the primacy of economic forces, or nothing. We may conclude that although it is often extremely difficult to confirm a social theory by the test of success, in so far as the test may be applied, the conspicuous failure of Marxist parties acting upon that theory in all industrialized countries gives only evidence against it.

VI

The fourth scientific test which we may apply to Marxism is that of prediction. As we have said earlier, the social sciences have not yet made much headway in their ability to give unconditional long-range predictions that come true, and it is doubtful whether they ever will. But this does not worry Marxists, because they believe that it is quite possible to foresee the future for at least two steps ahead, that is, up to the revolution and the classless society. In subjecting Marxism to the test of prediction, we are not therefore asking more of it than it is prepared to give. The question of timing, of when the revolution will happen, is of course crucial. How then do Marx's forecasts measure up by this test?

We may say at the outset that Marx was sometimes right and sometimes wrong if we look at the outcome of his short-run specific predictions. Such a conclusion is far from startling, since almost the same thing could be said about any social prophet.

As early as 1844 Engels, writing on the position of the working class in England, believed that England was on the threshold of a revolution. If this example is ignored, then the first of the early and notoriously wrong predictions of Marx and Engels concerns the events of 1848 in Europe. Shortly before the 1848 upheaval in France, Marx wrote that 'the German day of resurrection will be announced by the crowing of the Gallic Cock.' [14] At first sight this seems as ambiguous as any utterance of the Delphic oracle, but knowing the context we can make the pronouncement more specific. The crowing of the Gallic Cock was to be an uprising in France. Marx went on to say that although beginning as a bourgeois revolution, events in Germany would rapidly move on to

14. *Selected Essays*, p. 39.

the genuine proletarian revolution. The prophecy proved substantially false. An uprising did occur in France and there were, it is true, disturbances in Germany — every other observer had also anticipated them — although the only 'causal' connection was the inspiration of the French example. The German affair might perhaps be interpreted as a bourgeois revolution, but it was not followed by a proletarian revolution, and according to Marx himself, writing at a later date, even the bourgeois insurrection failed. Even an ardent Marxist has been constrained to note that 'for once the eagerness of Marx and Engels got in the way of their dialectic.' [15]

Two years later Marx had still not learned to temper his hopes with caution. His entire *Address of the Central Council to the Communist League* (1850) was written on the assumption that the revolution in Germany was imminent. Events during the summer of that year caused Marx's hopes to fade, and by September he was giving expression to extreme disillusionment and postponing the revolution for fifty years. In 1851, as he wrote (of France), 'there is damned little Red in the outlook.' [16]

Excellent theoretical reasons had been given beforehand for believing that the revolution they so much desired would take place in 1848 and 1850. Afterward Engels gave equally good reasons to show why the revolution had not occurred: feudalism and the petty bourgeoisie were strong, the bourgeoisie was weak, the industrial proletariat few, and farmers and peasants were in a majority.[17] But rationalizations and explaining away have only the most superficial resemblances to science, and resemble much more the optimistic forecasts usually made by leaders of all political parties on the eve of an election, and the simple post mortems by which the successful explain their success and the defeated their defeat.

Let us be charitable and forget these early examples, making allowances for Marx's youth and enthusiasm, and for his German patriotism. Fortunately there are many other examples from the maturer years of Marx and Engels by which to test their accuracy.

15. T. A. Jackson, op. cit. p. 434.
16. *Selected Correspondence*, p. 51.
17. *Selected Works*, 1942, II, p. 42–9.

In 1857 England was going through a trade depression, and Engels wrote: 'In 1848 we thought our time was coming and in a certain sense it came but now it is coming altogether, now it will be a fight for life.' Next year times were better, hope of the revolution had faded, and he wrote: 'I must say all the same, however, that the way the mass of over-production which brought about the crisis has been absorbed is by no means clear to me . . .' Marx for a while was less discouraged: 'It is at least consoling that in Russia *the revolution* has *begun* . . . on the Continent the revolution is imminent, and will also immediately [1858] assume a socialist character.' [18]

For years Marx and Engels continued in this way, living in the shadow of the expected revolution which never came. In 1860 they expected great things from an uprising of slaves in America, or of serfs in Russia.

> As in the eighteenth century the American War of Independence sounded the tocsin for the European middle class, so in the nineteenth century the American Civil War sounded it for the European working class.[19]

Believing thus, Marx was confident from the beginning of a Northern victory, but Engels was doubtful.

In 1863, after a rising in Poland, Marx believed that although their 'childish enthusiasm' of 1848 had all 'gone to hell,' 'the era of revolution has now fairly opened again in Europe.' [20] In the preface to the first English translation of *Capital,* Engels wrote: 'We can almost calculate the moment when the unemployed, losing patience, will take their own fate into their own hands.' A little later, in commenting on the Irish question, Marx came to the view (1870) that only when Ireland secured its independence (which again he took to be close at hand) would the English proletariat be emancipated, and that this in turn was the necessary condition for the emancipation of the proletariat on the continent of Europe.[21]

18. *Selected Correspondence*, pp. 86, 116, 117–18.
19. Ibid. pp. 124, 134, 136, 138–40.
20. Ibid. p. 144.
21. Ibid. pp. 228, 278, 280, 288. Mehring, op. cit. pp. 390–91.

England was, of course, the real test case. There, and only there, the conditions of revolution approaching these postulated by Marx's theory had existed for a long time, as Marx himself admitted in 1870.[22] But, obstinately, the British proletariat ignored the Marxist leadership and turned instead to trade unionism, with the result that Britain was one of the last countries of Europe to develop a socialist party. There are many expressions of annoyance at the British worker in Marxist writings: Britain was a living denial of Marx's thesis of revolution as a more or less automatic outgrowth of capitalism and industrialism.

Not only was Marx wrong when he ventured into these, and many other, specific predictions, but his whole system is a misreading of the future of industrial civilization. The course of subsequent history speaks for itself here, since hardly one of the developments he forecast have come true: the polarization of society with the disappearance of the middle class, the increasing impoverishment, the worsening trade crises, the growing 'industrial reserve army,' the decline of nationalism as a political force and its replacement by an international class struggle, the sharpening of the revolutionary ardor of the working class, and the violent, inexorable revolution.

It would, however, be a mistake to overstate the case against Marx. For one thing he was a shrewd observer and his insight was occasionally right, although his 'guesses' were not always justified by his analysis. Naturally, if one predicts crises and revolution constantly, one is almost bound to be right sometimes in this uncertain world; every war, every trade depression, and the Bolshevik revolution itself have been read by Marxists as confirmation of Marx's theory. Marxists also defend Marx, as Marx defended Hegel, by saying that although his conclusions may have been wrong here and there, his method of dialectical analysis is what is of most value. The defense is not a sound one. The more one reads Marx, the more one is driven to the conclusion that he had a considerable gift for nosing out the ramifications of economic interest, and it was this that usually made his thrusts and predictions come true, when they did come true. *But they often did not in fact follow from his theoretical analysis.* His twisting and turning to explain

22. *Selected Correspondence,* p. 290.

the economy on the basis of the labor theory of value is a choice example of this.

Nevertheless it was, for Marx, something of an achievement to observe the trend toward concentration of capital and control in industry, toward corporate monopoly and the crisis of boom and slump. It is relatively easy for us with the advantage of hindsight to see the exaggerations, the *non sequiturs,* the myopic concentration on the class struggle, the discounting of other tendencies at work in society, and so forth. Yet when full credit has been given to Marx's insight, and in particular to his emphasis on the historical nature of capitalism, the test of prediction shows that he frequently failed on minor issues, while his main predictions regarding later developments and the fate of capitalism have been quite wrong. Indeed, the very fact that Marx lived and published has injected a new factor into the situation, since the reactions to Marxism in the industrialized world tend to stultify Marx's very predictions.

It would be nearer the truth to say that Marx was not so much a scientist as a reformer: he did not predict as a scientist does; he *advocated,* and cast his predictions in a pseudo-scientific form, because of the prestige attached to science in the nineteenth century. By doing this he could show to his own satisfaction that the future he desired for society was also inevitable. There is about his whole system an air of revelation and very little of the cautious and qualified prediction characteristic of a scientific law. Marx's main prediction could perhaps be reframed in a scientific form, to run something like this: assuming all other things remain equal and there are no interferences, *then* this tendency in society — the class struggle — will lead to the overthrow of capitalism by the proletariat.

Thus stated it is a fair enough abstraction of a single tendency. One could make any number of similar abstractions of tendencies at work, some of them just as near, some as far from, reality as that of Marx. But alas for Marx's reputation, his abstraction has not proved to be realistic enough, other things *have* interfered, and his single tendency has not been allowed to work itself out unhampered.

VII

The major error in the Marxist theory, however, as we said in Chapter 6, is the confusion of 'laws' or trends in society with the uniformities of nature. The physical universe may fairly enough be regarded as subject to necessity or determinism or laws of uniformity. There seems to be some doubt about this today, for instance, in modern sub-atomic physics; but at any rate it was how the science of Marx's day looked upon natural laws. Nineteenth-century science was often dogmatic and self-satisfied, believing that it had found timeless and final truths.

The physical universe works independently of our volition and consciousness. The laws of its operation may be understood by man, and by adjusting to them man may adapt many of them to his purposes. Marx treated history as if it were also independent of man's will and purposes, and it was precisely here that he perpetrated his cardinal error.

The data of history and society are unlike the phenomena of nature: will and consciousness are of their essence, we are both the knower and the known because we are 'the reed that thinks.' Causality in nature is not purposive or teleological, infused with the wishes and intentions of man. Causality in history *is* teleological; man is pulled forward by his purposes as well as pushed by his environmental forces. Explanations of historical change must take note of the vital difference, and of the tremendous complexities thus introduced. No pattern of necessary change to which man must adjust has yet been found in history or society. As we have said, regularities of behavior may be altered by being pointed out to people, or even by being studied. 'Heavenly bodies ignore Newton, but investors do not ignore a business index.' [23] The scientific study of society yields us generalizations of a quite different order from the Marxist laws of motion, and the best that can be said of Marx is that, in his way, he was a kind of pioneer in applying semi-scientific methods to the study of society.

In Chapter 6 it was explained how it came about that Marx

23. Quincy Wright, *A Study of War*, Chicago, 1942, II, p. 1359.

identified the morally desirable goal for society with the naturally inevitable. Although its scientific flavor has contributed something to the spread of Marxism, its more powerful attraction lies in the moral judgments it contains. But this does not make Marxism science; it shows it for what it is, a political recipe for action which has hardened into a quasi-religion. Neither Marxist nor Hegelian theories are capable of scientific demonstration, nor can they be refuted by history and the appeal to the evidence, by the tests of success or prediction, or by any other scientific method, since in both systems the dialectic is only a magic spell, used to fuse together the necessary and the ethical. Marx's predictions were based not upon scientific study but upon the dialectic, which in Marx as in Hegel scarcely ever worked well — except after the event.

Only if Marx's iron laws are regarded as statements of tendencies, cautious and tentative in form, and even more cautiously applied to interpret social data, can Marxism conform to the canons of the scientific method. But so to dilute Marxism in the interest of science would be to rob it of its power as a fighting faith. Marxists are 'hot for certainties in this our life,' and are not to be put off with the dusty answers of scientific methods. The tragedy of Marxism is precisely this: the element of truth it contains has been elevated into dogma, a process which began with Marx himself in his self-confident youth. Although scientific methods cannot refute a protean philosophic synthesis such as Marxism, we may reasonably expect that time and events may sift out its truth and make the rest obsolete. But this statement is not a scientific prediction; it rests upon the avowed hope that the future of man will be more enlightened than his past.

Law, morality, religion, are to him [the proletarian]
so many bourgeois prejudices, behind which lurk in
ambush just as many bourgeois interests.
                                    COMMUNIST MANIFESTO.

In reality every class, even every profession, has its
own morality and even this it violates whenever it
can do so with impunity.   ENGELS.[1]

Religion is the moan of the oppressed creature, the
sentiment of a heartless world, as it is the spirit of
spiritless conditions. It is the opium of the people.
                                    ⸱MARX.[2]

8

Marxism, Morality, and Religion

I

BETWEEN MARXISM and scientific methods there is, on the whole,
very little in common except the use of the word science. But
there is an illuminating parallel between Marxism and organized
religions which is worth noting, not because of the exactness of
the comparison at every point, but because of the insight it gives
into the nature and attraction of Marxism.

First, one is struck by the use of religious language in the very
origins of the Marxist system. Marx and Engels at first considered
calling the Communist Manifesto a creed, a catechism, or a con-
fession of faith. Ever since then, no matter to which splinter group
they belong, Marxists have used the works of Marx and Engels
exactly as devout and literal-minded persons use the Bible or the
Koran. To settle an argument or justify a policy there is the same

1. *Selected Works*, 1942, I, p. 450.
2. *Selected Essays*, p. 11.

kind of reference to holy writ, the same practice of lavish quota-
tion of detailed texts.

If Lenin wished to prove a point he invariably clinched his
argument by quoting a remark of Marx or Engels. Stalin quoted
Marx, Engels, *and* Lenin. Ordinary communists floor their opponents by quoting all four of the fathers. To such lengths did
this invocation of texts go that it is usually impossible to find anything new in a speech of Stalin's dealing with theoretical aspects
of Marxism. Even Lenin himself did not greatly add to the content of Marxism as a philosophy or social theory, but he altered
the emphasis here, and extended the meaning there, and so gave
the original an application which better justified his own practical
policies. In doing this his method often was to select a text that
suited his purpose, or to elevate a minor and sometimes inconsistent work of Marx into a position of dominance. The net result,
however, is to make modern communism a body of revolutionary
precepts flexible enough to be adapted to any policy which the
leaders wish to follow.

Second, Marxism may be regarded as a revelation, as a gospel of
deliverance to the poor. The proletariat is a kind of Chosen People, who alone will possess the New Jerusalem. Lazarus and Dives
will exchange places. Marx, too, like the founders of some religions, was rejected by his well-to-do contemporaries. (Marx has
fared badly, however, in that he has not been greatly taken up
even by the industrial proletariat for whom he wrote.) He is
strangely like an ancient Hebrew prophet, and never in better
form than when playing Jeremiah to the Babylon of capitalism.
There is, moreover, the same apocalyptic note and sense of urgency
about his message.

Third, it is useless to expect a change in the hardened hearts of
the bourgeoisie, and thus the new order cannot come gradually;
only a cataclysm, the revolution, can bring it about. Immediately
thereafter will take place the great judgment — the dictatorship
of the proletariat — to separate the proletarian sheep from the
bourgeois goats.

Fourth, the struggle may be short or long, but beyond it there
lies the millennium. Marx's millennium is of this earth: the classless society. All previous history is merely a preamble; 'real' his-

tory will then begin in earnest, and ordinary historical laws will no longer apply. It is this reference to the end for which man and society are destined that, for both Marx and the prophets, gives history its meaning. There is also a golden age of the past. In some religions this is the Eden before the Fall, in political philosophy it has often been called the state of nature, in Marxism it is the stage of primitive communism. According to Engels social classes (sin) came into the world with private property, a view not unlike that held by some Christian sects; for instance, the Diggers in seventeenth-century England.

Fifth (this applies more to present-day communism than to the thought of Marx himself), the communist party is like a church hierarchy or priestly caste. The duty of obedience comes before everything else, and the party has built up throughout the world a remarkable reputation for enthusiasm, industry, and plain living. The party also has its saints and martyrs, and accords them an almost religious veneration. The cult of Lenin and Stalin is one of the features of Russian life that is so strange to the Western mind, which persists in regarding communism as a purely political or economic movement. If on the other hand these practices are seen as quasi-religious they are perfectly understandable.

Sixth (this also applies to modern communism more than to Marx's own thought), the way in which communist doctrines are held, interpreted, and enforced is astonishingly like the way in which some religious creeds are safeguarded. To the party is entrusted the message and the maintenance of its doctrinal purity. The current version of Marxist theory cannot be challenged and no dissent is allowed. Its truth is entirely taken for granted. Those who hold heretical views are denounced both as false prophets and as evil men. Doubt, which is virtue in the scientist, is grave sin in the believer. In the interpretation of communist doctrine, there is on the one hand the rigid orthodoxy known as Marxism-Leninism-Stalinism, which resembles nothing so much as a kind of secular scholasticism; and on the other is a variety of ever-splintering interpretations, the heresies known as 'deviations,' 'errors,' 'revisions,' and so on. (Is it too far-fetched to see in the recent Stalin-Tito breach a parallel to the fourteenth century, when for nearly forty years there was one Pope in Avignon and one in Rome, each claiming to be the 'true Pope'? Or may Tito be regarded as the Luther of a communist Reformation?)

Even in the teaching and study of Marxism there is a strangely religious flavor. If the student cannot 'see' the point at issue, the failure to do so is attributed to a defect of the will and he may be told first to make the act of faith and then his doubts will vanish. Trotsky emphasized the need to believe in order to understand, but the same disparagement of the intellectual approach is found in Engels himself:

> . . . how greatly superior the uneducated workers, for whom one can easily make comprehensible the most difficult economic analyses, are to our conceited 'educated people' to whom such intricate questions remain insoluble their whole life long.[3]

The same note is sounded by an American Marxist:

> Anyone who has taught Marxist economic theory to British coal miners knows that they grasp its intricacies more easily than do Oxford dons.[4]

Another, speaking of the dialectic, the inner, esoteric mystery of the Marxist religion, says:

> Just a moment's reflection is needed — and then the Great Light comes! [5]

Seventh, there is in both Marxism and religion the idea of inevitability, the same belief in ultimate victory, which is guaranteed by the eternal laws of history and the universe. Yet in both there is also the awareness that man must play his part in furthering the grand design, and so a complete fatalism is generally avoided. Marxism is thus a fighting creed, which challenges its adherents to change the world, and not merely to accept it piously.

Eighth, in Marxism as in religion, there is the same claim to universally valid truths. Marxism consists of 'the processes of his-

3. *Selected Works*, 1942, I, p. 243.
4. W. J. Blake, *An American Looks at Karl Marx, Elements of Marxian Economic Theory and Its Criticism*, New York, 1939, p. 114.
5. T. A. Jackson, op. cit. p. 307.

tory made conscious.' The theory is true, and there is no argument about it; he who is not with it is against it: there is no middle position. Like religion it therefore claims a prior loyalty, over the loyalty which the citizen owes to the bourgeois state. It follows from this, of course, that other doctrines are false, and hence we have the old scholastic argument in new guise: error has not the same right as Marxist truth.

Ninth, Marxism is not only a social theory, it is also a point of view on the world, a *Weltanschauung,* which like religious faith meets a deep craving in man, and enables him to integrate his life. In an age such as the twentieth century, when all creeds are in the melting pot and men are running hither and thither for security and certainty, the world view of communism makes it especially attractive, and in a psychological sense helps to explain some of its appeal.

In one respect Marxism goes beyond not only a scientific theory, or a political program, but even beyond most religions: it is a *complete* system of thought. In its philosophic basis of dialectical materialism Marxism functions as a metaphysic, a theory of knowledge, and a new logic. In historical materialism it claims to have an explanation of history, a moral code, and a program of action which is a guide to both tactics and strategy. In its totality it explains the universe and man, and the relation of the two; it also explains man's social life, his science, his art, and his beliefs. There is nothing outside it; truly an amazing claim if Marxism is regarded as science, or even as a social philosophy, but a natural one if it is regarded as an all-embracing religion, suitable, say, for a completely theocratic state.

The analogy of Marxism with any or all religious faiths must of course be handled with great caution. An analogy does not *prove* anything, and we should not attempt to draw too much from the particular instances sketched above. At some points, too, the parallel can be maintained only by the distortion of a religious or Christian point of view, at others the comparisons are only formal and verbal, while the content shows up real differences. It can hardly be disputed, however, that communism has been made into a fanatical religion, and to most of its supporters is a substitute for other religions. Not surprisingly, therefore, to the outsider it looks like a highly organized religion. There are of course many differences between Marxism and religion, and to the believers in both camps these are far more important than the formal and often superficial likenesses. Before that question is discussed, however, something should perhaps be said about the Marxist theory of morals.[6]

II

The Marxist theory of morals may be simply stated. It is ostensibly one of strict determinism, with morality among those elements in the superstructure of society which are a reflection of the economic foundation. And since all societies have been class societies — the argument runs — the morality prevailing at any one time has been a rationalization of the interests of the ruling class. Like the legal and political systems, the moral code is designed to support the ruling class, and its precepts are then exalted into eternal laws of nature or reason. The process need not be, and usually is not, a deliberate conspiracy on the part of the bourgeoisie, who may be quite sincere in their beliefs, and dupes of their own ideology.

The Marxist theory that morality is only a matter of property interest means also that man is shaped wholly by economic interests and relationships, which in a sense is a doctrine that life is work, and this in turn accords closely with the spirit of early industrialism and its stern Puritan outlook. (Work, in Marx's view, is what has raised man from the animals.) The importance of all that large area of life outside of working hours and economic interest — for example, within the family — is left out of account. Marx's theory is thus incomplete, and the very most that could be claimed for it, even if it were true, is that it is true of only a part of the moral life.

A much more searching question, however, is this: cannot and does not the moral code transcend class interest? The Marxist reply is twofold: (a) the common element in all morals, as in politics,

6. An elaborate parallel has been drawn between communism and Roman Catholicism — unflattering to both — by Paul Blanshard, *Communism, Democracy and Catholic Power*, Boston, 1951.

law, and so on, is traceable to the fact that all past societies have been class societies; and (b) the oppressed classes are dupes, induced by propaganda to believe in the ruling-class morality. (Marx sometimes thought the proletariat would be shrewd enough to 'see through' bourgeois morality and to reject it.)

Such a reply is altogether too superficial, since in fact the severest critics of the bourgeoisie come from within that class, Marx and Engels themselves being outstanding examples. All moral codes (except the Marxist) recognize the distinction between interests and morals, between what is right and what is financially rewarding. A part of the moral code of the Western world has always been critical of some features of capitalism, even of private property itself, while within the bourgeois class ideas on what is right or wrong may often vary, as they do on the subjects of drink and divorce. In some fundamental respects the moral code is applicable to any kind of social structure and has already survived Hebrew pastoralism, Roman slavery, and feudalism, although no doubt the detailed application has often varied. The commandment 'thou shalt not steal' is not abrogated merely by extending the prohibition from private to public property, although Engels appeared to think otherwise:

> Does this law thou shalt not steal become an eternal moral law? By no means. In a society in which the motive for stealing has been done away with, in which at the most only lunatics would ever steal, how the teacher of morals would be laughed at who tried solemnly to proclaim the eternal truth: Thou shalt not steal! [7]

Neither is duty to one's neighbor superseded when the meaning of 'neighbor' is broadened to include all one's fellow citizens, or even all human beings. Finally there is the point that over a large area of conduct the moral code of the West is identical with that in the U.S.S.R., where, presumably, there are no exploiting classes.

For these reason alone it is hard to deny that all classes can and often do agree on many moral principles, and that such agreement is not merely common belief in ruling-class propaganda. One may well argue that it is *only* the moral code which does transcend

7. *Anti-Duhring, Handbook,* p. 248.

economic interests. Classes or any other groups may naturally have conflicting interests, as a result of which they may differ on what is right in some specific cases. But this does not constitute *a different kind of morality*. Classes and groups also have many common interests, which Marxist theory quite ignores.

A second serious question must also be raised; can morality alter only when the 'modes of production' are altered? This query, of course, is part of the wider problem of whether any elements in the superstructure, or mental life, of society may alter except under the influence of changing methods of production. Thus nothing less than the truth or falsity of the entire Marxist interpretation of history is involved — a question that has been discussed in Chapter 3, and need not be re-examined here. Suffice it to say that the many weighty objections which may be brought against the Marxist theory of history in general apply, *a fortiori*, to the particular case that changes in morals can come about only as the result of economic changes. When the economic foundation of society alters there will be some changes in the detailed application of moral principles: that is the grain of wheat in the Marxist chaff.

A third difficulty with Marx's moral theory (already dealt with in Chapters 2 and 4) is that of bridging the gap between the self-interested individual and class loyalty. There is no answer to this in Marx, except that given by every moralist from time immemorial: exhortation and the call to duty. Soviet Russian practice gives the same answers, as when in the Second World War the appeal was made not to class or other selfish interest but to the traditional values of duty, loyalty, and patriotism in order to stimulate the fighting spirit of the Soviet peoples.

A fourth objection arises from Marx's idea of 'progress' in morality. If morality is class determined, in what sense can the judgment be made that one moral code is better than another? The Marxist reply is that as methods of production change, new ruling classes are thrown up. A rising class will develop a morality which favors its interest, and will reject unsuitable elements in the code of the older ruling class. A society built upon slavery rationalizes the rightness of slavery, as in ancient Greece, and stresses such virtues as obedience to masters. Feudal society, while condemning slavery, believes in the essential rightness of feudalism, and stresses order and hierarchy in society. Feudalism in turn was readily seen as wrong by the bourgeoisie, who naturally stress individualist ideas associated with mobility of labor and freedom of contract in business; and these translated into moral terms become freedom of choice and opinion, individual instead of group responsibility, and so forth. Now to Marx that moral code is better or higher which represents the interests of the new class that will take the place of the older class. Thus the morality of feudal society was better than that of slavery, and capitalist morality is better than feudal. Hence Marx could call capitalism progressive compared with its predecessor.

This is all very well so far as it goes, if one ignores the omissions and the historical distortions; but the main issue has clearly been dodged by Marx, as it was dodged by Rousseau and others in the eighteenth century who conceived of man as 'naturally good' but corrupted by society. The higher morality is defined as merely the interests of the class which will inherit the future. If morality is *defined* in this way there is no more to be said. Right and wrong cease to have any of the ordinary meanings attached to them, and become today merely the expedient in terms of what is to the interest of the proletariat — the class of the future. Success then becomes the criterion of morals, as of truth, a position which is very near that of Hegel, in whom there was always a tendency to identify what is with what is right. History, like necessity, makes its own rules; this is more often expressed as necessity knows *no* law. Such a definition is also very like that of Hitler, in which right was defined as what promoted the interests of the German people. Marx's argument is also circular. Only by assuming that his forecast is true, that is, that the proletariat *will* inherit the future, can the proletariat be called progressive, and hence its morality be called 'better.'

We can see from this that in labeling capitalism immoral, Marxists ought to mean merely unprogressive, or out of date. (It was of course progressive, and hence moral, in its earlier stages.) There is also no point in passing judgment upon the capitalist as a person, since he is only doing what to him seems right. But this strict position is seldom maintained by Marxists, who, from Marx onward, can hardly find language strong enough to express their condemnation of bourgeois actions; and in judging they invariably appeal to traditional moral standards. Similarly, communists often fail in practice to worship success (other than communist success) with its corollary that power alone gives right; and in speaking of the classless society they describe it in terms of high social ideals which any good liberal may accept. Ordinary moral standards emerge also in the selfless behavior of many communists, both in the rank and file and in leaders such as Marx and Lenin.

Marxist practice is thus often inconsistent with its own moral theory (a subject which is treated more fully below). But there is still another way in which Marx left open an escape from moral determinism. It lies in the same kind of dualism that may be seen in every part of the Marxist system, including his theory of knowledge and his interpretation of history, namely, the allowance for man's interaction. Man is a product of circumstances (determinism), yet circumstances are modified by man (interaction). Hence his remark that 'the educator must himself be educated.' Allowance for interaction of this kind ruins the sense and consistency of a simple theory of moral determinism, just as it ruins the economic determinism of history.

When Marx adhered to his theory of a class-determined morality he was led to an extraordinarily hopeful view of man's potential virtue once private property is abolished. (Presumably a kind of classless morality also prevailed under primitive communism before man was corrupted by private property.) Marx spoke as though all crime — or even sin, if one may use that word in connection with Marxism — would disappear in the classless society. Engels expressed this simple faith when he wrote: 'Prostitution is based on private property and falls with it.' [8]

True, many crimes are crimes against private property; and a portion of all crime has its predisposing economic circumstances, such as overcrowding and poverty. We may also take for granted that some crimes will vanish if private property is socialized — for instance, if there is no market in stocks and bonds there can be no dealings in fraudulent securities (except on a black market). Yet granting in full the Marxist assumptions of public ownership

8. *Principles of Communism,* p. 18.

and a high standard of living for all, no one, however slight his knowledge of human nature or criminology, could possibly expect this to give us an entirely new morality. Marx's very impatience and his dreams of a better society often led him, as they led many of the Utopians of his day, to see the proletariat through rose-colored glasses. He himself could work prodigiously, without any hope of immediate gain, and he thought the proletariat, too, would be above sordid aims. He could not seem to realize that the workers are no better than anyone else; they want the same things as other classes, and respond to the same incentives.

The elaborate Soviet legal and penal system shows how varied and frequent offenses against public property may be, while in addition most of the ordinary 'bourgeois' type of crime still continues in the U.S.S.R., that is, offenses against the person and against private property in consumer goods. In short, all that one can say about the classless society is that the 'causes' of some types of crime and the temptations to some types of sin will have been removed. We may be quite sure that no institutional reorganization is going to do more than that. Sin, selfishness, and crime did not come into the world with capitalism, nor will they go out with it.

If Marx's theory is true and morality is merely a cover for class interest, he thus effectively dismisses the moral 'ought.' As long as Marxists subscribe to this kind of theory they should not be surprised if they find themselves opposed by those who believe in some other basis for moral values. Marx's theory clearly also involves the relativity of all morals. Marxism is not unique in defining morals in naturalistic or non-moral terms, or even in its relativity. It is unique, however, in placing morals entirely on a class basis, and in asserting that what is inevitable is also right.

Marx's so-called theory of morals and his related remarks on crime are perhaps the most cavalier and least-thought-out parts of his system. The purpose of his savage outbursts against bourgeois morality is easy to understand. He raged against the common notion of his day that there was something eternal about the capitalist economy, and hence he castigated also the ideals of moral rightness and of natural rights, and even the divine law, which were often used to justify private ownership, laissez-faire, the existing income distribution, and so on. Some Marxists admit as much when they say that in moral principles there are both an eternal element and a relative element, that Marx merely concentrated on the relative element, and that when he did this he was usually correct.[9] There is a lot to be said for such a modest appraisal, although it would hardly find favor in Moscow.

Few theories are wholly wrong, and even in Marx's moral theory there is an element of truth. Psychology has taught us that individuals do often rationalize their behavior and produce excellent moral reasons for doing what they want to do or what will benefit them. Many observers other than Marx have also noticed a class element in morals. Mill, for example, wrote: 'Wherever there is an ascendant class, a large portion of the morality of the country emanates from its class interest, and its feelings of class superiority.' [10] Also, the content of the moral code must usually be socially useful, although this need not always be so. For instance, the dietary rules of the ancient Hebrews served a useful hygienic purpose in a different age and climate; but although they may not serve any hygienic purpose today, they are retained with great tenacity. But Marxism gives no explanation of why they are retained, since on Marxist principles they should be altered with the changed methods of production.

Much the same considerations apply to the 'Marxist view of human nature' of which so much has been made. It comes down to very little: that self-interest has dominated human behavior through history, but that once capitalism is abolished, man will transcend self-interest and be 'naturally' good. Marx, like every other radical reformer, was thoroughly indignant at man's present and past lot, with invincible faith in man's future potentialities.

Although Marxism has no complete moral theory, and even the partial theory has been pushed to an untenable extreme, there is a residue which we shall do ill to ignore. The emphasis on the social content of morality, and on the emptiness of vague principles that give no help in dealing with pressing everyday problems; the warning that when the spectacles of self-interest are worn

9. Jack Lindsay, op. cit. pp. 209–12.
10. *On Liberty* (Everyman's), p. 70.

we can so easily adapt our morals to our inclinations; and the strictures on the inhumanity of so much of the philosophy of competition: all these are useful hints from whatever source they come. They embody ideas that today are commonplace, but Marx helped to make them so.

III

Marx's ostensible theory is one thing, but his practice and the bulk of his writings are another. That is why it is never wise to take Marx's theory of morals, such as it is, at face value. Few communists do in fact take it so in their propaganda; for the most part they rest their case on a moral judgment common to all classes, and seldom indulge in moral cynicism, except as a matter of routine in explaining the actions of class enemies. The one kind of behavior which Marxism cannot explain, on its own principles of economic determinism, is that of Marxists themselves. Alternative explanations of Marxist ethics as a species of 'romantic destructionism' or as sheer naked power without any ideals at all seem to me quite wrong.[11] Explanation of Marxism as non-moral cannot account for the attraction of Marxism to so many high-minded people. For another thing, it gives democracy an all too easy moral victory over Marxism by painting the latter all black; and for a third, it tends to play down the great challenge of Marxism to democracy: the demand that men should construct a *just* society.

It is more important, if we are to understand the appeal of Marxism, to look at practice rather than at theory. For example, where Marx in the *Communist Manifesto* spoke of the bourgeois attitude toward marriage and the family, he was not enunciating any theory of class-determined morality; what he was really indignant at was the exploitation — poverty, long hours of toil, mother and children all working — which made it impossible for the worker to enjoy a decent family life. It is strictly an *argumentum ad hominem,* to refute the bourgeois charge that communists wish to destroy the family, and is not really a discussion of family morals

11. F. H. Knight, *Freedom and Economic Reform*, New York, 1947, pp. 87ff.

at all. Engels, in outlining his history of the family, strongly condemned the double standard of sexual behavior for men and women and looked forward to the day when there would be no economic exploitation of woman by man, when love between equals would be the only tie holding the family together.

Some communists have occasionally dismissed all moral standards — although few if any of the top leaders have ever done so — including those concerning relations between the sexes; and in the first years after the revolution the Bolsheviks broke with the Western code at some points. Campaigns were carried on against all traditional ideas, and with lenient laws the abortion, divorce, and illegitimate-birth rates soared. But these were exceptional and temporary episodes, due partly to the early Bolshevik belief that the family bolstered up the psychology of private property.

Lenin, too, had, perhaps unknowingly, lent some support to Bolshevik practice by his ambiguous references to a 'revolutionary morality.' But he certainly made up for this later by expressing strong and prudish views and, as is well known, his private life was austere and disciplined. He severely denounced 'free love' and what he called 'the glass of water' theory of sex, which he said was 'completely un-Marxist, and moreover, anti-social.'

Today there is a good deal of evidence to show that the Russians have swung from their former Bohemianism to an almost puritanical attitude toward sex; the laws on marriage, divorce, and abortion, for instance, are nowadays stricter than in some Western countries. Even the marriage ceremony itself has been made more solemn and dignified. Moral discipline and training are much emphasized in school education (co-education in secondary schools was widely abolished in 1943), the virtues of patriotism, self-reliance, and diligence are deeply inculcated — together of course, with indoctrination in communism.[12] Again, the reliability of loose-living communists is regarded with deep suspicion by party leaders everywhere, since what is demanded is dedication and self-control to the point of austerity, so that in all things the party interests may be given first place. Lenin had set the example:

> You know young Comrade . . . ? A splendid boy, and highly talented. And yet I feel that nothing good will come out of

12. *Soviet Studies*, April 1950, pp. 319ff.; *Russian Review*, April 1950, p. 87.

him. He reels and staggers from one love affair to the next.
That won't do for the political struggle, for the revolution.[13]

Moral indignation is a marked feature in the writings of Marx
and Lenin and in much of the later Marxist literature. The Marxist critique of society can perhaps best be understood as chiefly
moral, a view which may be supported by putting the question:
why do people become communists? In the last resort they usually
give the injustices of capitalist society as their chief objection
to it, the sense of injustice, as in Trotsky, often having been
aroused in childhood. They pass essentially moral judgments and
their standards are liberal and humanitarian. They may give other
reasons on the surface, such as the economic inefficiencies of capitalism, but this detached scientific appraisal is not what has power
to move people to passionate action, and is never more than a secondary reason or a rationalization.

That sensitive people both join and leave the communist party
for moral reasons is plainly the evidence of the six eminent ex-
communists in *The God That Failed,* and of many others.[14] These
high-minded Westerners, fired by all the humanist ideals of liberal
democracy, begin their pilgrimage to the modern Holy Land full
of generous admiration for the 'Russian experiment.' They are
prepared to make full allowance for all the special and difficult
Russian circumstances. But misgivings come with closer experience
of party methods inside the Soviet Union, and great numbers of
the pilgrims have returned sadder but wiser men.

What do we find has caused the change in outlook? The answer
is nearly always the same: it was the ruthless disregard in the Soviet
Union of all humanitarian ideals. No one with ordinary human
standards of morality and decency could fail to be distressed and
repelled by the inhumane manner in which opponents are dealt
with in the U.S.S.R. No lover of liberty could possibly live amid
such stifling of the human spirit. Bertrand Russell was the first
of these well-known visitors — he was of course much too cool-
headed ever to become a communist — to make the journey to
Moscow, shortly after the First World War, while the revolution

13. *Reminiscences of Lenin,* cited in R. Schlesinger (ed.), *The Family in the
U.S.S.R.,* London, 1949, p. 77.
14. Richard Crossman (ed.), *The God That Failed,* London, 1950.

was not yet over; and his evidence is typical and unmistakable.[15] He, like most of us, was not averse to the aims the Russians profess to have in mind: the classless society, the higher standards of living, the industrialization, perhaps even the economic planning. But the methods employed and the price paid, in terms of regimentation and actual suffering, made Russell, as they must make all humane people, reject Soviet Communism. If the problematical, or even certain, good must be purchased at that price, then we would rather go without than pay the price.[16] (It is somewhat easier, however, for us in the comparatively wealthy and free democracies to take this higher moral line. Had we never enjoyed freedoms we could hardly be expected to miss what we never had.)

Now the Russians, like everyone else, do not act as they do without a theoretical explanation of their behavior; and that brings us to the essential principle of Marxist moral practice, the doctrine that the end or result justifies the means, a view usually attributed to Machiavelli and, perhaps unjustly, to the Jesuits. It may be regarded also as a perversion of the insight of the utilitarians into the importance of probable or actual consequences.

The doctrine easily follows from Marx's view that the interests of the proletariat are a higher form of morality. Since by definition the communist party acts only in the interests of the proletariat, whatever the party does is thus morally justified. Admittedly there can be some confusion here, and two quite different ideas are easily mixed: (a) whatever the party or proletariat does is right, by definition; (b) some of the means adopted, though admittedly wrong in themselves if judged by ordinary canons of morality, are nevertheless to be condoned as the shortest or the only means that can promote the good end in view.[17] The two ideas are extremely difficult to separate in practice, but the latter is the one most often put forward to justify communist action. It is undoubtedly more subtle and less outrageous than the alternative view, and enables the communist to stand on higher moral

---

15. B. Russell, *The Practice and Theory of Bolshevism,* London, 1948.

16. Ibid. pp. 102ff.

17. Lenin harbored both views: '. . . our morality is entirely subordinated to the interests of the class struggle of the proletariat,' and 'morality is what serves to destroy the old exploiting society, to unite all the toilers around the proletariat.' *Lenin, Selected Works,* 1951, II, Part 2, pp. 483, 485.

ground. Some support is lent to this by the statement of ideals incorporated in the Stalin constitution of 1936. Many parts of the constitution are clearly ignored in practice, but within the Soviet Union they still seem to be widely regarded as ultimate goals.

Communist behavior and conscience are easier to explain on the means-and-results principle than on any other. Marx himself, while professedly seeking good ends for society, did not hesitate to stir up hatred and could be ruthless, even cruel, in some of his polemics. The same tendency was strongly marked in Lenin, not so much because he was self-important, or wished power for himself, as because he regarded himself as 'an agent of history.'

Two instances may be given from Soviet behavior of the appeal to 'bad' means to secure good ends: (1) The decree legalizing abortion in 1920 was admitted to be evil, but was defended as necessary for practical reasons: to prevent the death of women at the hands of quacks by putting the operation into the hands of qualified surgeons. At the same time propaganda against abortion was carried on, and doctors were not allowed to perform the operation 'with mercenary aims.' [18] (2) The suffering caused by liquidating the kulaks as a class, and by forced collectivization of farming in the famine year of 1932, was afterward admitted to have been real and terrible; but has been justified because the purpose was good.

'The Cause' is everything, and human life must not stand in its way. What does it matter if some of the suspects are innocent? 'So mighty a form,' as Hegel wrote of the Great Man, 'must trample down many an innocent flower — crush to pieces many an object in the path.' The ruthless 'social engineering' must go on, to construct the kind of society the leaders have in mind.

It is [thirty] years since the Communist Party obtained undisputed political power in Russia. Still the victims tramp down to death. There is no end to the suffering, the river of blood flows on . . . To those, who really seek a better social order — and are not merely seeking in political action relief from the explosive violence of their own natures — I would say with assurance: *This is not the road.*[19]

18. R. Schlesinger, op. cit. pp. 271, 371ff.
19. E. F. M. Durbin, op. cit. p. 218.

Critics of the regime are regarded as diseased flesh on the body politic, to be removed by a surgical operation. A little judicious pressure — social, economic, legal, or extra-legal — is applied to the critic or unbeliever and he soon renounces his skepticism or heresy. But this is a medieval way of describing Soviet methods. A more modern and illuminating version is this: any difference of opinion that arises (and there is no institution about which genuine questions cannot arise) is not met by rational argument or by appeal to the evidence. *It is not met at all.* Instead, the matter is regarded as one of psychology. The *questioner* is treated as if his attitude were a symptom of neurosis, a defect of character, exactly as Lenin dealt with opponents in some of his writings.[20] The heart of the process is best described in such books as Arthur Koestler's *Darkness at Noon,* and best of all perhaps in George Orwell's *1984.*

Communist parties outside Russia have often used the same ruthless methods, and all for the same ostensibly high-minded purpose. As Professor Laski put it:

> the passion for conspiracy, the need for deception, the ruthlessness, the centralised and autocratic commands, the contempt for fair play, the willingness to use lying and treachery to discredit an opponent or to secure some desired end, complete dishonesty in the presentation of the facts, the habit of regarding temporary success as justifying any measure, the hysterical invective by which they wrought to destroy the character of anyone who disagreed with them, these . . . have been the normal behavior of Communists all over the world.[21]

Russian groups such as the Nihilists justified terrorism and assassination as proper political methods against the Czarist regime, and (in certain circumstances) the Bolsheviks were prepared to use the same weapons. In a similar way the party now justifies every kind of method both inside and outside the Soviet Union. Nothing has a right to exist which stands in the way of a communist objective: the possession of adequate power to carry out policies im-

20. I. Berlin, 'Political Ideas in the Twentieth Century,' *Foreign Affairs,* April 1950, pp. 364ff.

21. H. Laski, *Communist Manifesto: Socialist Landmark,* London, 1948, p. 89.

poses the only limit. It has been well said that 'Communism is the doctrine of humanitarianism driven to an extreme in the pursuit of offensive and defensive methods.' [22]

This explanation, in terms of means and results, enables us to dismiss the superficial and misleading explanation that all communists are fiends, lost to all morals and decency. It is not a question of ideals versus power, but one of power used amorally in support of a moral ideal. Nor is it only 'spiritual wickedness in high places'; it is just as much a case of ignoring Kant's maxim to treat men as ends, not merely as means, and of forgetting to use methods compatible with the goals desired.[23] We can then see communists for what they are: single-minded fanatics so devoted to their cause that they will stoop to conquer by any methods. They are thus brought, where of course they belong, into the fold of common, erring humanity.

The tradition of using evil means to promote good ends is not confined to Russians. A lack of scruple in promoting national objectives is common in all history, although never, except perhaps in Nazi Germany, has it been carried so far as in the Soviet Union. Cavour noted that his methods of unifying Italy would hardly stand scrutiny, and Bismarck altered the Ems Telegram to provoke the war of 1870. But we are all tarred with the same brush. Which of us has not been tempted to turn a lenient eye when our own cause has been promoted by dubious methods? Where is the party or nation which has not to greater or lesser degree brought forward the same Machiavellian argument of the end justifying the means? Did we not in such instances as the blockade of Germany in World War I, the mass bombing and the atom bombing in World War II, use the argument that these were bad, but necessary since they would shorten the war? If the answer is yes, then we are not far from the Soviet argument used to justify the methods employed in the collectivization of agriculture in the 1930's. Had Russia not mechanized and collectivized agriculture, and had she not concentrated on building heavy industry at the expense of consumer goods, it is arguable that the U.S.S.R. would

22. I. Berlin, loc. cit.
23. But see the denial of any separation of means from ends in Howard Selsam, *Socialism and Ethics*, New York, 1943, pp. 309ff.

have been completely overrun by the Nazis. Many people in the West did, in fact, give an *ex post facto* justification of Stalin's methods on just those lines during World War II. It was along similar lines that observers such as the Webbs could write off the worst aspects of the Stalinist regime as merely 'temporary misery.' [24]

We may thus explain the principle of communist behavior; we may trace its origin to the conspiratorial and terroristic tactics of an illegal party; we may notice that the same principle is common to all fanatics; we may even take note of all the special historical factors which make it easy to see why the Russian leaders today behave as they do. To explain is not to condone. If we are to retain any moral sanity at all we can only condemn the principle and the communist practice that is based upon it. We must go even farther, and condemn every trace of the same doctrine whenever we see it being espoused and practiced in the democracies.

IV

We have now to ask the question: what is the relation of Marxism to religion, and more particularly to Christianity? To many people this may be the most important question of all, and even for those who are not especially religious or Marxist, it is one worth exploring.

As to the hostility of Marxists to all religions there can be no doubt, and since Marxism is primarily of the Western world, that hostility has been directed mainly toward Christianity. The anti-religious tradition began with Marx and Engels and has been faithfully carried on by all communist leaders inside and outside the U.S.S.R., as well as by the rank and file of party members. To some extent it is merely an anti-clerical polemic, based on the accusation that the churches have usually been on the side of the ruling class. We may sympathize with the anti-clerical protest while regretting that the baby should have been tossed out along with the holy water.

But this is hardly to scratch the surface of the question, since Marx and his followers have gone much farther than to censure

24. S. and B. Webb, *Soviet Communism: A New Civilization?*, London, 1935, II, p. 601.

the churches for their class alignment. Marx himself had sloughed off all religious belief while he was still a student, long before he had formulated his social philosophy. In the preface to his doctoral dissertation he had brashly announced his 'detestation of all the gods.' Besides regarding all religion as 'the opium of the people,' he enunciated the propositions that 'the criticism of religion is the basis of all criticism,' and 'man makes religion, religion does not make man.' [25] Even this does not altogether dispose of our question, because an infidel may well propound scientific or social theories to which true believers may subscribe. A more searching query is therefore: is the Marxist philosophy essentially irreconcilable with religion? Or simply, can a man be a communist and a Christian at the same time?

Consider first of all the Marxist theory of the origin of religion, formulated most clearly by Engels and repeated by Lenin. It is a theory of religion in general; there is scarcely any special account of Christianity in Marxism. The view, quite briefly, is that religion arose as a means of placating the mysterious and hostile forces of nature. 'The first gods arose through the personification of the natural forces of nature,' i.e. religion originated in fear, and was at first a form of animism, a kind of pre-scientific account of natural phenomena. As man came to understand nature, and brought natural forces under control, religion has been continued as a means of placating the equally mysterious and harmful social forces. Engels put it most plainly:

> All religion however is nothing but the fantastic reflection in men's minds of those external forces which control their daily life . . . In the beginnings of history it was forces of Nature that were at first so reflected . . . later, social forces began to be active.[26]

A modern Marxist suggests that the belief in immortality is also a social problem, originating in insecurity, which will disappear as man controls nature and lives in harmony with his fellows.[27]

We must remember that all theories about the origin of primi-

25. *Selected Essays,* p. 11.
26. *Anti-Duhring, Handbook,* pp. 299–300.
27. Edel, in *Philosophy for the Future,* p. 414.

tive religions are little more than speculation. A more important criticism is that to place the origin of religion in fear of nature is on the whole contradictory to Marx's main theory that all the elements in the superstructure of society, religion included, are determined by the modes or methods of production. In any case, the objections to this strict determinate relationship make it untenable. A religion may continue regardless of how the modes of production change, so that Christianity has thus flourished in all three of the Marxist historical categories of slavery, feudalism, and capitalism; while, alternatively, under any given method of production many religions may be found, as in the Roman Empire or the United States.

Further, to explain the continuation of religion by the need to placate social forces is not altogether consistent with the account of religion as a rationalization of ruling-class interest. Christianity, like many other religions, began not in a ruling class but among the poor and lowly, and was probably practiced most seriously when it was confined chiefly to them, as it was for the first hundred years of its history.

The Marxist theory of religion, like Marxist ethics, is in fact neither fully thought out nor consistent, so that little purpose would be served by criticizing it in detail. The essence of the Marxist attack upon religion and morality was that they seemed to justify the existing social and economic order. As Marx observed:

> The social principles of Christianity have had eighteen hundred years in which to develop . . . [they] justified slavery in the classical world and they glorified medieval serfdom, and if necessary they are quite willing to defend the oppression of the proletariat . . . The social principles of Christianity transfer the reparation of all infamies to the realms of heaven and thus justify the perpetuation of these infamies on earth.[28]

Religion, to the Marxist, is thus a refuge for the ignorant and the weak, a method of escape from reality, a promise of 'pie in the sky.' The ruling class throughout history merely uses religion to safeguard its privileged position. The clerics know which side their

28. Cited in Mehring, op. cit. p. 131.

bread is buttered on, and throw the halo of sanctity around class privileges, preach submission to one's betters and contentment with one's humble lot; and since the exploited are generally foolish enough to believe them, the churches become a milder and less expensive method of keeping the proletariat in order than a police force. The Bible is used, in Kingsley's phrase, as 'a constable's handbook'; and Christianity becomes what Sorel savagely called the 'morality of mendicants.'

History does indeed furnish examples of this kind of clerical behavior — after all, churchmen, like everyone else, are not above opportunism — and of the quieting social effect of other-worldly religion. Methodism in the eighteenth century, like the Salvation Army in this century, no doubt did siphon off much social unrest. With something like this in mind, Cobbett called Methodists 'the bitterest foes of freedom in England.' But the whole view is one-sided. To take only one example on the other side: non-conformity in England contributed greatly to trade unionism, co-operatives, Chartism, and working-class education, as did Christian Socialism within the Anglican fold. An interesting by-product of this may be observed in England: the association of religion with working-class movements prevented working-class hostility to religion, and was and is an obstacle to the spread of Marxism in the Labour movement.

Although in general Marx ignored the long tradition of social criticism within church and sect, he made an incidental reference thereto of some interest. He did admit that small sects might occasionally oppose the existing order (although not by force) and genuinely try to revive the ancient notions of real brotherhood. The point is not reconcilable with his main theory and seems as though it might open the door to an admission that religion, in itself, need not be opium. It is also not clear from Marx's account of religion whether a different kind of economic organization, based, say, on public ownership, might not in the future throw up a religion of its own, rooted in other soil than economic insecurity and class rule, and of value in the same way that classless morality would be intrinsically 'good.'

Marxists believe that their social theory rests upon the philosophic foundation of dialectical materialism. We may then ask: is dialectical materialism incompatible with religion? Now, all varieties of materialism and philosophic idealism are essentially nothing more than descriptions of the physical universe. For that reason, as Susan Stebbing said, they are equally foolish when extended into philosophies to cover all of life. In so far as they go beyond description, and they usually do, they must rest upon philosophic arguments and ultimately upon assumptions that are unverifiable. The assumptions, and denials, of all materialist philosophies normally have no room in them for a spiritual view of the universe, and this is also true of dialectical materialism.

Marx himself, with some inconsistency, often made allowance for the free play of mind. If Marxist materialism is regarded as common-sense realism and nothing more, then strictly speaking this, if taken with Marx's dualism, might allow room for the active mind, or 'spirit.' But the point is theoretical only and Marxists do not allow the spiritual to slip in through that crack. To the orthodox Marxist religion is not only a reactionary ideology, but all religious presuppositions are nonsense. He is constrained to believe that there are only two possible philosophies, idealism and materialism; that they are opposed and that materialism is fundamentally anti-religious. As he sees it, dialectical materialism has no room for the supernatural; and it is impossible to see how such a view could be made compatible with most religious outlooks and certainly not with Christianity.

The same conclusion emerges if we examine the Marxist attitude toward science. Some scientists — Eddington, for example — have believed that science confirms theology, but Marx and Engels apparently thought that science had made God unnecessary. As Engels put it: 'in the evolutionary conception of the universe, there is absolutely no room for either a creator or a ruler.' [29] Modern Russia, as Edouard Herriot said, 'has bestowed on science all the authority of which it deprived religion,' and religion is regarded as an enemy of science as well as of dialectical materialism. The Russian attitude expresses a faith in the ability of science and technology to raise production and the standard of living. But whether it is based on science or on dialectical materialism (the two are usually said to be synonymous) the Russians take their

29. *Selected Works,* 1942, I, p. 399.

philosophy to be fundamentally and totally an enemy of all religion. Hence the strong Soviet campaigns against 'religiosity' or 'religious prejudices' in schools and elsewhere, although they sometimes try not to humiliate and antagonize religious supporters of the regime.[30] The incompatibility of religion and Marxism may also be easily deduced from an examination of the Marxist doctrine of truth and morals as class-determined and always partisan. The denial of the very existence of contemplative knowledge may likewise be put among the elements in the Marxist system which cannot be reconciled with religion.

One may, however, separate the Marxist social theory from dialectical materialism, as suggested in Chapter 2, and be a Marxist of sorts. Only by making this kind of distinction is it possible to explain how some Western Christians can accept both the Marxist social analysis and Christian doctrine.

What of the social theory itself, the historical materialism — which is after all the heart of Marxism — is this incompatible with Christianity? Marx's main point here is his law of dialectical economic necessity by which history moves ineluctably toward the revolution. We may ignore for the moment the precise mechanism of this process, the sharpening of the class conflict, and so on. Does this law of necessity deny the Christian doctrine of man's free will? It seems to me that it does, for the Marxist holds that there is really nothing man can do about the inevitable movement of events except to help it along slightly. The Christian must surely hold that the future is open and indeterminate for two reasons: because it could be whatever man chooses to make it (man having free will), and because there is no telling at what point God may intervene.

The Christian could no doubt subscribe to a kind of statistical law of probability which made man in the mass predictable, on the basis of experience, but which allowed that individuals could make a free choice, and that some of them do. Marxists not only admit that some members of the bourgeoisie may desert their class to join the proletariat, but also make ample provision for 'traitors' and 'betrayers' within the Marxist movement. Similarly, it is no

---

30. *Anti-Religious Propaganda in Russian Schools,* Soviet Studies, April 1950.

denial of free will to be able to predict the number of murders or marriages in the United States in any one year with a high degree of accuracy. But the flaw in this argument is that statistical probability is not Marxism. (See also pp. 60, 215.)

The main conclusion thus stands: both dialectical materialism and the Marxist social theories, or 'iron laws' of history, are at variance with the basic beliefs of Christianity, or indeed with any spiritual view of the universe. If Marxism is toned down, and regarded only as a set of partial and sometimes enlightening social truths, then of course it is perfectly reconcilable with Christianity. But that is another matter, and again such residual elements of truth could scarcely be called Marxism.

The goal of the classless society toward which the Marxist believes that history is moving is not in itself something of which most religions need disapprove. Christianity could certainly adapt itself to a classless society founded on public ownership, possibly more wholeheartedly and with a less uneasy conscience than it has adapted itself to other economic arrangements throughout history. There are in Marxism, however, some implications on this point which the Christian must reject. He must deplore the simple optimism which sees so easy and Utopian a solution of man's problem; he must protest that nothing so simple as a change from private to public ownership will transform man from a sinner to a saint. Public ownership is not the same as Divine Grace, and even Divine Grace has a hard time transforming most people. The classless society may be good, but it is not the sole good and the Christian will not mistake it for the Kingdom of Heaven. He will see that not only must it fail to solve many of the problems of man's relationship to man, especially all those outside of working relationships, but also that it has nothing to say on something even more important: man's relationship to God. The Christian objections on the whole introduce a tonic air of realism into the fanaticism which sees the classless society as the be-all and the end-all of present efforts. Nevertheless many Christians are not neutral on social and political issues, but feel obliged to work for a better social order, so that communist and Christian are, or could be, in agreement about some social ends while differing widely on the meaning of those ends, and still more on the means to attain them.

At this point a few subsidiary questions should be mentioned: the first concerning violence. As we have seen, Marx did not idealize violence as such; his error may be called rather an error of judgment. Believing that the bourgeoisie would not yield their class position without armed resistance, he naturally believed also that overthrow by violence would be necessary, and this is now a prime article of the communist creed. The Christian will deplore the use of violence, but still he must make up his mind where he will stand should violent revolution or counter-revolution break out, just as he has always had to decide what his position on war should be. And violence is quite likely to break out in many parts of the non-democratic world before any substantial social reforms can be made. No church takes the perfectionist view of the Quaker and the absolute pacifist and condemns all war as wholly wrong. The theologian is quite familiar with the doctrine of the just war, although the usefulness of this medieval doctrine may be doubted in view of the fact that Christians are usually found on both sides in any war.

It is not then on the use of violence per se that the Christian and the communist part company, but rather on the advocacy of violence and the preaching of its necessity. This consideration at one time led J. Middleton Murry to argue that violence was the only issue between Christianity and communism.[31] Should the violence of civil war ever break out, the Christian and the communist may chance to be on the same side, as they were in World War II, but whereas to the communist his side will appear entirely and absolutely right, the Christian will always regard his choice as the lesser of two evils in an imperfect world, will cherish a real concern for his opponents, and will be ready to forgive them. He will not see them as class types but as individuals with immortal souls — something that is foreign to the communist outlook. And where social changes are at all feasible by constitutional methods — i.e. in the democracies — the Christian will reject the use of violence as an *unnecessary* evil.

31. J. Middleton Murry, *et al., Marxism,* London, 1935, p. 6.

Similar conclusions apply to the Marxist doctrine of class struggle. Class hatred ought, strictly speaking, to have no place in a
hypothesis as scientific as Marxism pretends to be. The capitalist
is as much a creature of the underlying economic forces as the
proletarian, exploitation is the nature of capitalism, and praise
and blame are out of place. We do not call cats immoral because
they prey on mice: it is their non-moral nature. This is all very
well in the abstract, but in practice communists invariably pass
harsh moral judgments upon the motives and behavior of capitalists, and actively foment class hatred as an integral part of class
warfare. Without ignoring the reality of class conflict — one of
many group conflicts in society — the Christian will take care not
to encourage hatred, even class hatred. More in sorrow than in
anger will he play his part in the struggle for social justice. No
doubt this is a difficult ideal, and the Christian does not always
succeed in living up to it, but it ought not to discourage him because he is forever carrying on within his own breast a struggle
of equal difficulty against his own sinful desires. Even in his opposition to communism, the Christian will resist the temptation
to foster hatred of communists as persons.

One often hears it stated that communism is a Christian heresy.
An examination of what this may mean should throw further light
on our main question whether a Christian can be a communist.
Marxism, like Christianity and Judaism, is firmly grounded in history, in time and place, and not in the eternal and changeless
world of Platonic forms. The Marxist view of history thus unquestionably bears a likeness to a Christian view of the age-old struggle
of good and evil, with God's purpose working itself out.

But the resemblance is superficial, and from the Christian standpoint there are several objections to the Marxist view of history:
(a) It is hard to see how economic forces working themselves out
even when man is unaware of them could be identified with the
will of God. There is no reason, for instance, why the Christian,
or anyone else, should not on occasion set himself against a social
trend or a so-called historical 'necessity' if it seems to him morally
wrong. (b) The Kingdom of God, in one sense, is here and now,
as well as in the future. (Perhaps the Marxist millennium has more
affinity with the Hebraic future, which seems to envisage a future

Kingdom on earth with no personal immortality.) (c) The Christian view, at least the more usual view, is that the Kingdom also transcends death, and after the Second Coming ordinary history comes to an end. The Christian finds complete redemption for mankind not in history but beyond it.

Marxism differs from these Christian beliefs in seeing the great struggles as over once and for all in the near future with the establishment of the classless society. The Christian has no guarantee of victory on earth for the right cause, and certainly not in the short run. And, as we have noted, he cannot fail to see that human nature is not 'redeemable,' though it may be improved, by social reforms. Redemption on earth, and by man's own efforts or those of impersonal economic forces, is so far removed from Christian doctrine as hardly to be called heresy at all. The gulf between the two doctrines may become more clearly recognized in our generation if, in face of the threat to all mankind from atomic warfare, the Christian is driven back to his last line of defense: salvation of his soul and a future life.

The 'heresy' of communism, however, usually means nothing so abstruse as the foregoing but simply the passion of the communist for social justice — to the neglect of his soul. Christianity is chiefly a gospel of personal salvation and personal ethics, with little to say on social problems. There is of course a doctrine of *personal* obligation and good will, and although this may give a helpful spirit of approach to social problems, and one not to be underrated, it is clearly not enough. Intellectual analysis and objective investigations are indispensable in attacking social problems. Good intentions cannot substitute for knowledge, since the harm done by well-meaning but ignorant people is notorious. Love for one's children is, in itself, not a sufficient guide on the subject of their upbringing.

Now, it is partly the Marxist criticism of existing society that has led the churches to re-examine their attitude toward society. Marxism has emphasized social justice and the social nature of man, the ubiquity of class interest, the equality of races, and internationalism. All these have given it a hearing, and the Christian has been compelled to take stock of the social implications of his faith on these great questions and has found himself in agreement with a substantial portion of the Marxist critique. He has come to realize the material and expensive basis of culture and virtue for the masses. Such realization has prevented an otherworldly absorption and an overemphasis on spiritual values to the neglect of the more lowly human virtues.

The agreement of Christian and Marxist has taken many precise forms besides those mentioned. Both reject skepticism and the Freudian and other purely psychological explanations of man. Both are repelled by the treatment of labor merely as a commodity, the Marxist theory of value being near in spirit to the medieval doctrine of the just wage — which may be one reason why some Roman Catholic intellectuals admire both Marx and Aquinas. (The compliment is not returned by Marxists, however.) Christian and Marxist unite also in being repelled by the premium society puts upon acquisitiveness, inequalities, and irresponsible economic power; by the competitive struggle of man against man, and the sordid commercialism of standards. That is to say, both fall back upon moral judgments of the economic system, the Marxist implicitly, while usually denying that he does so, and the Christian explicitly, because he sees the many points at which contemporary society conflicts with Christian values.

The wide recognition that there is no specifically Christian economic system, that Christianity is certainly not to be identified with nineteenth-century economic arrangements, is of recent growth in the Western world, and owes something, though not everything, to the influence of Marxism. The churches are more and more critical of many features of capitalist society, and the church is rare which cannot point to its outstanding Christian socialists, its labor and co-operative programs, or at the very least to resolutions passed at church assemblies affirming the need of justice and the sense of community in the social order. (In recent years, however, there seems to have been among Christian philosophers a reaction against the 'social gospel'; a return to more austere doctrine with new emphasis on man's innate sinfulness, and consequently more despair about man's efforts to solve any of his great problems.)

Although Marxism contains some ideas with which Christianity can agree, it is fairly clear why the two must part company. The

Marxist has elevated the passion for social justice into the whole truth, and this prevents him from seeing it in true perspective. To the Christian, social justice may be important but it is only one aspect of the good life. To Marx man is only a social animal, to the Christian he is that and more besides, and it is the 'more besides' which Marx not only ignores but also denies. Man is more than a child of the methods of production, he is also made in the image of God: a proposition that is quite foreign to Marxism.

If what is said above is true, how are we to explain those Christians who call themselves Marxists? Consider first the Christians outside the Soviet Union, who embrace Marxism as a matter of choice, not of compulsion. These would seem to be all cast more or less in the mold of the Dean of Canterbury, who, with naïve enthusiasm, has adopted just as much of Marxism as is compatible with his Christianity. (He had earlier embraced Social Credit as the practical expression of Christianity.) They are Marxists who would not long be *persona grata* if they lived behind the Iron Curtain. They are essentially extremes of the long Christian Socialist tradition. J. Middleton Murry in his early days was also a good example of this kind, when he argued that communism was necessary to the Christian; and so was John MacMurray, who could write that communism in Russia is the 'nearest approach to the realization of the Christian intention.' [32]

The attitude of the Russian Orthodox Church inside Russia may also be easily explained. That church, and perhaps all Eastern churches deriving Christianity *via* Byzantium, has always had an other-worldly and more mystical outlook, has been very little given to social services, and has tended to take more seriously the view that all authority is of God. Therefore providing it has no policy on political or social matters, the Orthodox Church is perfectly capable of coming to a more or less harmonious *modus vivendi* with whatever type of State exists. The traditions of linking church and state, and of church support for the social order, are strong in Russia. It should hardly be a matter for great surprise that a church which could prosper greatly under the Czars and throw the mantle of sanctity over their rule should come to terms with another despotism which, although more despotic and all-

32. J. MacMurray, *The Clue to History,* London, 1938, p. 206.

embracing, yet does at least *profess* to have a worthy end in view.

It would be a miracle if there were no anti-clericalism in Russia after the revolution and it is worth remembering that not the Bolsheviks but the Kerensky government broke the church's power by disestablishment and by separating the schools from church control. (The Bolsheviks of course went much farther.) The Russian church for its own purposes has made its peace with the Kremlin, more especially since 1941, and there are signs that it is reaping some advantages from this agreement, as the Kremlin in its turn tolerates and recognizes the usefulness of the church as an ally. The church in Russia is of course seriously circumscribed in its activities. For a long time freedom of *worship* only was grudgingly permitted, while evangelism and freedom of instruction in religion were not allowed. The strong propaganda campaign against the church and all religious ideas seems now to be less marked. Young people may now be taught religion, though not so freely as in most Western countries; clergy may be trained, some religious publications issued, and some welfare services rendered. Other churches than the Orthodox — for example, the Armenian and the Baptist — also exist but seem to be discriminated against.[33]

One should not be too cynical about the policy of *rapprochement* of the Russian church. It is at least something that the people in Russia are able to see an institution which predates communism and which, with the family, is the only social institution not completely assimilated by the state; and which serves, however weakly, as a center of loyalty that may be different from loyalty to the state. So long as men believe in another and higher power than the state, so long as they have access to ideas that are basically anti-Marxist, there is always the possibility that this will lead to criticism of the state and of Marxism.

The case of 'non-established' Christian churches in communist countries is somewhat different. At most they can live only in uneasy sufferance under communist governments, and their members may sometimes feel obliged to resist, as they did in Nazi

---

33. I. B. Barron and H. M. Waddoms, *Communism and the Churches, A Documentation,* London, 1950; Waldemar Gurian (ed.), *The Soviet Union, Background, Ideology, Reality, A Symposium,* Notre Dame, 1951, pp. 153–94.

Germany. In countries without a communist government, the churches may well conceive it to be their duty to point out just how and why Christian principles are at odds with communist theory and practice. It is no part of their duty, however, to instigate an international war in defense of the faith.

Some churches are better equipped than others to carry conviction to the peoples of the world in the struggle against communism. Charges of party dictatorship do not ring wholly true when brought by churches which themselves are authoritarian; nor is the appeal to liberty more than a hollow sound if a church approves non-communist dictatorships solely because they have left it alone in its privileged position. Above all, a church that is not willing to adopt an attitude of helpfulness toward social reform, and to trust itself bravely to the masses rather than to the 'classes' for its support, cannot hope to fight communism successfully. A good way to insure the victory of communism, and with it the victory of anti-religion, is for the churches to sit tight on privilege and refuse to countenance social and economic change. But if they carry out their mission in the spirit of their founder, the Christian churches can be a bulwark against tyranny, communist or any other kind.

*So Two cheers for Democracy: One because it ad-
mits variety and two because it permits criticism.
Two cheers are quite enough; there is no occasion
to give three. Only Love the Beloved Republic
deserves that.*

E. M. FORSTER.[1]

9

Democracy and Marxism

I

THE PRECEDING CHAPTERS have offered a survey and assessment of
Marxism, omitting only Marx's economics, which, owing to its
instrumental character, is not essential to the understanding of
his main theories. To carry out a survey and assessment of Marxism is tedious but not intrinsically difficult. The works of Marx
and Engels, of Lenin and Stalin, contain the authoritative exposition, and if these are examined with care and perseverance the
framework of communist theory can be discerned and laid bare
for critical analysis.

It is, however, much harder to give an account of the theory of
democracy, since there are no authoritative books, no agreed interpreters whose word is law. Democracy is a word that may be,
and usually is, used in a number of ways, until it has almost come
to mean all things to all people. Being one of the prestige words,
democracy is often a kind of label put onto whatever cause people
happen to favor.

The oldest usage of the word democracy, which comes to us from
ancient Athens, has a political reference. Democracy is a form of

1. E. M. Forster, *Two Cheers for Democracy*, London, 1951, p. 79.

264

government or political system in which, as we say, 'sovereignty' rests with the people. Democracy is also increasingly used in the modern world in a second way, with an economic and social reference. Here the emphasis is not on political method but on the substantive content, in particular upon social justice, economic security, lack of special privileges, and the like. Democracy is also coming to be used in a third and wider sense, being spoken of as an attitude or disposition or way of life. On this usage one may speak of a democratic personality or family or university, in contrast to an authoritarian person or institution.

All of these meanings or usages are in common currency today, and to that extent all are justified. Nothing but confusion can result, however, unless we first specify which usage we are following when we engage in a discussion of democracy.

The first of the three usages is primary in time, being at least as old as the Greeks, and is also basic in the sense that the other meanings have been derived from it. Following this usage we may look upon democracy as a political system having certain special features which mark it off from other political systems. By general agreement (outside the communist world) a democracy is a political system in which representatives are freely elected on a basis of adult suffrage; by freely elected we mean that there exists the usual range of political liberties (including speech, press, assembly, and organization) which make the elections meaningful by giving the electorate a free choice among candidates and parties; the representatives in their turn enact the laws and decide the policies for the time being, and when they are divided in their opinions the decision normally goes by majority vote. In these terms, democracy as a unique political system may be defined in one proposition: the ability of a people to choose and dismiss a government. To call anything else political democracy is only to abuse words. However, such a political system is by no means as simple as it sounds, and its implications could be explored in great detail, a task which would be out of place here.

Corresponding to democracy as a political system, there is also an elaborate theory to explain the operation of the system and to justify it. In the same way, Marxism stands for a theory or set of theories — as examined earlier in this book — while the system which embodies the theory is that of the Soviet Union and other communist countries, and the communist movement throughout the world.

The question we now come to is this: how is Marxism related to democracy? Since the question is a complex one, it must be broken down into several parts in order that intelligent answers may be derived. There is first the question whether Marxist theory (and practice) are incompatible with the theory (and practice) of democracy, and if so in what respects. Secondly, there is the more practical question of what attitude a democratic government should adopt toward communism and toward the Communist Party. And finally there is the relation of the democracies to the Soviet Union.

To answer the first question, the different parts of the Marxist system of thought must be separated. To begin with, consider dialectical materialism, which is said to provide the philosophical foundation of Marxism. In Chapter 2 it was pointed out that the function of dialectical materialism in the Marxist system is to give plausibility to the idea that the physical universe and history move by identical laws, unaffected by the motives or intentions of man; and so to lend an air of science to Marx's historical analysis. But it is pseudo-science, since the laws of natural science cannot be translated directly into social terms. It is also quite possible to separate metaphysics from any particular social theory, so that in a sense dialectical materialism is irrelevant to the Marxist historical and social analysis. If this is true, as it seems to be, then dialectical materialism is no less irrelevant to the theory of democracy.

In Chapter 2 we went even beyond those conclusions, and suggested that dialectical materialism is not so much false as nonsensical, chiefly because of its use of the dialectic. Dialectical materialism, of itself, therefore bears no more relation to democracy than does any nonsense theory. It is only significant inasmuch as it is held by Marxists as part and parcel of the more important social theories. The relation of dialectical materialism to democracy will thus not be considered further.

When the more specific social theories of Marxism are considered it becomes plain that not only are they hostile to the presuppositions of democracy, but they also make it difficult to work the democratic political method successfully. Let us take some examples.

Marxism as a grand-scale philosophy of history has obvious anti-democratic implications. The theory of an inevitable law of history, a dialectical economic process to which mankind can only conform, is stultifying to a free society. Democracy involves a faith in a future which is open and which can be, in time, what man chooses to make it, whereas Marxism casts the immediate future in an iron mold. So far as the Marxist philosophy of history is believed, even though it is false, to that extent it tends to weaken the will to democracy, encourages a fatalistic submission to communist movements, and postpones freedom of choice for mankind until the far future and the arrival of the classless society. Anyone who really believes in the inevitable victory of communism is lost as a democrat.

But the big guns of the Marxist attack are aimed more directly against democracy. It will be recalled from Chapter 5 that Marxist political theory describes the state as a class state, a mere instrument of exploitation in the hands of the bourgeoisie. Legal and political systems are called forceful instruments of class rule, with the moral code cunningly devised to operate by persuasion to serve the same class interests.

Democracy is thus regarded by Marxists as a sham, because, despite all the fine talk about equality before the law, the common good, and freedom for all, it gives the substance of freedom to the rulers but only 'formal' freedom to the proletariat. The workers are only 'formally' free and equal, because of their economically exploited position, as shown by their low wages, poverty, insecurity, and their inability to do more than vote every few years for a 'choice of masters.' 'The political business of the worker just consists in paying taxes.' Or in Lenin's words: 'To decide once every few years which member of the ruling class is to repress and oppress the people through Parliament — this is the real essence of bourgeois Parliamentarianism.' The liberal state is a 'paradise for the rich, a snare and deception for the poor,' the freedom it gives is like the 'freedom for the slave owners' in ancient Greece.[2]

---

2. *State and Revolution*, pp. 186, 218. *Towards the Seizure of Power*, I, pp. 189ff. *Revolutionary Lessons*, p. 76.

The capitalists control the economic power, and in turn control the state in their own interest. They also control the press and all organs of propaganda, and so being able to manufacture public opinion as they wish they control elections and can afford to allow 'free' speech and voting as harmless toys with which the deluded proletariat may amuse themselves. Behind the scenes 'the stock exchange and the banks rule.' From those premises the Marxist conclusion follows: that 'real' liberty is impossible under capitalism and the only way it can be achieved is by the overthrow of capitalism and of bourgeois democracy. No other article in the Marxist creed is held with greater tenacity.

Sometimes, however, a slightly different case is presented, as a concession to the existence of a substantial portion of political democracy: although some political liberties may be exercised by the workers, it is not really very important; what matters is economic liberty, which is denied to the proletariat by the facts of capitalist ownership. A poor man, clinging to an uncertain job, cannot be free but is always in bondage to his stomach and hence to his employer. In any event, the same orthodox conclusion is drawn: that only by overthrowing capitalism will the workers achieve 'economic democracy' and the substance of political freedom.

This, then, is the main line of the Marxist critique of democracy. There is no possible way of operating a constitutional democracy smoothly if this kind of theory is widely believed by the citizens, and Lenin's advice to communists to get into a parliament in order to disrupt it is a natural deduction for anyone who regards bourgeois democracy as a sham.

Nevertheless the Marxist critique may usefully be examined. Marxists can of course find real instances in all democracies of class pressures upon government, and the farther back one goes into history the more numerous the instances become; naturally so, since democracy did not spring full-fledged into being, but has been steadily developing through the years. For that reason, too, Marxists are fonder of citing the past, as revealed in the works of Marx and Engels, than of making fresh analyses of contemporary society.

A plausible case for the Marxist critique can very easily be made. Who can deny on the one hand the tender solicitude of government for business, and on the other, the shorter shrift which labor has so often got as its portion? Who can deny the enormous influence of money and a monied press in molding public opinion and influencing elections and legislatures? Who would feel so confident of receiving justice under the law even today if he were destitute?

Yet even when one has selected all the class elements within the democracies — conditions so much better documented by others than by Marxists — such a case is slowly but surely becoming obsolete. The redeeming feature of the democracies is that they are aware of the existing anomalies and are steadily reducing them; so that to say with the Marxist that the liberal democratic state of today is only a class dictatorship, or that 'formal' freedom exhausts the content of democracy for the mass of the population, is a farcical exaggeration which scarcely calls for refutation. One comment suffices. Civil servants are not lackeys of the capitalists, as Lenin thought; their increasing number shows how the welfare state is growing, not how the bourgeoisie is grinding the faces of the poor.

One may go deeper with the inquiry. If Marx's general theory is right, and the economic foundation is all-important, can politics matter at all? Two conclusions are possible. One is that drawn by non-revolutionary socialists such as the Fabians: the political system can be consciously and flexibly adapted to changing economic conditions, and as long as that is done there need never be a violent break with the past. But such a conclusion is distasteful to Marxists and instead their conclusion is that under capitalism the chief purpose of the struggle for political power is to strengthen the class consciousness of the proletariat. Democratic politics has merely an instrumental and temporary function, to enable the proletariat to capture the state machinery in order to 'smash' it. The Marxist theory thus reduces democracy to a mere stage before the inevitable dictatorship.

It was of course only too easy in early nineteenth-century England to believe in the ineffectual state and the harsh realities and power of economic life. The state that Marx analyzed was, in truth, grossly class-biased, as was the Russian state against which Lenin inveighed. But historically it is political action that has come in to redress the balance and to make wealth and economic power more and more responsible for public welfare. And every partial political control has also enlarged the area of man's freedom by lessening dependence on purely unplanned and unregulated economic forces. It is, among other reasons, just because the conscious social controls have increased steadily in number and scope since Marx's day that his predictions have proved to be so wide of the mark.

Because he believed so little in the efficacy of political power Marx did not anticipate any danger to freedom from a state, even a classless 'state,' which controlled the economy, and hence it is understandable that Marx should have contributed nothing to the solution of this great twentieth-century problem. Yet the objection to central planning would seem to be greater on political than on economic grounds, and this opinion appears to be gathering weight among democrats the world over.

The popular criticism leveled against Marxism is that it tends to degenerate into a form of 'statism.' At first sight the criticism appears wide of the mark, for the virtue of Marx's political theory, like that of most of the early socialists, is the entire absence from it of any glorification of the state. Marx and Engels, motivated by their hatred of the bourgeois state, often wrote as though no coercive power of any kind would exist in the classless society, and Lenin carried the anarchic trend to its farthest limits in his *State and Revolution*. But unless Marx is to be written off entirely as a utopian (which is a legitimate interpretation, based upon his few remarks that have any relevance to the classless society), the statism is implicit in the requirements of total planning, the monopoly of economic and political power in the same hands. Any sense of the reality of economic life, and all human experience hitherto, testify to the inherent tendency of Marxism to lead to an all-powerful state; and the justice of the charge is confirmed by present-day communist regimes. Although Marx and Hegel appear to be poles apart in their attitude toward the state, nowadays the Russian followers of Marx look upon the Soviet State with a sense of awe that even Hegel could have approved. Democracies are properly suspicious of the totalitarian tendencies of Marxist theory and practice.

But what makes dogmatic Marxism an enemy of *contemporary* democracy is the denial of the autonomy and efficacy of politics *here and now* in any of the liberal democracies. Democracy can be stretched to mean many things, but when it ceases to mean that through political action a free people can shape the policies they desire, including the economic policies, then with Marx we must lapse into sheer economic determinism. This is only another way of saying that the difference between Marxist and democrat is that the latter believes it is possible to achieve economic change by peaceful political means, but that nothing short of revolution will satisfy the Marxist.

The 'revisionists' had a keener understanding here than Marx and Lenin. Lenin had written that 'the toiling masses are *barred* from participation in bourgeois parliaments . . .' The statement was nonsense, based upon the working example of no capitalist democracy, and in convenient forgetfulness of Engels' observation that communists thrived on legal methods. Marx was indignant at the Gotha Program, since, although not saying so in as many words, it amounted to a rejection of his theory of the class state, and an affirmation that the state could be used for the benefit of all classes including the workers. The leaders of the Social Democratic party in Germany were aware that they could reasonably expect substantial reforms once the workers were enfranchised. The Social Democratic party, it is true, continued to suffer from a split personality: in practice its program was one of reform, but a section of its membership continued to profess adherence to Marxist theory. Nevertheless the party remained firmly gradualist and democratic in its conduct until the Russian revolution. In the end doctrinaire Leninism drove a section of the proletariat (the communist party) into open hostility toward democracy, while under the influence of revisionist leaders the rest of the workers rallied to the support of constitutional government.

The idea that government is conducted by a ruling class, whose interests are always identified with the national interest, was not invented by Marx but had been an accepted commonplace long before the nineteenth century. Sir Thomas More had defined government as 'nothing more than a certain conspiracy of rich men procuring their own commodities under the name and title of a Commonwealth.' James Harrington had taken it for granted (in 1656) that 'power follows property.' Even with the rise of modern democracies, the idea that political power *should* follow property took a long time a-dying, and for that matter still lingers on at the

municipal level of government, in the remnants of property quali-
fications sometimes attached to the vote. But the Marxist accusation that government is merely another arm of the bourgeoisie or,
in Lenin's words, 'the millionaires' national committees called governments,' has become a less and less adequate description of democratic government.

The one thing which Marxism cannot explain in modern democracies is the hostility of business toward its alleged puppet, the
state. On ordinary empirical grounds, however, the explanation is
easy: the enmity arises because the democratic state is used to benefit all classes, to weight the scales in favor of the weak, and to subject the economy to political direction.

An incidental point of some importance arises. In one sense,
those who are nearest in spirit to Marx are not the social democrats,
Fabians, or Keynesians, who wish to use political power to modify
and improve the going economic system, but the *laissez-faire*
economists and their spiritual descendants of the present day.
There is little difference on this point between Marx and, let us
say, Professor Hayek.[3] They unite in their deification of economic
power and their belief in the futility of political action to build a
free and just society. Marx and Hayek would, of course, give quite
different reasons for their distrust of the state — Hayek the impossibility of improving upon 'consumers' sovereignty,' and the
dangers to freedom from economic planning; and Marx the useless-
ness of expecting political action to make any real improvements
on behalf of the mass of the people so long as private ownership
prevails. Both hold fast to an economic determinist view of the
state.

II

To Marx, the economic forces worked themselves out through
the class struggle. Now, as shown in Chapter 4, the sharpening of
the class struggle and the increasing impoverishment which Marx
expected have not in fact come about, and there is consequently
no sign that the capitalist democracies will ever pass through the
period of revolution predicted by Marx. It may be worth digressing
briefly, to sketch a picture of present-day economic society which is
more realistic than the Marxist abstract dichotomy of classes.

3. F. von Hayek, *The Road to Serfdom*, Chicago, 1944.

Perhaps the great depression during the 1930's was the period when, if ever, the danger of proletarian revolution was most to be apprehended, yet nowhere did the revolution occur. In Britain the number of votes cast for the communist party remained negligible, while in the United States the communist vote actually declined. If there is such a thing as a concensus, it is that never again will depressions be allowed to become really severe. The United States and Canada have both officially adopted the Keynesian principles, the former in the Employment Act of 1946, and the latter in the 1945 White Paper on Employment and Income. The specific measures so far proposed are not likely, in themselves, to avert another slump, yet nevertheless once the state has assumed responsibility for a high level of employment, income, and prosperity, more than half the battle has been won. Citizens will rightly expect their government to take adequate remedial measures, and no democratic government will be able to refuse, especially now that the economists are widely publicizing the view (perhaps a little too confidently) that they know how to avert a serious slump, and how to keep on increasing the real income per capita.[4] Should the economic situation require drastic measures, as it may well do, these could lead very far indeed away from the kind of capitalist society we have had in the past. Lord Keynes himself foresaw that prospect and did not dodge it.[5]

Marxism is here, again, at sharp odds with democracy, since it teaches that the democracies cannot prevent the crises of boom and slump. Engels was eloquent on the subject:

> Bourgeois economics can neither prevent crises in general, nor protect the individual capitalists from losses, bad debts and bankruptcy, nor secure the individual workers against unemployment and destitution. It is still true that man proposes and God (that is, the extraneous force of the capitalist mode of production) disposes.

All later Marxists have constantly chanted the same refrain: '. . . capitalist society is always an endless horror.'[6] Within the

---

4. E.g. Benjamin Higgins, *What Do Economists Know?*, Melbourne, 1951.
5. *General Theory of Employment, Interest and Money*, Ch. 24.
6. Engels, *Anti-Duhring, Handbook*, p. 301; *Lenin, Selected Works*, 1951, I, Part 2, p. 574.

framework of capitalism, crises can never be abolished, but will continue to get worse and worse, until the final catastrophic collapse.

As capitalist society changes its character, however — and it is changing all the time — many of the worst objections to it tend to disappear, in particular those stemming from unemployment and gross inequality. 'Prosperity demoralizes the workers,' as Marx noted, and since increasing impoverishment and the 'industrial reserve army' are nowhere in evidence, Marxism loses its trump card. Political action then becomes a matter of degree, a little more or less of public ownership, social security, or piecemeal planning, in the interest of equality and the general welfare. Revolutions are not made by this pragmatic approach to the problems of society.

Since industrial society is nothing if not dynamic and experimental it would be more than remarkable, it would be miraculous, if subsequent development had fitted into the iron prognosis drawn up by Marx a century ago. (The society which Marx studied was moreover largely that of the *early* nineteenth century; that is, many of the Reports and Blue Books which he used referred to the past, and not to the second half of the century, when he studied and wrote.) The increasing economic influence and the growing political influence of the 'working class,' and of the organized farmers, are two of the outstanding features of the modern world, especially in the more industrialized countries. And these are not revolutionary groups. As we know well, one of the best innoculations against revolution is a flourishing trade-union movement which can see that it is making substantial gains. Marx would no doubt take the stand that all these things do not really lead to a change of system per se, but that is only a matter of definition. What matters is that the going economic and social system under which we now live, whatever it may be called, is quite unlike the society analyzed by Marx and even more unlike the future which he anticipated.

Today, comparatively few people labor under what Engels described as the 'bourgeois illusion of the eternity and finality of capitalist production.' The Amsterdam Council of Churches in 1948 spoke for the times in its announcement that Christianity is not necessarily linked to *laissez faire,* thus emphasizing the essentially transitory nature of all economic systems. Marx's general instinct was sure when he pointed out that nineteenth-century capitalism was merely a passing phase in world history. Its rise may be traced through mercantilism back to the Middle Ages, and its transformation, slow at first, has been proceeding at an accelerating rate during the present generation. But it is not traveling the route of class struggle and revolution mapped out for it by Marx.

Marx turned to the study of economic history to find the proof for his class-struggle theory. The social scientist of today, however, turns to society not with a thesis to prove but with a question: are the rigidities arising from property relations so serious that industrial society cannot adapt its institutions and ideas to the changing modes of production quickly enough to make a peaceful transition to the future? In less Marxist language: is the social lag between technology on the one hand, and institutions and beliefs on the other, capable of being reduced peacefully?

The question used to be discussed in terms of whether socialism can come peacefully or whether it must be by violence: a debate which today has a curiously old-fashioned flavor. Conditions have passed the controversy by in all advanced capitalist countries, and in some of the others as well. (The old debate may be relevant to some countries; much depends on the strength and reality of the democratic tradition. Naturally there can never be any *guarantee* of peaceful change, especially if, as may well be true, 'it is the conservatives rather than the radicals who produce revolutions.' [7]) Unfortunately the controversy is being kept alive by Marxists on one extreme and by over-zealous conservatives on the other, both groups persisting in describing our present order as free enterprise or free competition, as though the underlying reality had not changed from the *laissez faire* advocated by Adam Smith. These extreme schools of thought tend to think in stereotypes (although different stereotypes) of what may be called 'the folklore of capitalism.'

The mixed economy we have at present is partly 'socialized' and partly in private hands, partly free and partly controlled. Anyone

7. Joseph Roucek (ed.), *Twentieth Century Political Thought*, New York, 1946, p. 61.

who fails to recognize this, and to make it the very basis of his analysis, is looking at the world through glasses as opaque as those worn by the Marxist. A system and an age are passing away and the resulting conflicts in society are being resolved in other ways than by means of a sharpening class struggle. Nor is it accurate to describe present society as socialist, for the kind of society that is coming about in the Western democracies is a long way removed from socialism as it has traditionally been understood. In Britain many an old-time socialist has been disillusioned by the course of events, while many a younger conservative finds the changed social climate quite congenial. The same process goes on in nearly every country regardless of the political party in power, and serves to show how free societies can adapt themselves peacefully to meet changing conditions. Democracy today is not merely liberalism but liberalism with something added, which may be described as social welfare and the public interest.

We are thus justified in saying that whatever kind of economic society is evolving (regardless of the label pinned on it) is bound to be collectivist to some large degree, and subject to political planning in a number of spheres, if it is to be based on modern technology with its possibilities of a high standard of living. How large the private sector of the economy will remain, and whether it will be a *free* society, preserving and extending the best in our heritage, we do not know. But we can keep a free society if enough people want it strongly enough. We need not be slaves of technology or of social trends.

III

Lenin and Stalin have extended Marx's theory of the class state to justify the existence of only one political party, a system that has been established in the U.S.S.R. In doing so they have used several arguments. One of these is that only one party is possible, 'the Communist Party, which does not share and cannot share the guidance of the state with any other party.' [8] Nor is this merely

8. Stalin, *Leninism*, p. 42; *Handbook*, p. 851.

while the revolution is in progress — which would be excusable (after all, revolutionists usually tend to treat all opposition as treason) — but it is meant to apply as long as the Soviet state endures; until the never-never land of the classless society and plenty is reached, when 'the Party will die out.'

That there must be only one party is an assertion, not an argument. It can hardly be profitably discussed, since there is simply no way of proving or disproving it; and in any case the communists never try the alternative to see whether it would or would not work. There is little use in pointing out that the democratic socialist countries disprove the necessity for a one-party state, since the stock communist reply consists in a denial that they are socialist at all. The British Labour Government (1945–50), for instance, was labeled a reactionary capitalist regime — an impression not shared by Mr. Churchill or by the North American press. The communist annoyance with countries like Britain arises because these countries flout the Marxist thesis that capitalism can be transformed only by violence. The American annoyance, on the other hand, is derived from the businessman's myth that any overhaul of capitalism must be communism.

But the real communist argument for the single party is a matter of Marxist definition. Political parties are regarded merely as representative of economic classes and since — when reduced to the simplest terms — there are only two classes, the proletariat and the bourgeoisie, therefore there are only two real parties: the communist party represents the working class while all other parties represent the interests of the bourgeoisie. After the revolution, since there will be only one class (more strictly, no class) there will then be no need for more than one party. It is a typical piece of rigid and deductive Marxist reasoning.

Following the same line of thought, Lenin used to argue that in the democracies there is really only one party (excluding communists where they exist, and they do exist, contrary to Lenin's belief) since there is agreement by all the so-called parties on fundamentals. If Lenin were right, then reasoning by analogy we could expect a number of parties to appear in the communist proletarian state; all of them agreeing on, say, the principle of public ownership but differing on such 'nonessentials' as the relative proportions of consumer or capital goods to be produced by the Five Year Plans. But there are as yet no signs of any such open differences within the U.S.S.R. (The Nazis, so it is said, predicted that ultimately, when all were in agreement, two parties would be permitted.)

The charge that democracies contain only one party divided into the 'ins' and the 'outs' deserves some attention. Others besides Marxists have declared that party differences are purely artificial, as meaningless as the struggles between the Big Enders and the Little Enders in Lilliput.

In the first place, even if it were true, and party platforms scarcely mattered, the existence of a number of parties led by different persons engaged in a fight for office would still be of high value. If power tends to corrupt — about which there can be little doubt — it is wise to shift 'office holders' from time to time.

In the second place, the communist charge ignores all party divisions except the economic. Now it was true that before the advent of socialist parties the older parties did not challenge the principle of private ownership of the means of production. The case is usually made, for example, that the Liberals and Conservatives in nineteenth-century Britain did not differ on 'fundamentals,' in the sense that they agreed upon private ownership and enterprise, and that the same is true of similar parties today in Canada and the United States. Even here, however, doubt arises. It all depends on what is regarded as fundamental. These parties *feel* their differences to be vital, and would strongly resent being forced into one party. And if they feel that way it seems foolish to argue that parties do not matter. Once more we see that only by assuming that economic differences alone are important can the Marxist case be sustained. But to do that is to beg the whole question.

A third and more important objection, however, is that democracies do in fact contain parties and other minorities, which do not subscribe even to the most fundamental beliefs of the great majority, and the existence of such critical opposition is one of the tests of democracy. Parliament may be something of a distorting mirror, in reflecting all opinions and group interests in the country, but it is a counsel of despair and cynicism to smash it on that account, and to ignore all the other channels by which public opinion influences legislation.

A democracy becomes endangered whenever frustrated minorities put their principles before the 'rules of the game.' That is why, in the last analysis, every democratic socialist must, if he is a democrat, put the democratic method before his socialist objectives should he ever be placed in the invidious position where he is forced to choose between the two. A democracy becomes more stable as its opposing parties approach each other in outlook and come to share the moral premises of democracy (or, alternatively, as they agree to keep strongly felt differences outside of politics); but that is a long way from proving that party differences are of no great importance. As a common religious faith is not required by different countries before they can agree on international law, so uniformity is not required within any particular country before it can become democratic. The only concensus that is indispensable to the working of the democratic method is the agreement to differ, and not to persecute. And it is at this very point that the one-party system differs so profoundly from the democracies and creates the strong presumption, which is confirmed by all experience, that no democracy — in any ordinary non-communist sense of the word — is possible without at least two political parties and a wide range of civil liberties.

The special case of socialist and non-socialist governments alternating in power may be mentioned. It hardly seems possible to socialize a country under one regime and to 'de-socialize' it under another, although it is not impossible to 'de-nationalize' specific undertakings. Yet that is to express the general problem in an unreal and extreme form, since no democratic socialist government has gone very far with a socialist program. All democratic governments are both socialist and capitalist nowadays, depending on one's yardstick, and the difference is hardly more than a question of degree. During the tenure of office of one party the rate of socializing is more rapid, while under another there is a period of consolidation, not of a complete unscrambling of the eggs. As the argument in the preceding section has shown, much of the welfare and regulating program is almost forced upon a society based upon specialization, interdependence, and modern technology, and subject to all the moral pressures engendered in a democracy.

IV

Earlier chapters of this book have shown many points at which the Marxist theory conflicts with the theory of democracy, but for the sake of convenience the chief points may be summarized here.

The Marxist philosophy of history is in contradiction to the democratic theory that a free society has an open future. The Leninist theory of imperialism makes impossible almost any trading or other economic relations of capitalist democracies with poorer parts of the world because it teaches that these relations are invariably 'exploitive.' The Marxist theory of truth teaches the class-partisan nature of all ideas, including those of economic theory. The ethical theory of Marxism is that whatever serves the interests of the proletarian struggle is right — and it easily follows that any methods, even the most undemocratic, are justified so long as they promote this end. The Marxist theory that economic forces determine all the other institutions and ideologies of society is at odds with the democratic use of political action to build the free and just society.

The Marxist diagnosis of the liberal state as merely the political arm of the bourgeoisie, if accepted by large numbers of people, tends to hamper the smooth working of constitutional democracy. Marxism teaches that the class struggle is everything, that class differences are irreconcilable; yet the one thing calculated to destroy democracy is the existence of bitterly hostile class parties that put their objectives before the maintenance of democracy.

Marxism teaches that since liberal democracy is a sham, it must be overthrown by the class-conscious proletariat (or, in later communist theory, by the party, on behalf of the proletariat); that the overthrow can only be by violent revolution (or perhaps today by a *coup d'état*); and that the communist party will then proceed to suppress all other parties and set up a dictatorship instead. Early Marxism had presupposed an element of democracy in the 'dictatorship' phase, but modern communist practice by subordinating

the proletarian state to the party has violated every democratic belief in the dignity and moral responsibility of free men. And to
make matters worse it has done this behind the moral façade of its
ultimate utopianism.

Marxism teaches all this as scientific truth, and that those who
oppose it are class enemies of the proletariat. These are the chief
issues on which the Marxist social theory conflicts most openly with
the theory of democracy. They establish the case beyond dispute
that the two theories are quite irreconcilable. Only on two important issues could the Marxist and the democrat find themselves in
agreement, the first being that of the ultimate goal of the classless
society of 'plenty.' But this in turn is so universal an ideal, and so
remote from realization in any near future, and hence so utopian,
that it is of no practical importance in helping to bring Marxist
and democrat into the same camp.

The second issue arises because in one sense the Marxist professes
not to be anti-democratic at all, but to be in favor of democracy,
while asserting that it is impossible under capitalism. A recent
study of the theoretical foundations of democracy, to which both
Marxists and non-Marxists contributed, turned up an astonishing
amount of seeming agreement:

> Probably for the first time in history, 'democracy' is claimed
> as the proper ideal description of all systems of political and
> economic organization advocated by influential proponents.[9]

Although one side was talking of 'proletarian democracy,' the
other was talking of Western democracy, whether in its capitalist or
socialist variety. Yet both sides were also agreeing upon an ideal
democracy, while disagreeing only on the economic foundation required to support it. The dispute over the necessary and sufficient
conditions for democracy could theoretically be settled by an appeal to empirical evidence, but it cannot be so settled as long as the
Marxist stand is one of definition and dogmatic assertion. In practice, therefore, it is precisely the doctrinal position which drives the
Marxist into implacable enmity to capitalist democracy — and
most of the democracies of the world are still far more capitalist

9. *Democracy in a World of Tensions*, UNESCO, Paris, 1951, p. 527.

than socialist. The Marxist wants all or nothing, and thus rejects the piecemeal changes, the mixed economy, the agreement to work within the constitutional framework. To him these are not good in themselves, but are useful only as preliminaries to the dictatorship of the proletariat.

The first question has thus been answered: in what respects does Marxist theory conflict with democracy? The second question may now be dealt with: what attitude should a democratic government adopt toward Marxist theory and teaching? If Marxism is taken as a body of ideas — whether on philosophy, history, or contemporary society — the question is easily disposed of. Democracies are not and cannot be in the business of thought control, and so long as there is free discussion of ideas, i.e. so long as a country is democratic and civil liberties exist, Marxism like all other theories must be left alone by governments. When wrong thinking becomes a crime the light of democracy will be extinguished.

That is the main, the fundamental principle. It can, however, be reinforced by secondary considerations. In the first place, a number of philosophies whose principles are hostile to democracy already circulate in the democracies. They all compete for adherents in the market place of ideas, to find their own level in the intellectual life of free countries. In the second place, wherever in democracies Marxism has been in free competition with other ideas it has shown no ability to shoulder out competitors. If the theory of democracy should fail and be forgotten, it will not be because Marxism or any other argument defeats it, but because democracy as a form of government does not cope adequately with its practical problems of liberty, security, and justice.

V

Marxism is more than a number of social theories, however. In its contemporary form of Marxism-Leninism-Stalinism it is also a political and social movement, organized in communist parties throughout the world, almost all of them joined together and dominated by the Russian party. For that reason another question arises, of keen contemporary interest: what should be the attitude of a democratic government toward the communist party? At this point, too, the additions made to Marxist theory and practice by Lenin and his successors become far more relevant.

The nature and objectives of the party are clear enough. Its nature is conspiratorial and monolithic. In so far as it is orthodox and 'Stalinist' the party everywhere can be regarded only as controlled and directed by the Politbureau (now the party Presidium) according to the policy that best fits or seems to fit with the foreign policy of the U.S.S.R. The party's objectives are also plain: the overthrow of 'bourgeois democracy' in whatever country it operates, the suppression of opponents, and the establishment of the dictatorship of the proletariat, which for all practical purposes is the dictatorship of the party. Since the U.S.S.R. is the leading communist state there is every likelihood that most foreign communist parties, if successful, would bring their own countries into subservience to the U.S.S.R. The experience of Eastern Europe amply bears out the conjecture. Even in the case of Yugoslavia the intention of Moscow domination was strong enough, until owing to a peculiar combination of circumstances Tito was able to make a break, and to do so successfully.

The tactics of the party, too, may be summed up in one phrase: whatever methods lie to hand will be used to further the cause. If legal methods serve, these will be employed, but if they do not, then others will be used, including, if necessary, revolution or a *coup d'état*. The party has no intention of playing the rules of the democratic game: all that counts is winning, and if the party wins it will change the rules and put an end to the game.

Here we are out of the realm of philosophy, ideas, and free discussion, and into the realm of political and possibly violent action. Quite obviously, regardless of what ultimate humanitarian end the communists profess to have in mind, the nature, tactics, and program of the party are destructive of the democratic political method. A person can no more be a party member and a democrat than he could be a Nazi or a Fascist and a democrat.

Should a democratic society, which is characterized by toleration and free circulation of ideas and parties, adopt a tolerant policy toward the communist party? To many people this appears to be the most important question of contemporary politics. And it is by no means an easy question to answer wisely.

There are three fundamental considerations, which may give some help in arriving at an answer:

(a) Communist practice in a number of countries bears out the theory that if the party achieves power it will set up a dictatorship, establish the one-party state, and crush all opposition. Experience gives no ground for believing that the party merely 'talks tough' but would in time settle down in office as another democratic party.

(b) Plainly, to allow the party to operate and grow is therefore to risk the destruction of the democratic method, the very method which makes all parties and the free society possible.

(c) It follows that the party cannot logically claim toleration as *of right*. One can demand to join in the game only if one agrees to abide by the rules, or to change them only by mutual agreement.

Yet these three considerations, although valid, do not settle a matter that is both complex and difficult. The question, when generalized to include all groups whose philosophy is anti-democratic, may be put thus: should democracy tolerate everything *except* the intolerant, or everything *including* the intolerant? One school of thought, inclining toward the former view, holds that democracy on its own principles cannot tolerate the intolerant without asking for its own destruction by groups which take advantage of the principle of freedom in politics only to destroy it. All rights to toleration are forfeited by groups who will not extend toleration themselves; Rousseau had the same point in mind when he wrote, 'Tolerance should be given (only) to all religions that tolerate others.' [10] No society or system, so it is said, is under any obligation to commit suicide. And further, that as by law a man is not allowed to sell himself into slavery, so no society should be allowed to do so. An analogy is also drawn from economic life: while freedom of competition is the principle of business, the democratic state does not allow corporate monopolies to destroy competition; and so a democracy must legislate against a party which would destroy freedom. In short, a democracy is perfectly entitled to take such legal action as may be needed to enforce tolerance and freedom, and may quite consistently make the communist party illegal.

But there is also a school of thought which believes that a de-

10. Rousseau, *Social Contract*, Ch. xv.

mocracy would contradict its own principles of liberty and tolerance by taking action restricting the activities of any group, even
the most intolerant. Democratic liberties and rights are not extended only to the 'deserving,' or we should forever be lost in the
disputes over who are the 'deserving.' The fundamental principles
and ideas of democracy itself should not be exempt from criticism,
but evidence against, as well as for, should be freely permitted or
even encouraged. Liberty is not only the abstract right to differ
but in the realm of politics presupposes the actual power to oppose, to propagandize, and to organize a political party.

The philosophic issue involved is subtle, and many intelligent
and impartial people come down on different sides of the argument. One can only record a personal opinion. I see no inconsistency of *principle* in sometimes taking steps, legislative or other,
to enforce toleration and freedom in a democracy. Indeed it may
often be the duty of a democratic state to suppress the 'liberties'
of some people in the interest of the liberties of others, as in laws
against racial and other forms of discrimination. Again, there is
nothing illogical in suggesting that force or the threat of force
should be met with the force of law; although many difficulties
may arise in drawing the line between ideas and action, between
opinion and conduct, between violence and beliefs that logically
imply the use of violence.[11]

Yet, at the same time, such analogies are not entirely convincing.
In practice a democracy is generally wise to tolerate all views, organizations, and political parties. It seems a poor sort of democracy
that is compelled to suppress any party or group, even the most
intolerant and anti-democratic.

Nor is it always necessary or wise in real life to press any one
principle to its logical conclusion. To push even the best of principles always to its limits, at the expense of other principles, may
make dangerous absolutists of us all. Despite the fact that the communist party may have no just claim to toleration, and that democracy is under no duty to tolerate it, that need not be the end
of the question. Democracies can, and usually do, tolerate a number of intolerant cranks, of obstinate minorities, on what is known
as the 'lunatic fringe' of politics. If the main part of the body

11. Cf. Alf Ross, *Why Democracy?*, pp. 231ff.

politic is healthy, such deviations are not likely to have serious detrimental effects. It will therefore depend very much upon circumstances whether the threat of force, or the incitement to action, is regarded as serious enough to justify legal proceedings against the communist party. So long as the party is small and exercises no great influence, expediency may well be our guide, and the decision to take legal action to outlaw the party need not always be taken.

The principle of expediency (if principle it can be called) is after all commonly followed in real life, although whenever it is followed, awkward cases are bound to arise. But awkward cases can never be avoided whenever any general principles are applied to particular cases. It might be perfectly possible, in this instance, to outlaw and control the communist party in countries where it is negligible, as in Canada, the United States, and the United Kingdom, but when the party has grown large and powerful it may have passed beyond effective legal control. How are we to resolve this dilemma?

In practice there is no easy solution but it is easy to find one in theory. The best long-run approach is certainly to take a course of action that prevents the dilemma from arising. There are many things seriously wrong in any country where the communist party can command wide-scale support, so wrong that banning the party will not go far toward solving the problems. To meet the communist challenge so that it does not become serious means to create the kind of conditions in which communism does not thrive and gain mass allegiance. We must remember that the party does not usually (although it may sometimes) invent the grievances, injustices, and inefficiencies which can arouse mass action. The experience of the democracies and of other nations is surely conclusive: normally in the countries where real efforts are made to meet and solve the economic and other problems the party is not a serious contender at the polls for political power. Of all the Western democracies, only in Italy and France is the communist party at all powerful.

The conclusion follows that the policy which is wisest for one country is not a rule of thumb to be applied everywhere indiscriminately regardless of local circumstances. The tolerant attitude which may be appropriate in the more stable and prosperous democracies may be an invitation to disaster in other states. Prime Minister Nehru and his party, for instance, can make real progress in tackling the tremendous problems of India, within the framework of constitutional democracy, only if they are given plenty of time. The economic and social conditions of India are such that if the communist party is permitted to grow, and if it is well financed and well led, it could spread like wildfire. The Congress Party may well be justified in setting up legal barriers against the spread of the communists. The stricter measures required in India, say, may be quite out of place in North America or Britain.

VI

There is one other complicating factor often raised these days — the issue of loyalty to the state. It is one thing to criticize the government, or to advocate social and economic reforms, but it is a different matter to betray one's country. The argument is that communists have a prior loyalty to the Soviet Union and for all practical purposes are mere agents of Moscow. This is true, at least since the shift of policy in the Soviet Union in the 1920's, and providing the party concerned is 'Stalinist.' The argument does not, however, apply to any purely national or Titoist brand of communism, which puts patriotism above Moscow, and above all it does not apply to the wide variety of philosophic Marxists — Trotskyites and others — who are outside any party. The practical question then arises: can a dividing line be drawn between communists who are loyal to Moscow, and Marxists who are not? If it can be drawn, then we may divide communists into two categories — 'Stalinists' and others — a division which many people in the Western world are now beginning to make but which greatly complicates the legal problem.

The issue of loyalty turns almost wholly on the needs of military security. If these are to guide policy (and security must obviously be the concern of every government) then the policy should be to safeguard 'official secrets,' and to maintain an efficient counter-espionage service. It means treating the individual party member, assuming he can be identified, as a bad security risk when his position gives him access to information with military significance. Such is broadly the policy of countries such as Britain and Canada today, and on the whole it seems to work satisfactorily.

The policy is one of taking precautions against Soviet agents, not of taking fright at Marxist ideas. It does not necessarily imply that the party itself should be driven underground but it does imply due administrative and legal procedures to protect every accused person, as well as safeguarding the security of the state. And such procedures become all the more essential as the party tactics change — to eliminate membership cards and records, and so on — and so make it more difficult to identify a party member.

What is said above will be brushed aside by many on the grounds that we are already in a stage of cold, or perhaps lukewarm, war; and that the emergency is acute enough to justify stringent war measures. If this extreme opinion is acted upon, the resulting action is likely to crush not only the communist party but also many civil and political liberties. Already most of the democracies have gone far in violating a number of traditional legal concepts: the substitution of administrative discretion for due legal process; the presumption of guilt without full proof, instead of assuming innocence; and the punishment (by firing or demoting) of people for crimes which they *might* commit in the future, instead of for offenses actually committed. Democracy cannot endure for long in the atmosphere of war, or perhaps even in the 'garrison state' of a long, cold war.

The danger is that we might drift into a secret-police state, and undermine that confidence in free speech and independent citizenship which is so essential to the free society. Only under the utmost provocation, that is, in time of war, ought democracy to play that insidious game. In time of peace we can hardly do better than remember Woodrow Wilson's words:

If there is one thing we love [in the United States], it is that every man should have the privilege, unmolested and uncriticized, to utter the real convictions of his mind. I believe that the weakness of the American character is that there are so few growlers and kickers among us. We have forgotten the very principle of our origin, if we have forgotten how to ob-

ject, how to resist, how to agitate, how to pull down and build
up even to the extent of revolutionary practices.

VII

If the communist party is not normally best treated by being
outlawed and driven underground, is there a better way in which
its threat can be met? The answer is implicit in what has gone
before, but may be stated more explicitly. To do so, we must first
of all recognize why people are attracted to Marxism; and this is
not by any means the agreed subject that it is often taken to be.
A distinction must be made between the appeal of Marxism to the
few and its attraction for the masses.

One sometimes hears it argued that the attraction of communism is quasi-religious, that in an age with all values in the melting
pot, communism is a new and invigorating faith to replace the
older, declining faiths. There may be something to this, and certainly many people who embrace communism make it a substitute
for other religions. The usefulness of the diagnosis is the emphasis
on the psychological. In a time of grave social troubles and
heightened international tensions, there will always be perplexed
and frightened people anxious to embrace confident and ready-
made answers to all their queries. Man needs purpose and hope,
a unified view of life, and if he cannot find them in one place he
will generally seek them in another. The drifting, the unstable, the
disillusioned, those who are 'destitute of faith but terrified at
scepticism' may therefore well be potentially fertile soil for communism.

This kind of explanation never covers more than a small proportion of Marxists, however, and never accounts for the mass support. Even if it were true that communism merely rushes in to fill
a vacuum of doubt and despair, it by no means follows that the
best way of meeting the problem is to outlaw the party. To take
legislative action to safeguard any beliefs savors too much of the
inquisition. Those with a better faith than Marxism ought to
examine afresh why they fail to hold adherents, to offer more
convincing evidence for their beliefs, and to state their case more
persuasively.

As noted earlier, Marxism makes an even stronger appeal on moral grounds. This helps to explain why it is taken up by people with sensitive social consciences, since there will always be points at which the charge of injustice may be brought against even the best and most prosperous community. For this reason, too, prosperity and democracy alone will never entirely eliminate Marxism.

They can, however, go most of the way, so that even if the party exists, as it may well do, it will be a negligible movement, gathering to itself the cranks, the high-minded but unrealistic, the unstable temperaments, the maladjusted. Such a party is no great danger to democracy and is never likely to come anywhere near forming the government. It will be the kind of absurd party which in fact now exists in Canada, Britain, and the United States.

To explain the *mass* support we must also take social conditions into account. The common theory that communism arises from poverty, although oversimplified, does direct attention to the fact that certain social conditions are favorable to the spread of Marxism, or of any other reformist or revolutionary gospel.

Communism offers people a way out that looks both realistic and hopeful. Rejecting all escapism, it offers a simple and plausible explanation for the world's troubles and an even simpler cure. The analysis may be erroneous, the cure fantastic, but no one can deny that Marxism deals with the real world, with bread and butter and moral feelings, with standards of living, and also with a sense of purpose. When we look around us, we see that communism has not gained mass support in most of the democracies. The quasi-religious and the purely moral appeals, though strong in themselves, have given rise to mass parties only in countries where economic and social conditions are favorable. These 'favorable' conditions include much more than poverty; they include also such factors as economic instability, personal frustration and insecurity on a wide scale, bad or ineffectual government, and above all the upsetting of the old and stable ways of life in a period of swift social changes or war. In this receptive ground Marxism flourishes widely, for Marxist denunciations of injustice, and its confident promises, find an echo in hearts quite unmoved by the pseudo-science of its theories. It is toward the feeling of injustice, not merely to poverty; to hope and not to despair; to the feeling that things could be better and to the promise of abundance, and not merely to resentment over bad government or economic inefficiency, that the Marxist aims his propaganda. Marxism cannot deliver the oppressed masses in, for example, a country such as Britain because there are no oppressed masses. But it can appeal to the masses in many countries, once they come to believe their poverty is due to oppression and is curable by the overthrow of a small class of 'rulers,' such as foreign colonial powers or native landlords.

It is thus not difficult to understand why communists have won mass support for their program in colonial or peasant countries already disrupted by the impact of industrialism and Western ideas, and in recent years also by war; or in those Western countries where social reforms are blocked, where class lines run deep, and which are so notoriously badly governed that their grave economic and social problems seem beyond solution by traditional means. One is not surprised that China turned communist once the party was shrewd enough to base itself on the peasantry, or that Italy is on the borderline, but one is surprised that China did not turn communist years ago, or that Italy did not go the whole way in the midst of the breakdown and distress of the postwar years. Mass support for the communist party, as in France or Italy, does not necessarily represent a conversion to Marxist philosophy, but is much more a vote cast against the terrible economic and social conditions in these countries, and against the inadequacies of alternative parties. To center attention on the communist party in such countries — as by legal prohibitions — may possibly prevent these countries from turning communist for the time being, but can be successful for long only if at the same time the democratic state deals with the underlying troubles as well as with the symptoms.

We must never forget, then, that communism is successful only where the real problems of the real world are not being otherwise faced and met. In any reasonably just and efficient democracy, where complaints are attended to and reforms are not blocked, where insecurity is banished and fraternity is possible, where a spirit of hope is abroad in the land, Marxism is no serious mass danger. Communism, like slavery, is 'a weed that grows in every soil' but it crowds out the crops only in the uncultivated field.

Marxism has nothing to offer democracy on the positive side,

nothing constructive to say on curing the ills of democracy —
apart from killing the patient to save him from his disease. A case
can be made, however, for having Marxists about, on the argument that if there were no devil it would be necessary to invent
one. The useful function of the Marxists is that of gadflies, of
captious and irresponsible critics. They may irritate, but they also
prevent complacency and stagnation. Their information is heavily
weighted in the direction of the faults and follies of democracy,
but they shake us from our apathy, force us to re-examine our
beliefs and the grounds for holding them; and above all they continually challenge us to build a better society by arousing us to
awareness of our faults. They remind us that social justice is a not
wholly solved riddle of democratic politics. Tension and conflicts
do exist in society, and perhaps always will, and it is useful to have
them drawn to our notice. We always need to be reminded to look
for the selfish interests cloaking themselves in the guise of patriotism and high moral principles. Fortunately, communists also offer
us, in the U.S.S.R., a perfect object lesson on what to avoid. Free
countries on the borders of the Soviet Union have always known
too much about their totalitarian neighbor to be anything but
suspicious of it.

By tolerating communist parties the democracies naturally pay
a certain price. A class struggle is fomented and emotions of hatred,
envy, resentment, and aggression are stirred up; cynicism is created
by concentrating always on the worst motives of people, by emphasizing only economic power, and by preaching the hopeless-
ness of expecting reforms from 'class' governments. The democratic
political method and its institutions — of voting, political parties,
and parliament — are all ridiculed, and thus become handicapped
in their working. The price is high, but so, too, is the price of
banning. No doubt it is a matter of opinion which is worse at any
one time. The democrat may be emboldened, however, to take the
risk of tolerating, on the practical ground that in no democracy
has the communist party ever yet been voted into power. (The only
partial exception is Czechoslovakia, but even in that unfortunate
country, with the Russian bear breathing down its back, the party
obtained supreme power not at the polls but by a *coup d'état*.)

VIII

A final point to be dealt with briefly is the relation of the democracies to the U.S.S.R. The point is put into perspective if the inquiry is widened to include the relation of the democracies to any authoritarian regime, or to any potential enemy. If that is done, at once it becomes apparent that the problem is a common one in the sphere of international politics and was not brought into the world by the rise of Soviet Russia. There is of course the complicating factor of the communist party, already discussed, but even this had its analogues, one of them being prewar Nazism, according to which every German living abroad was expected to give his first allegiance to Berlin.

Since the problem is one of international politics, it can be treated only at that level. Pending the establishment of an international organization strong enough to enforce the peace — for which democrats are in duty bound to work — all nations can only fall back upon the instruments of diplomacy, alliances, and preparedness. At every point practical considerations of national security and power must be taken into account. The North Atlantic Treaty Organization is one such instrument of collective security, the purpose of which is to safeguard the countries within it from the possible aggression of the U.S.S.R.

The world is divided into two enormous power blocs, headed respectively by the United States and the U.S.S.R. In between are a number of neutral countries such as Eire and Sweden, who, while doubtless sympathetic to the Western alliance, are unconcerned enough to wash their hands of its fate; while others, such as India, are desperately trying to postpone a decision to join either side. Whether a global war will break out depends almost wholly on the two Titans, who thus hold the fate of the world in their hands. Countries without atomic bombs hardly count today from a military point of view, despite the presence in the United Nations of so many 'sovereign' states. Each of the Titans tries in various ways to push or pull the uncommitted countries onto its side.

The evidence is overwhelming that the alarm and despondency felt throughout the West is inspired mainly by fear of Russia's intentions. Why the Russian leaders behave as they do, and what they intend to do in the future, are thus among the most important questions facing the democracies. The subject is much too big to be explored in detail here, but there seems to be general agreement on a few main points, which may be recalled and noted.

The most obvious feature of the present world situation is that the U.S.S.R. professes to have a great fear of the West. It is never easy to understand another country, but we may make the attempt to see on what grounds the fear of the West is based, and why the U.S.S.R. takes such a hostile position.

First, there is all the normal hostility between great powers when, as today, the Soviet Union and the United States are rival world leaders. This explains much more than is usually supposed. International tension would exist (as it has always done) regardless of the political complexion of the great powers concerned, and whether Russia were aggressively imperialist under a communist, Czarist, democratic, or any other flag.

Second, there is the influence of Marxist-Leninist-Stalinist theory, which for a generation has led the Russians to believe that the capitalist countries, in their desperate attempts to avert a proletarian revolution, or to avoid serious economic depression, will very probably be driven to launch a war against the Soviet Union as the way out of their difficulties.

Third, experience seems to confirm the Russian view that they are living in a hostile world. The West has forgotten, but the Russians will never forget, the civil-war period immediately following their Revolution, when American, British, French, Czech, and Polish troops all fought in support of the anti-Bolsheviks. The Munich agreement of 1938 is interpreted as a deliberate attempt on the part of the West to turn Germany against Russia. Memories of the later attack by Nazi Germany, with the thinly veiled approval of many Western statesmen, are always present in Russian minds; and like the French they are deeply apprehensive of an armed and independent Germany.

Fourth, there are the 'vested interests' of Soviet rulers, the 'new class' of which Djilas has spoken.

The new class may be said to be made up of those who have special privileges and economic preference because of the administrative monopoly they hold . . . To be an owner or a joint owner in the Communist system means that one enters the ranks of the ruling political bureaucracy and nothing else.[12]

The point here is that this class not only benefits from the system, but also cannot afford to relax its controls because it is not sure — even at this late day — that the mass of the Soviet people would support the monopolistic party rule. Although no doubt there has been a relaxation, a 'thaw,' since the death of Stalin, a substitution of collective for single dictatorship, any substantial broadening down of political and civil liberties is scarcely to be looked for in any forseeable future. A little freedom is a dangerous thing, as the Soviet rulers learned from Poland and above all from the desperate rebellion in Hungary in 1956. Consequently, the outside world must always be painted as an implacable enemy, from whom nothing but a temporary truce is possible.

Add to this that the Soviet Union was treated for the most part as an international outcast until the middle 1930's (as communist China is today) and the fact that many spokesmen in the West are often violently anti-Soviet as well as anti-communist (some people have gone to the length of calling for a preventive war) and it is not difficult to understand that, seen through Russian eyes, the West has been an enemy camp since 1917. NATO is a defensive alliance from the Western point of view, but any defensive alliance always looks like an offensive coalition to the other side.

Theory and experience and survival itself thus tend to confirm the Russian leaders in their suspicion and fear of the West. This almost pathological apprehension helps to explain a great deal in Russian behavior: for instance, the careful insulation of their citizens from ideas and contact with the outside world, and the policy of giving to the people of the U.S.S.R. the kind of propaganda picture of the West which distorts social reality in the

12. Milovan Djilas, *The New Class: An Analysis of the Communist System*, New York, 1957, pp. 39, 61.

U.S.A. or Britain beyond all recognition.[13] Even with the best will in the world, one country seldom finds it easy to convince others of its good faith.

To account for the behavior of a ruling class is rarely simple — Marxist theory to the contrary — and still less can a simple explanation be given of the behavior of a nation. But among the other factors that must enter into any explanation of Russian behavior, both inside and outside Russia, the following cannot be ignored. Russia has had a traditionally small middle class, a background of subservience and ignorance among the masses, and very little experience with democracy. The Russian political heritage is one of absolutism, secret political police, and — to a considerable degree — terrorism and violence. Even the practice of extorting confessions from political prisoners was an amiable custom of old Russia, being used, for example, by Nicholas I against Bakunin. Conspiracy is second nature to the Bolsheviks themselves, and they fall naturally into the habit of suspecting conspiracies against them everywhere. Possibly the greatest tragedy of the modern world is that 'socialism' was introduced into a politically backward country, in the name of Marx but by a band of fanatical revolutionaries.

From Russian history there come the sensitive national pride and jealousy, the idea of Slavic destiny and leadership, and the dislike of the West, as seen, for instance, in the works of Dostoevsky. This feature in the Russian character has now been identified with the success of communism, and is carried to fantastic lengths in the rejection of all Western influence, in the claims of priority and superiority for Russian science, inventions, and so on. In Berdyaev's words:

> Socialism in Russia, even when atheistic, bears the impress of religion. The Messianic idea of Marxism which was connected with the mission of the proletariat, was combined and identified with the Russian messianic idea.[14]

The Soviet Union has the most *self-conscious* and messianic cul-

13. Frederick C. Barghoorn, *The Soviet Image of the United States*, New York, 1950.

14. Cf. Nicholas Berdyaev, *The Russian Idea*, London, 1947, pp. 98, 249.

ture in the world, if 'culture' is the right word for the stifling of criticism and — except for natural science — a 'blank page' of culture from 1932 to 1955.[15] Finally there are the tremendous influences of World War II and the terrible price which the U.S.S.R. paid for victory, and the always vital factor of leadership — that has gone through such changes with the death of Stalin. All these and many other influences would have to be explored and weighed in order to give an adequate explanation of why the Russian rulers behave as they do.[16] Fortunately this fascinating and vital subject is being studied extensively in a number of scholarly centers in the Western world, and in time no doubt the U.S.S.R. will appear less of a 'riddle wrapped in a mystery inside an enigma.'

Reference to Marxist theory, to Bolshevik experience and suspicion, and to Russian history and psychology may explain a good deal, but in the end, and perhaps most important of all, are the plans and policies of the present Russian leaders. Here we leave the realm of rational explanation and are compelled to speculate. Do the leaders themselves believe in the Western bogey? Are they really so blind as to believe the democracies have aggressive intentions? Are the men of the Presidium determined at whatever cost to subjugate the rest of the world to their system? Or are they primarily concerned with the success of communism within Russia, and unwilling to risk all on a world war? Are they still inspired by the original dreams of Marx and Lenin, of raising the standard of living and building the classless society? There are a variety of answers to these and other questions about the U.S.S.R., and evidence can be (and has been) adduced for (and against) all of them. But since nobody can be certain, further speculation would be futile.

IX

We are often told that behind the conflict of power between Russia and the West there is a irreconcilable ideological conflict;

15. Isaiah Berlin, 'The Silence in Russian Culture,' *Foreign Affairs,* October 1957.
16. Cf. John S. Reshetar Jr., *Problems of Analyzing and Predicting Soviet Behavior,* New York, 1955.

that two fundamentally different philosophies and ways of life are at stake; and that the tension can be resolved only when one or the other ideology is stamped out by war. On the one side, obvious to all, is the philosophy of communism, the confused and odious ideology upon which the U.S.S.R. and its satellites are, or profess to be, united. On the other there is something called 'Western civilization.' Exactly what kind of *Weltanschauung* the West stands for is not easy to say; and no wonder, since within it there is something to everyone's taste. It is a rich *smorgasbord* of philosophies, religions, political, economic, and social systems. Is there, behind this surface diversity, agreement among the Western allies upon any kind of fundamental principles?

Private enterprise or free competition is often said to be the basic principle that unites the West. Yet Yugoslavia and Norway are dissenters, and several other countries in the Western camp have had socialist governments at one time or another, and may have them again at the next election; while almost everywhere the capitalist countries have diluted the pure milk of private enterprise and competition. Western Europeans, for the most part, have no intention of fighting an atomic war in defense of private enterprise; and still less is this slogan (or principle) likely to attract support from the masses in the uncommitted countries of the Far East.

Is the West united on the principle of national sovereignty? Curiously enough it is the communist countries which have become notorious for their beating of the nationalist drums, whether in Russia, Yugoslavia, or China. But even more important is the fact that the really strong popular support for a merging of national sovereignties, for schemes of federalism, and for eventual world government comes from within the Western countries themselves. To say that the West stands for complete national sovereignty and the Soviet Union for internationalism is not only to distort the truth but also to invite Western democrats to desert their own side *en masse*.

Is religion something that unites the Western allies? Hardly any part of the globe is more secular in outlook than the Western world. Secularism is often associated with the enjoyment of creature comforts, the good things of this world. In our day the emphasis is on a constantly rising standard of living, measured in such terms as more leisure and a larger output of goods and services. If judged by their actions (and their advertising) the Western peoples seem to attach paramount importance to these material standards. But on this very point the West and the Soviet Union are, for once, in agreement, since both make a fetish of higher productivity and standards of living.

An even more difficult question arises. On which religion are we united — the Jewish, the Moslem, or the Christian? Is Turkey not in the alliance? Is Israel not a friendly neighbor? And if the Christian, which of the innumerable bodies into which Christendom is divided? No doubt if we all belonged to the same church it would unite us; but we do not.

There has been a strong move afoot to put up a fourth uniting principle called 'Western values.' But as one philosopher has said:

> These western values are supposed to consist of toleration, respect for individual liberty, and brotherly love. I am afraid this view is grossly unhistorical. If we compare Europe with other continents, it is marked out as the persecuting continent.[17]

Western history has often shown us the opposite qualities: intolerance, blind obedience to authority, and ruthless self-interest. Values of all kinds can be found in our blood-stained past, but which ones we select depends entirely on our *present* beliefs, and it is precisely the unity of these present beliefs which may be questioned.

Are we bound together by a belief in peaceful change as opposed to violence and revolution? Peaceful political change is a principle adhered to only in the democracies — how does one get a change of government or policy in Spain or the Argentine? — and so is included within the wider principle of democracy. The claim that democracy is the unifying principle of the West, although stronger than the others, is not without weaknesses. A number of democracies stand aloof from the Western alliance, while one of the allies (Yugoslavia) adheres to an ideology similar to that of the

17. B. Russell, *New Hopes for a Changing World*, London, 1951, p. 118.

Soviet Union; one is authoritarian in a clerico-Fascist way (Spain); and South Africa — which must also be counted in the Western camp — introduces an embarrassing racial complication. Clearly we cannot, without qualification, equate the West with democracy.

Nevertheless, the more powerful of the Western nations *are* democracies. The United States, Britain, Canada, for example, do substantially believe in and practice the democratic principles of constitutionalism, political freedom, toleration, and maintain the traditional cultural and civil liberties. Enough other countries are with them on these matters to justify the claim that in a broad general sense the Western cause is the cause of democracy. If the Western allies should triumph, democracy would gain enormously in prestige and influence, and communism in turn would suffer the ignominious fate of Nazism and Fascism.

The agreement is not unanimous, however, by all the nations in the alliance, but is only a kind of majority-nation opinion; and even that does not extend beyond political democracy. One should not, like the Marxists, decry political democracy merely because one believes it is not enough, but it is as well to realize that the Western world differs widely on how far democracy should be extended into the economic and social sphere. Any one interpretation, if pushed too far, may endanger the solidarity of the alliance.

What, then, does unite the West? The answer is simple. It is fear of a possible enemy, the threat of possible aggression, and so the Western nations have allied and armed for self-protection. This may seem a negative sort of union, and of course it is negative to those who favor liberating crusades on behalf of great principles, and the enthusiasm which belief in cosmic ultimates can give. What is often forgotten, however, is that resistance to a common enemy has usually been the chief bond between allies, a classic example having occurred in the Second World War, when the democracies and the Soviet Union fought together against the Nazis.

Such an alliance also has its positive side, since when all the exceptions are allowed for, the Western cause remains, broadly speaking, the cause of democracy. Moreover, each nation within the alliance is also protecting its independence, its way of life, its own ideals, however these may be defined. And while defending what is our own we defend also the essential principle of diversity.

A great deal of nonsense is talked about the need for a faith to unite the West against communism. Many people are frantically looking around for a faith or an idea that can command general assent and inspire the West to the fervor of enthusiasm formerly displayed by the Nazis, and now by communists. But it is more than doubtful whether such an ideal set of values or ultimate principles can be found to command general agreement. Nor is it possible to adopt beliefs merely because they would be useful in the cold war: beliefs on such a scale can be manufactured to order only in the totalitarian states. The very search for a Western faith is a tacit admission that we are not already agreed upon our ideology. The common impression that an ideological conflict has lead to international friction is probably mistaken. It seems nearer the truth that the friction and fears came first, and the clash of ideologies has been called upon in order to bolster morale. There is no logical chain of necessary reasoning from Marxist theory, in all its ambiguity, to the behavior of Soviet imperialism; and neither is there any necessary connection between democracy and political crusading in the international field.

If the preceding argument is sound, then it is misleading and self-deceptive to speak of ideological Western unity where none exists, because such talk tends to gloss over the differences within the Western alliance and to assume that all are democratic, or share some other common philosophy, solely because they are anti-Soviet and reject communism. Moreover, an uncompromising ideological attitude will keep us fighting forever all over the globe, since as soon as one 'bad' principle or philosophy is destroyed another is bound to spring up and offend us. Already there has been friction among the allies, caused by this talk of 'our' ideology. Even the total preparation for an ideological war, and the atmosphere of conformity created, are giving rise to a tendency which, if carried far enough, could convert the West into military states indistinguishable from military tyrannies.

But the most serious immediate danger is this: for the West to adopt the language and attitude of Russia, with constant emphasis on a messianic message, is to make it almost impossible to come to any sort of peaceable *modus vivendi*. Questions of moral principle should not be ignored in international relations and elsewhere in politics, but if it is a mistake to ignore them it is an even worse mistake to elevate every clash of interest into a conflict of sacred principles. In that way we become intransigent, publicly committed beforehand on every issue, until every compromise, every trivial concession, every negotiation is interpreted as surrender, betrayal, or appeasement.

What we tend to forget is that it is not necessary to agree on our metaphysics first in order to agree on policies and to live together without fighting. Differences on ultimates divide Jew from Gentile, Catholic from Protestant, Moslem from Hindu, atheist from believer. And none of these differences is likely to be settled in any foreseeable future. But the slumbering volcanoes need not erupt. We have learned to live together within the democracies, despite the gulfs that divide us, united in our common humanity, in the desire for law and order, and in the procedural agreement to differ.

So in the international sphere. An international community does not necessarily presuppose that we all think alike on fundamentals. We are all united in our will to survive, and it is (or ought to be) perfectly possible to live in a world at peace without deciding whose ultimates are right. War will settle not which side is right but merely which is the more powerful; although victory will no doubt lend prestige to the ideas of the winner.

In the last few years the job of Western statesmanship has been to build the military strength of the West as a precaution against the uncertain intentions of the Soviet Union. On the whole, that job has been done. The great aim now must be to relax the international tension and avoid war. Not at any cost, since we are prepared to fight if attacked, but at the same time with a flexible policy compounded of the inevitable give and take. Each side will keep its basic principles, but that still leaves room to seek agreement on 'second order' principles, on working agreements short of war.

World war is not inevitable unless the Kremlin has world ambitions to be pursued by force of arms, and that is the whole point in dispute. We cannot be sure. One can never be certain when dealing with minds in the Marxist blinkers exactly what prescription they will deduce from their texts. A tenable theory is that they believe their own propaganda. If so, they may rely on the dialectic of history to bring about the inevitable decline of the West. Shortly before his death Stalin taught that the capitalist countries would probably end by fighting one another, and Malenkov once remarked (hopefully) on the growing 'antagonisms' between the United States and its allies. The Soviet leaders may well believe that time is on their side, because of simple population growth, and by reason of their confidence that the continuing Soviet economic development will be enough to prove the superiority of their system, and to serve as a magnet to draw other countries to them. Marxist theory can always be flexibly interpreted — as noted often in earlier chapters — and hence could be used to justify a policy of waiting, and of trying to win neutral countries by any methods short of war. It is not an unreasonable hypothesis, and is presumably that upon which the Western policy of firmness and containment is based.

If, of two neighbors, one is aloof, suspicious, and almost pathological in his fears and fanaticism, and the other is relatively normal and well balanced, the establishment of friendly relations depends almost entirely on the second neighbor. He is the one who must make the overtures, and keep on making them with understanding and almost infinite patience, in the hope that his surly neighbor will eventually become tolerable to live with. If an examination of international politics shows anything, it is that while Russian behavior and attitudes are responsible for most of the international tension, any initiative toward relieving the strain can come only from the comparatively enlightened democracies. And if the initiative is to be taken, then Western policies are in need of revision at some points.

There should be less thinking exclusively in terms of military strategy, or in terms of cold war itself, as though this were the only foreign policy issue, especially in dealings with many countries in the non-communist world. Considerations of military strategy should be confined to the key areas and not allowed to dominate foreign policy everywhere. Again, for the Western countries to eschew communism for themselves is one thing, but to keep up a display of overt hostility to the Soviet system is another since it serves to weld the Russian rulers and people together. Great restraint and patience are required to follow such a policy, when there is no sign of any reciprocal softening of propaganda by the Russians.

Further, it is not reasonable to put impossible conditions upon the Russians, for example to expect them to withdraw from the spheres of influence now occupied on their frontiers. To grant withdrawal would be equivalent — as the Hungarian rebellion showed — to permitting the satellites to join the Western camp. Again, the official policy of the Western nations is settled: they will not launch any war of liberation. The numerous exiles and refugees who have sought asylum in the West have every right to expect generous and humane treatment. Their lot is tragic, like that of their occupied homelands, but, unfortunately, suffering does not qualify them for the statesman's craft in a world that requires sober thought and steady judgment.

Above all, the best chance of bringing a divided world together in a comity of nations lies in specific and co-operative efforts — Western and Russian association in UNESCO, in United Nations Technical Assistance; the travel and interchange of persons; and world trade, including trade with China and the Iron Curtain countries. (The West is by no means guiltless here, since trade and travel have been discouraged by the democracies as well as by Russia.) It is an economic axiom that trade benefits both sides and is a road to prosperity. Perhaps nothing can diminish the fanaticism, envy, and resentment of the communist countries, but if anything at all is likely to do so it is prosperity. Yet, no matter how Western policy may shift its emphasis toward negotiation and co-operation in order to convince the Russians of Western good will, the outlook is not bright. But such a change is the only hope; to cling to the older, more militant policies can only perpetuate mutual hostility.

X

At one level the division of the world is between two power blocs, while many neutrals sit with differing degrees of comfort and uneasy consciences on the fences. At a deeper, and in the long run perhaps more significant, level the division is between the wealthy democracies and the rest of the world, which is miserably poor. The test of democratic statesmanship is not, therefore, only how negotiations with the U.S.S.R. are handled, but what kind of leadership is given to the Middle and Far East, to Africa and South America.

Marx was wrong about the social trends of industrial societies. Instead of the domestic class war, what has occurred is a division of the world into poor and rich nations, and the gap between them is if anything growing wider — on a globe where the population is increasing by 25 millions a year, and mostly in the poorer countries.

Class war has not appeared in the leading democracies, because they have gone through an industrial and agricultural revolution which has raised productivity almost beyond the dreams of avarice, and because the growth of democracy has insured that the benefits are widely spread. Similar developments must go on in many other countries before they, too, are immune to communist agitation, and if the democracies do not lead this technological and social revolution abroad, the communists can hardly fail to take over.

Communism has in fact a number of advantages in bidding for support in the poorer countries. It appeals to elemental feelings, the hunger for bread and land; to easily stirred emotions of anti-colonialism and hatred of landlords. It is aimed at people with almost 'nothing to lose but their chains' living in societies with a more rigid and often oppressive class structure. Conveniently it ignores the terrible urgency of the problems arising from 'the population explosion.' The cure which it advocates for poverty is simple enough to reach even the most ignorant: behind the primal act of revolution lies the millennium of plenty and equality. Nor does it matter, for propaganda purposes, that the promises cannot be redeemed, the expectations gratified, since by the time a nation wakes up to the grim reality its people are already in chains and can no longer demand that the contract be fulfilled.

The ideals of democracy have a universal and powerful attraction: they are generous, humane, hopeful, and international.

Communist parties in the poorer countries capitalize on these ideals, posing as national liberators and as the conscience of civilization.

The handicaps of the Western democracies are serious, and not always fully realized. Some of these — such as the publicity which attends discussion of public policy — are inherent in the democratic system, while others are written into the historical record. Asia and Africa, for instance, are far more inclined to be suspicious of the Western world than of Russia. Russia has been aloof and is not known, its interference by means of communist parties is, so to speak, a 'proxy' fight, and so does not arouse the same suspicions of 'imperialism,' while, as Toynbee has emphasized, throughout most of the Christian era the West has been the aggressor in relation to the rest of the world. The West is still tainted with colonialism in spite of the fact that many former colonies have achieved independence and many more are traveling the same road. All too often, too, the West, under military necessity, has been associated with the 'old regimes' against which the social revolution is proceeding, whereas the communists can be counted upon to make the most of every popular movement against the old regimes.

Communism today goes beyond philosophy and even beyond a political movement. It is also an economic and social program of rapid industrialization: the promise of a short cut, via a temporary dictatorship, from poverty to abundance. The program makes irrelevant nearly all that Marx wrote in his diagnosis of the future of industrial society, and transforms communism into a policy adapted almost wholly to the circumstances of underdeveloped and/or colonial areas. Hence the mere refutation of Marxist-Leninist theory, through necessary, will never defeat a communist party or frustrate communist foreign policy designs.

A grave weakness therefore of democratic policy, only recently and still insufficiently recognized, has been the framing of an alternative to the communist program: how to promote industrialization and social reform quickly, under democratic leadership and within a framework of constitutionalism. Dictatorship is a method that may be used anywhere, but it is not at all easy to make democracy work even where the underlying conditions are favorable. For the communists the problem of methods is settled, since, not being hampered by democratic scruples, they can force industrialization through ruthlessly, without reckoning the cost in terms of human suffering. Discontent is crushed, not met by argument, concession, or compromise. Should the Soviet Union continue to forge ahead with its economic development, then many countries may look to it as a model, seeing only the end result of national power and modern industry, while forgetting the generations since 1917 who had to pay the heavy price.

The democracies have one great advantage. Not being handicapped by the rigid Marxist categories of analysis, they ought to be far ahead of the Soviet Union in their understanding of the thinking and needs of the poorer countries. It is a great mistake to assume that communist governments are always wise, rational, and successful in either their propaganda or policies.[18] The democracies also have an advantage, not fully exploited, in that their borders are not sealed off, so that Asians and others may come and see what life is like — instead of relying on propaganda and escorted tours. The 'red tape' curtain which hangs around some of the democracies is still much more permeable than iron, and there is no reason why the tape cannot be trimmed here and there.

The spectacle of two power groups competing for the allegiance of the uncommitted countries, and treating them like pawns in the game of power politics, is not a nice one. For that reason alone the prime mistake to be avoided by the democracies is to proffer aid solely on grounds of self-interest, of acquiring allies, and of keeping Asia, say, out of the communist camp. To give assistance subject to tests of political conformity is a policy that is doomed to failure. National independence and forms of government must be respected, and nowhere more so than in countries where nationalism came late; and aid and trade must be embarked upon because of the principles of democracy itself: the sense of duty to

18. Michael Lindsay, in *China and the Cold War*, Melbourne, 1955, gives many examples of where adherence to dogma has blinded communists to reality.

others, the recognition of their human dignity and racial and national equality, and of their full right to accept or reject whatever is offered.

Most of the underdeveloped countries are interested in Russia or the West only insofar as they themselves are affected by Russian or Western policies. They are not convinced by mere protestations of good will and unselfish intentions, and often have no concern with a democratic or a communist ideology, both of which may be 'foreign.' Their practical interests lie in independence, in trade and investment, in the necessities of life, and in the benefits which modern technology can provide. Any kind of ideology or system which brings or promises these things is likely to capture their imagination and allegiance. The Western democracies are fortunately placed in this respect, since they have the resources, skills, and machines which the poor people of the earth so desperately want.

Investment and technological and all other forms of aid to the underdeveloped countries are less suspect as militarism or 'imperialism' when they come through international agencies, as through the United Nations, or when they are the joint affairs of several nations, as in the Colombo Plan. The generosity behind the U.S. Point Four Program is doubtless genuine, but it is difficult to make it appear so in the eyes of the recipient countries, and it is no use for a donor country to expect displays of public gratitude. Although the measures already carried out have done far more for the recipients than Russia has done for all its satellites and the neutrals combined, yet only the most complacent could regard the steps so far taken as anything but tragically inadequate in view of the almost bottomless need.[19]

The democracies, in the last decade, have shown their readiness to make the necessary sacrifices for rearmament. But this is not what carries conviction to the poor and uncommitted countries, since they can easily interpret it as the rich fighting to hold what

19. One should not minimize Soviet economic aid in this day of 'competitive co-existence.' See Joseph S. Berliner, *Soviet Economic Aid*, New York, 1958.

they have.[20] The best way to show that democracy is worth defending, and worth copying is, over the long pull, to make the equally necessary and possibly even greater sacrifices required to assist and strengthen, economically and politically, the have-not nations of the world. The democracies must make themselves the source of help and hope and aspiration for the hundreds of millions of awakening peoples.

It is all a race against time, and the outcome is uncertain. We may never be willing to give up much of our overflowing abundance; and even if we do we cannot be sure that democratic deeds will be more effective and persuasive than communist agitation and promises. But we ought to try: our principles give us no honorable alternative.

20. John K. Galbraith's book *The Affluent Society*, New York, 1958, sketches a wealthy North America which must seem quite out of this world to the poor nations of the earth.

A Guide
to the Literature of Marxism

THIS BRIEF GUIDE has been compiled for the use of the general reader and for those students who wish to read somewhat further in Marxism. It is not meant, however, for the specialist, and for that reason only English-language sources are given. There is no great disadvantage in this, since all important works on Marxism have in fact been translated into English.

1. A NOTE ON BIOGRAPHIES.

(a) *Marx and Engels*. It is rather surprising, in view of the historical impact of Marx and Engels, that so few biographies of these men have been written.

The standard biography of Marx is still Franz Mehring, *Karl Marx, The Story of His Life*, translated by E. Fitzgerald, London, 1936 and 1948. Although Marxist in outlook, it is not entirely un-critical. Since it was written in 1920, its bibliography is now partly superseded.

A similar work is Otto Ruhle, *Karl Marx, His Life and Work*, New York, 1929.

A sympathetic short life is Max Beer, *The Life and Teaching of Karl Marx*, London, 1929

A first-rate short biography, emphasizing ideas more than personalities, is that by I. Berlin, *Karl Marx, His Life and Environment*, London, 1939 and 1948.

My personal preference leads me to place the study by E. H. Carr, *Karl Marx, A Study in Fanaticism*, London, 1935, at the top of the list of Marx's biographies in English for the general reader and beginning student.

The recent biography by L. Schwarzchild, *The Red Prussian*, New York, 1947, has the sole virtue of containing some new material, but it contains so much abuse that its interpretation of Marx's character is misleading.

The only biography of Engels in English is Gustav Mayer, *Friedrich Engels*, London, 1935. There are a number of shorter biographies of Marx, only one or two having any merit.

(b) *Lenin, Stalin, et al.*

D. Shub, *Lenin: A Biography*, New York, 1948. By a former Menshevik; useful, but dull reading.

Bertram D. Wolfe, *Three Who made a Revolution: Lenin, Trotsky and Stalin*, New York, 1948. Easy to read.

L. Trotsky, *Stalin: An Appraisal of the Man and His Influence*, New York, 1941. Assumes the truth of Marxism, but is, naturally enough, unflattering to Stalin.

I. Deutscher, *Stalin: A Political Biography*, New York, 1949. Probably the best work on Stalin.

I. Deutscher, *The Prophet Armed: Trotsky, 1879–1921*, New York, 1953. A lively work dealing with Trotsky's rise to the peak of his influence in Russia. *The Prophet Unarmed: Trotsky, 1921–1929*, New York, 1959, relates the story of his fall and exile. A third volume is planned.

E. H. Carr, *Bakunin*, London, 1937. The life of Marx's great rival in the First International.

G. P. Maximoff (ed.), *The Political Philosophy of Bakunin: Scientific Anarchism*, Glencoe, Ill., 1953.

George Woodcock, *Pierre-Joseph Proudhon*, London, 1956. The life of the greatest early French socialist, who had a considerable influence upon Marx.

2. GENERAL WORKS AND SOURCES.

(a) *Original Sources.* The most convenient sources for the most important works of Marx and Engels are:

Selected Works of Marx and Engels, 2 vols., London, 1942. Another *Selected Works* in two volumes was published in Moscow and London, 1951, with some different selections.

Selected Correspondence of Marx and Engels, 1846–1895, London, 1934. Marx and Engels were prolific letter writers, and many of the letters in this volume are much quoted and sometimes throw light upon disputed points of Marxist theory.

Handbook of Marxism, ed. by Emile Burns, New York, 1934. Contains also some of the writings of Lenin and Stalin.

Capital, *the* Communist Manifesto *and Other Writings by Karl Marx: with an Essay on Marxism by V. I. Lenin,* ed. by Max Eastman, New York, 1932.

Marx and the Marxists, The Ambiguous Legacy, by Sidney Hook, New York, 1955. A short but varied selection of communist documents.

Lenin, *Selected Works,* 2 vols., Moscow, 1947 and 1951. Probably sufficient for any but the specialist, for whom there is a *Selected Works of Lenin,* 12 vols., New York, 1936–9; and other extensive collections.

Stalin, *Leninism, Selected Writings,* New York, 1938. A collection of writings and speeches of Stalin, to 1926, abridged from the longer two-volume work, *Problems of Leninism.*

Trotsky, *Selected Works,* edited by Max Schacktman, 7 vols., New York, 1936; *The Revolution Betrayed,* New York, 1937; *Trotsky's Diary in Exile, 1935,* Cambridge, Mass., 1958. Trotsky learned nothing, even from his exile.

Many of the separate writings of Marx, Engels, Lenin, Stalin, Mao Tse-tung, and of numerous other Marxists are available in pamphlet or book form from International Publishers, New York, and Lawrence and Wishart, London. Beginning in 1953, the latter have brought out the collected works of Stalin in 16 volumes. They are tiresome reading but enlightening for the Stalinist period of the Soviet Union, especially when contrasted with post-Stalin 'debunking.'

Mao Tse-tung, *Selected Works,* 4 vols., New York, 1954–6. These selections take his work only to 1945. Among his later writings are: *On Practice,* New York, 1953; *On Contradiction,* New York, 1953; *Let a Hundred Flowers Bloom: 'On the Correct Han-*

dling of Contradictions among the People,' ed. by G. F. Hudson, New York, 1957. Mao Tse-tung is obviously a more intelligent man than Stalin was.

History of the Communist Party of the Soviet Union (Bolsheviks), New York, 1939. Often ascribed to Stalin.

(b) *Assessments.* Many general surveys of Marxism have been made, some of them propagandist and quite misleading for the student. From the better, i.e. more objective and reliable, I choose the following.

G. D. H. Cole, *The Meaning of Marxism,* London, 1950.

E. F. M. Durbin, *The Politics of Democratic Socialism,* London, 1940. Contains a careful critique of Marxism.

W. Gurian, *Bolshevism: Theory and Practice,* New York, 1932.

Sidney Hook, *Towards the Understanding of Karl Marx,* London, 1936. Very generous to Marx's inconsistencies.

R. N. Carew Hunt, *The Theory and Practice of Communism,* rev. ed., New York, 1957. One of the best surveys; fuller on the practice than on the theory. The same author's *Marxism Past and Present,* New York, 1954, strengthens his theoretical analysis.

Herbert Marcuse, *Soviet Marxism, A Critical Analysis,* New York, 1958. An interesting analysis, which takes seriously the dialectic as a tool.

Klaus Mehnert, *Stalin verus Marx,* London, 1952. Shows briefly how Stalin turned, especially during World War II, from Marx to nationalism.

Alfred G. Meyer, *Marxism,* Cambridge, Mass., 1954; and *Leninism,* Cambridge, Mass., 1957. Able studies with a historical approach.

H. and B. Overstreet, *What We Must Know about Communism,* New York, 1959. A chatty and popular book.

H. B. Parkes, *Marxism: An Autopsy,* Boston, 1939

John Plamenatz, *German Marxism and Russian Communism,* London, 1954. A first-rate detailed analysis of changes in the theory.

K. R. Popper, *The Open Society and Its Enemies,* Princeton, 1950. The enemies are Plato, Hegel, and Marx.

B. Russell, *The Practice and Theory of Bolshevism,* London, 1920 and 1948. Has stood the test of time.

Rudolph Schlesinger, *Marx: His Time and Ours,* London, 1950. A full-scale critique. somewhat heavily Germanic.

Joseph A. Schumpeter, *Capitalism, Socialism, and Democracy*, London, 3rd ed., 1950.

Edmund Wilson, *To the Finland Station*, New York, 1940.

3. DIALETICAL MATERIALISM.

Marx himself can scarcely be said to have given any systematic exposition of dialectical materialism, but the following contain his more important remarks on the subject. Engels was more interested and wrote at greater length, often very superficially. Later Marxist writings are not much more than glosses on Engels.

(a) *Expositions.*

V. Adoratsky, *Dialectical Materialism*, New York, 1934.

M. Cornforth, *In Defense of Philosophy*, London, 1950. A Marxist onslaught upon positivism, pragmatism, and other schools. *Dialectical Materialism: An Introductory Course*, London, 1952.

Engels, *Anti-Dühring*, London, 1935; *Ludwig Feuerbach and the Outcome of Classical German Philosophy*, New York, 1934; *Dialectics of Nature*, New York, 1940.

D. Guest, *A Textbook of Dialectical Materialism*, New York, 1939.

T. A. Jackson, *Dialectics: The Logic of Marxism and Its Critics*, London, 1936. This must be one of the longest, most logic-chopping, and most abusive books ever written on the subject. It even outdoes Lenin's *Materialism*.

Lenin, *On Dialectics* in *Selected Works*, 1947; *Materialism and Empirio-Criticism*, New York, 1927.

Jack Lindsay, *Marxism and Contemporary Science*, London, 1949.

Marx, 'A Critique of the Hegelian Philosophy of Right,' in *Selected Essays*, trans. by H. J. Stenning, New York, 1926.

Marx, *The Poverty of Philosophy*, New York, 1936.

Marx and Engels, *German Ideology*, trans. by R. Pascal, New York, 1939.

G. P. Plekhanov, *In Defense of Materialism*, London, 1947.

Stalin, *Dialectical and Historical Materialism;* as a separate pamphlet, or in *Leninism, Selected Writings*, op. cit., or in Ch. 4 of *History of the Communist Party of the Soviet Union (Bolsheviks)*, New York, 1939. Stalin can hardly be called a philosopher, and he was wise to refrain from writing much philosophy.

The following three are by Marxist scientists, and all attempt the impossible task of showing how Marxism can benefit science.

J. D. Bernal, *Marxism and Science*, London, 1952.

J. B. S. Haldane, *The Marxist Philosophy and the Sciences*, London, 1938.

H. Levy, *A Philosophy for a Modern Man*, London, 1938.

(b) *Assessments*.

H. B. Acton, *The Illusion of the Epoch: Marxism-Leninism as a Philosophical Creed*, London, 1955. An excellent critique.

Max Eastman, *Marxism: Is It Science?*, London, 1941.

P. Geyl, 'Dialectic in History,' *Journal of the History of Ideas*, January 1949.

For a sympathetic account of Hegel's philosophy see two books by G. R. G. Mure, *An Introduction to Hegel*, Oxford, 1940; and *A Study of Hegel's Logic*, Oxford, 1950.

Sidney Hook, *From Hegel to Marx*, London, 1936.

J. M. E. McTaggart, *Studies in the Hegelian Dialectic*, Cambridge, 1922.

Alexander Philipov, *Logic and Dialectic in the Soviet Union*, New York, 1952. Shows how formal logic was rehabilitated in the Soviet Union in 1950.

K. R. Popper, 'What is Dialectic?' *Mind*, vol. 49, 1940.

J. Somerville, *Soviet Philosophy*, New York, 1946.

Gustav A. Wetter, *Dialectical Materialism*, New York, 1958. A complete, monumental work.

On science and dialectical materialism in the U.S.S.R.:

Eric Ashby, *Scientist in Russia*, Baltimore, 1947.

Julian Huxley, *Soviet Genetics*, London, 1949.

Conway Zirkle (ed.), *Death of a Science in Russia*, Philadelphia, 1949. This book outlines, with selections from Russian documents, the steps by which scientific genetics was forced to give way to the views of the Lysenko faction.

T. D. Lysenko and others, *The Situation in Biological Science*, New York, 1949. Stenographic report of the genetics debate at a Soviet Scientific Conference.

Soviet Science, a symposium arranged by Conway Zirkle and Howard A. Meyerhoff, Washington, 1952.

4. ECONOMIC INTERPRETATION OF HISTORY AND THE CLASS STRUGGLE.

(a) *Expositions*.

The economic interpretation of history and the class struggle runs through almost everything that Marx and Engels wrote. The shortest and most eloquent statement of Marx's theory of history is the Preface which he wrote to his *Critique of Political Economy,* and which may be found in any copy of his *Selected Works.* More extended treatment is found in:

Marx, *The Poverty of Philosophy,* translated by C. P. Dutt, New York, 1936.

Marx and Engels, *The German Ideology,* New York, 1939.

Engels, *Anti-Dühring,* London, 1935. See also letters on historical materialism in *Selected Correspondence,* 1934; and *Selected Works,* 1942 and 1951.

Engels, *Origin of the Family, Private Property and the State,* London, 1940.

For more particular reference to the class struggle, or for the application of the Marxist analysis, showing Marx at his most plausible and stimulating, see:

Marx, *Communist Manifesto.* (There are innumerable editions.)

Marx, *The Class Struggles in France, 1848–50; The Eighteenth Brumaire of Louis Bonaparte* (1851); *The Civil War in France* (*1870–71*). These may be found in *Selected Works,* 1942 and 1951.

Marx and Engels, *Germany: Revolution and Counter Revolution, 1851–52,* London, 1933. The work consists of a collection of articles which appeared in the *New York Tribune* when Marx was its European correspondent. The articles were written by Engels, but at first were credited to Marx.

Engels, *Condition of the Working Class in England,* trans. by Chaloner and Henderson, Oxford, 1958.

Engels, *Principles of Communism,* a new translation by Paul M. Sweezy, New York, 1952.

Engels, *The British Labour Movement,* London, 1934.

G. P. Plekhanov, *The Materialist Conception of History,* London, 1940; *Fundamental Problems of Marxism,* London, 1941; *The Role of the Individual in History,* London, 1940. Plekhanov was a Menshevik, a scholarly gentleman of the old school of Marxists. His works were much admired by Lenin, who often recommended them to his followers.

A few of Lenin's shorter writings dealt with historical materialism; for example, his pamphlet: *The Teachings of Karl Marx,* London, 1931.

Stalin's most succinct account is contained in his *Dialectical and Historical Materialism,* op. cit.

C. Caudwell, *Studies in a Dying Culture,* London, 1949.

(b) *Criticisms.*

E. R. A. Seligman, *The Economic Interpretation of History,* London, 1902.

Karl Federn, *The Materialist Conception of History,* London, 1939.

L. Robbins, *Economic Basis of Class Conflict,* New York, 1939.

M. M. Bober, *Karl Marx's Interpretation of History,* Cambridge, Mass., rev. ed. 1948.

See also General Works and Sources.

5. MARXIST ECONOMICS.

(a) *Expositions.*

Marx, *Wage-Labour and Capital* in *Selected Works,* 1942 and 1951, and in Algernon Lee (ed.), *The Essentials of Marx,* New York, 1946.

Marx, *Value, Price and Profit,* London, 1931.

Marx, *A Contribution to the Critique of Political Economy,* Chicago, 1911.

Marx, *Capital,* 3 vols., translated by S. Moore and E. Aveling, London, 1909–13; also *Capital,* 3 vols., Chicago, 1933. There are a number of English editions of Volume I.

The first volume was in fact the only volume of *Capital* brought out by Marx during his lifetime. After Marx's death the faithful Engels put together two more volumes from Marx's notes, and these were first published in 1885 and 1894 respectively.

The rest of Marx's material (intended as the fourth volume of *Capital*) was later brought out in 3 volumes by Karl Kautsky, under the title of *Theorien über den Mehrwert,* Stuttgart, 1905–10. In 1952 a large part of the Kautsky material was brought out in English under the title: Karl Marx, *Theories of Surplus Value,* translated by G. A. Bonner and Emile Burns, London, 1952.

Engels, *The Housing Question,* in *Selected Works,* 1951, vol. I.

K. Kautsky, *The Economic Doctrines of Karl Marx,* London, 1925.

W. H. Emmet, *Marxian Economic Handbook,* New York, 1925.

M. Dobb, *Marx as an Economist—An Essay* (pamphlet), London, 1946; *Political Economy and Capitalism,* London, 1937, New York, 1939; *Studies in the Development of Capitalism,* London, 1947.

Paul M. Sweezy, *The Theory of Capitalist Development,* New

York, revised ed. 1956. The most comprehensive Marxist discussion
of Marxist economics, including imperialism.

Political Economy in the Soviet Union, translated by E. A.
Kazakevich, New York, 1944.

Eugene Varga, *Two Systems: Socialist Economy and Capitalist
Economy,* New York, 1939.

Stalin, *Economic Problems of Socialism in the U.S.S.R.,* Moscow,
1952 (a pamphlet that does a good deal to restore economic studies to
respectability and sense within the Soviet Union. Whatever the reasons for it may be, Stalin similarly intervened in the linguistics controversy, to rescue the study of philology from the sterility into
which it had fallen. Stalin, *Marxism and Linguistics,* New York,
1951).

(b) *Assessments.*

E. von Böhm-Bawerk, *Karl Marx and the Close of His System,*
new edition by Paul M. Sweezy, New York, 1949. The classic refutation of Marx's economic theory.

B. Croce, *Historical Materialism and the Economics of Karl
Marx,* New York, 1914.

H. W. B. Joseph, *The Labour Theory of Value in Karl Marx,*
London, 1923.

A. D. Lindsay, *Karl Marx's Capital,* London, 1931 and 1947.

Joan Robinson, *An Essay on Marxian Economics,* London, 1947.

[Books on the economics of non-Marxian socialism — whether
written by Marxists or not — have been omitted from this guide. The
literature is abundant, and any economist can advise the student.]

6. MARXIST VIEWS ON NATIONALISM, COLONIALISM, AND THE
   PEASANTRY.

(a) *Original Sources.*

Dona Torr (ed.), *Marx on China, 1853–1860:* Articles from the
New York Daily Tribune, London, 1951.

Marx, *The British Rule in India; The Future Results of
British Rule in India,* in *Selected Works,* 1942 and 1951.

Marx and Engels, *The Russian Menace to Europe,* ed. by Paul
W. Blackstock and Bert F. Hoselitz, Glencoe, Ill., 1952; *Letters to
Americans, 1848–1895,* New York, 1953.

Marx, *Relations between the Irish and English Working
Classes,* in *Handbook.* See also letters 'On Ireland' and 'On
Colonies' in *Selected Correspondence.*

Engels, *The Peasant Question in France and Germany*, in *Selected Works*, 1951, II.

Lenin, *The Agrarian Question and the Critics of Marx, The Iskra Period*, vol. I, New York, 1929.

Lenin, *Imperialism; The Highest Stage of Capitalism*, London 1940; *The Imperialist War (1914–18)*, New York, 1940; *The Right of Nations to Self-Determination*, New York, 1940.

Stalin, *The International Situation, 1927*. Deals with China; may be found in *Handbook*.

Stalin, *Marxism and the National and Colonial Question*, English edition, Moscow, 1940.

Dona Torr (ed.), *Marxism, Nationality and War*, London, 1940. Two small booklets, mostly quotations, from which it is hard to disentangle any consistent argument.

Lenin and Stalin wrote further on these subjects. See *Selected Works*.

(b) *Assessments*.

W. K. Hancock, *Wealth of Colonies*, Cambridge, 1950.

L. Robbins, *The Economic Causes of War*, London, 1939.

David Mitrany, *Marx against the Peasant*, London, 1951. Contains a useful bibliography.

7. Party, Revolution, and Dictatorship of the Proletariat.
(Including the Marxist theory of the state.)

(a) *Sources*. Marx's whole theory is meant of course to point the way toward the revolution, and everything he wrote is oriented to that purpose. The references to the role and nature of the party, the use of violence, the timing of the revolution, and what will follow thereafter must for the most part be found scattered throughout his works. A few specific works may, however, be listed.

The Communist Manifesto itself is the classic statement, but this must be supplemented by the *Address of the Central Council to the Communist League (1850)*. His political ideas are also found in the important *Critique of the Gotha Programme*, 1875. (All are in *Selected Works*.)

The ideas of Engels may be found in his *Origin of the Family, Private Property and the State*, London, 1940; and in his short article *On Authority (Selected Works.)*

Almost everything that Lenin wrote deals with these important subjects, and it would be a work of supererogation to list them in detail. See *Selected Works*, where in numerous writings Lenin deals with party and tactics, the seizure and maintenance of power, and so on. In particular, however, mention should be made of:

Lenin, *State and Revolution* (1916), New York, 1932. The plainest and most utopian of his views.

Lenin on Trade Unions and Revolution 1893–1917, ed. by T. T. Hammond, New York, 1957.

Lenin, *The Proletarian Revolution and the Renegade Kautsky,* London, 1918; written in reply to K. Kautsky, *Terrorism and Communism,* London, 1920. Trotsky wrote his reply to Kautsky in his pamphlet, *Defence of Terrorism* (1920).

Many of the speeches of Stalin, his reports to party congresses, etc., also deal with the subjects of party, revolution, and international affairs.

K. Kautsky, *The Class Struggle* (Erfurt Program), Chicago, 1910; *The Dictatorship of the Proletariat,* London, n.d.

Rosa Luxemburg, *Reform or Revolution,* New York, 1937.

A good deal of information may be found in the extremely tendentious book: *History of the Communist Party of the Soviet Union (Bolsheviks),* New York, 1939.

(b) *Assessments.*

I. Berlin, 'Political Ideas in the Twentieth Century,' *Foreign Affairs,* April 1950.

Eduard Bernstein, *Evolutionary Socialism,* London, 1909. A kind of Fabianism. Abused as 'revisionist' by Kautsky, Rosa Luxemburg, Lenin, and other communists.

E. H. Carr, *The Bolshevik Revolution, 1917–23,* 3 vols., London, 1950–53. Vol. I has a note on Lenin's theory of the state, and on the Bolshevik doctrine of self-determination. Vol. III has a note on the Marxist attitude to war.

S. H. M. Chang, *The Marxian Theory of the State,* Philadelphia, 1931. A survey, but not a criticism, of all aspects of the Marxist theory of the state.

Peter Gay, *The Dilemma of Democratic Socialism; Eduard Bernstein's Challenge to Marx,* New York, 1952.

Hans Kelsen, *The Political Theory of Bolshevism; A Critical Analysis,* Berkeley, 1948; *The Communist Theory of Law,* New York, 1955.

8. PHILOSOPHY OF HISTORY

Marx and Marxists have written nothing that is specifically labeled 'a philosophy of history' in the now fashionable sense of that phrase.

Nevertheless a philosophy of history is contained in Marxist thought, and may be assembled from the many references throughout almost all of Marx's writings. On the general subject of philosophy of history the following works are useful.

Isaiah Berlin, *Historical Inevitability*, London, 1954.

J. B. Bury, *The Idea of Progress*, London, 1924.

M. R. Cohen, *The Meaning of Human History*, La Salle, Ill., 1947.

William H. Dray, *Laws and Explanation in History*, London, 1957.

S. W. Dyde, *Hegel's Philosophy of History*, London, 1922.

P. Gardiner, *The Nature of Historical Explanation*, London, 1952.

G. W. F. Hegel, *The Philosophy of History*, trans. by J. Sibree, New York, 1900.

Herbert Marcuse, *Reason and Revolution: Hegel and the Rise of Social Theory*, New York, 1941. This is perhaps the best account of Hegel's thought.

G. J. Renier, *History, Its Purpose and Method*, London, 1950.

Toynbee may most conveniently be read in the two-volume abridgement *A Study of History* by D. C. Somervell, New York, 1946, 1957. The best answer to Toynbee's more ambitious speculations has been given by P. Geyl, in 'Toynbee's Systems of Civilization,' *Journal of the History of Ideas*, January 1948; and *The Pattern of the Past: Can We Determine It?* by Geyl, Toynbee, and Sorokin, Boston, 1949.

9. MARXISM, MORALITY, AND RELIGION.

It is not possible to point to a systematic treatment by Marx and Engels of either morality or religion. The student must consult the *Selected Works,* especially the philosophical writings of Engels. A few books on these subjects are:

(a) *Expositions.*

Lenin, *Religion*, New York, 1933 (pamphlet).

V. Venable, *Human Nature: The Marxian View*, New York, 1945.

Howard Selsam, *Socialism and Ethics*, New York, 1943.

K. Kautsky, *Ethics and the Materialist Conception of History*, Chicago, 1913.

K. Kautsky, *Foundations of Christianity*, New York, 1925.

(b) *Assessments.*

I. B. Barron and H. M. Waddams, *Communism and the Churches: A Documentation,* London, 1950. (Contains also the Vatican decree of wholesale excommunication of communists in Italy in 1949.)

John C. Bennet, *Christianity and Communism,* London, 1949.

Paul Blanshard, *Communism, Democracy and Catholic Power,* Boston, 1951.

J. M. Cameron, *Scrutiny of Marxism,* London, 1948. A useful little critique of Marxist ethics.

W. Gurian (ed.), *The Soviet Union, Background, Ideology and Reality,* Notre Dame, 1951.

D. M. MacKinnon (ed.), *Christian Faith and Communist Faith,* London, 1953.

John MacMurray, *Creative Society: A Study of the Relation of Christianity to Communism,* London, 1936.

J. Middleton Murry, *et al., Marxism,* London, 1935.

R. Schlesinger (ed.), *The Family in the U.S.S.R.,* London, 1949.

N. S. Timasheff, *Religion in Soviet Russia,* New York, 1943.

The Church under Communism, The Second Report of the Church of Scotland, New York, 1953. (The First Report, 1951, was *The Challenge of Communism.*)

The Truth about Religion in Russia. Official statement of the Moscow Patriarchate on the position of the Orthodox Church, London, 1943.

Charles C. West, *Communism and the Theologians,* London, 1958.

A few of the more balanced books by ex-communists:

Edith Bone, *Seven Years Solitary,* London, 1958. A good personal account of a human spirit rising above the cruelties of communist imprisonment.

R. H. S. Crossman (ed.), *The God That Failed,* London, 1950.

André Gide, *Retour de l'U.R.S.S.,* Paris, 1936; *Retouches à mon retour de l'U.R.S.S.,* Paris, 1937.

Douglas Hyde, *I Believed,* London, 1950.

Arthur Koestler, *Arrow in the Blue,* 1952; *The Invisible Writing,* London, 1954.

10. BOOKS ABOUT THE SOVIET UNION

'Soviet Studies' must now be regarded as a major industry in the

U.S.A., and the number of books on one or other aspect of the subject is beyond counting. The list given here contains only a tiny selection of the most helpful.

Raymond A. Bauer, Alex Inkeles, and Clyde Kluckhohn, *How the Soviet System Works; Cultural, Psychological, and Social Themes,* Cambridge Mass., 1956.

E. H. Carr, *A History of Soviet Russia,* London, 1950–58. The first 3 vols. are on *The Bolshevik Revolution, 1917–23,* vol. 4 is *The Interregnum, 1923–24,* and vol. 5 is *Socialism in One Country, 1924–26.*

Merle Fainsod, *How Russia Is Ruled,* Cambridge, Mass., 1953.

Leo Gruliow (ed.), *Current Soviet Policies: The Documentary Record of the 19th Communist Party Congress and the Reorganization after Stalin's Death,* New York, 1953; and *Current Soviet Policies: The Documentary Record of the 20th Communist Party Congress and Its Aftermath,* New York, 1957.

John N. Hazard, *Law and Social Change in the U.S.S.R.,* London, 1953; *The Soviet System of Government,* Chicago, 1957.

Samuel Hendel (ed.), *The Soviet Crucible; Soviet Government in Theory and Practice,* Princeton, 1959. A book of widely varied readings, with bibliography.

Alexander G. Korol, *Soviet Education for Science and Technology,* Cambridge, Mass., 1957.

Barrington Moore Jr., *Soviet Politics: The Dilemma of Power,* Cambridge, Mass., 1951.

Alan Moorehead, *The Russian Revolution,* New York, 1958. A very readable account.

Joseph Revai, 'On the Character of Our People's Democracy,' *Foreign Affairs,* March-April 1949, October 1949.

W. W. Rostow, *The Dynamics of Soviet Society,* New York, 1953.

R. Schlesinger, *The Spirit of Post-War Russia,* London 1947; *Soviet Legal Theory; Its Social Background and Development,* New York, 1945.

Ernest J. Simmons (ed.), *Continuity and Change in Russian and Soviet Thought,* Cambridge, Mass., 1955. A compendium of 26 papers of high quality.

The Land of Socialism Today and Tomorrow. Reports and speeches at the Eighteenth Congress of the Communist Party of the Soviet Union (Bolsheviks), 10–21 March 1939, Moscow, 1939.

A. Vyshinsky, *Law of the Soviet State,* New York, 1948.

Among numerous other authors whose works may be consulted are Raymond A. Bauer, Abram Bergson, Nicholas Berdyaev, Frederick Barghoorn, Edward Crankshaw, David J. Dallin, John Gunther, Leopold H. Haimson, A. Inkeles, George F. Kennan, Walter Kolarz, Nathan Leites, Gerhard Niemeyer, Julian Towster, and Warren B. Walsh. Excellent books are put out by centers of Russian Research such as those at Columbia University and Harvard University.

11. DEMOCRACY AND MARXISM

(a) *The History of the Communist Movement.*

Max Beer, *Fifty Years of International Socialism*, London, 1937.

Franz Borkenau, *The Communist International*, London, 1938. Covers the Third International, and more important national communist parties.

G. D. H. Cole, *A History of Socialist Thought*, 4 vols., London, 1953–57. A new standard work. Vol. II deals with *Marxism and Anarchism, 1850–1890,* vol. III with *The Second International, 1889–1914,* vol. IV with *Communism and Social Democracy, 1914–1931.*

Alexander Gray, *The Socialist Tradition from Moses to Lenin*, London, 1946.

J. Lenz, *The Second International*, New York, 1932.

Arthur Rosenberg, *A History of Bolshevism*, London, 1939.

Hugh Seton-Watson, *From Lenin to Malenkov, The History of World Communism*, New York, 1957.

(b) *On Communism and International Problems.*

Gabriel A. Almond, *The Appeals of Communism*, Princeton, 1954. An elaborate study of why people join and leave the Communist Party.

The Anti-Stalin Campaign and International Communism, A selection of documents edited by the Russian Institute, Columbia University, New York, 1956. The chief document is Khrushchev's speech at the 20th Party Congress, February 25, 1956, denouncing Stalin for his 'Cult of the Individual.' The speech has been widely circulated in other editions as well.

Max Beloff, *Soviet Policy in the Far East, 1944–51*, London, 1953.

William Benton, *This Is the Challenge*, New York, 1958.

Joseph S. Berliner, *Soviet Economic Aid*, New York, 1958.

Howard L. Boorman, *et al.*, *Moscow-Peking Axis, Strengths and Strains,* New York, 1957.

Chester Bowles, *Ideas, People and Peace,* London, 1957.

Milovan Djilas, *The New Class: An Analysis of the Communist System,* New York, 1957. By an ex-Titoist; to be read with caution.

C. Grove Haines (ed.), *The Threat of Soviet Imperialism,* Baltimore, 1954.

George F. Kennan, *Russia, the Atom and the West,* New York, 1958.

Michael Lindsay, *China and the Cold War,* Melbourne, 1955.

Charles P. McVicker, *Titoism, Pattern for International Communism,* New York, 1957. Despite the title, it deals with the nationalist communism of Tito.

Imre Nagy, *On Communism, In Defense of the New Course,* New York, 1957. By the ex-premier of Hungary.

Henry L. Roberts, *Russia and America,* New York, 1956.

Benjamin I. Schwartz, *Chinese Communism and the Rise of Mao,* Cambridge, Mass., 1951.

Index